VOLUNTEERS HANDBOOK ®

Stories, Stats and Stuff About Tennessee Football

By Ward Gossett
Foreword by Phillip Fulmer

Printed in the United States of America by
Mennonite Press, Inc.

ISBN 1-880652-76-5

PHOTO CREDITS All photographs were supplied
by the University of Tennessee Sports
Information Department and the *Chattanooga
Free Press* unless otherwise labeled.

All names, logos and symbols attributable
to the University of Tennessee which appear
in this book are trademarks of the University
of Tennessee and have been reproduced with
the permission of the University of Tennessee.
This notice is for the purpose of protection of
trademark rights only, and in no way
represents the approval or disapproval of the
text of this book by the University of
Tennessee.

ACKNOWLEDGMENTS

One doesn't undertake the task of writing about Tennessee football without poring over the works of Tom Siler, Ed Harris, Ben Byrd and Russ Bebb, or the current group of Knoxville-based scribes that includes Jimmy Hyams, a long-time friend.

My wife, Becky, my daughter, Jenifer, and my son, Josh, were most understanding about the numerous research trips to Knoxville, the extra time sifting through microfilm at the *Chattanooga Free Press* and the hours I sat in my study writing or simply staring at the wall.

No one could ever begin to write a book on Tennessee football without the help of the UT sports information department, Haywood Harris, Bud Ford and especially Tom Mattingly, who welcomed me with open arms and on more than one occasion pointed me in the right direction.

I am indebted, too, to Phillip Fulmer, who answered an endless stream of questions, to Doug Dickey, who patiently rehashed "ancient history" with me, to Johnny Majors, who put up with my sometimes stupid questions as I learned the ropes of covering Tennessee football, and to the players themselves.

I thank the folks at Midwest Sports, first for asking me to write this book, then making me look pretty good (my editor, MeLinda Via, in particular) when it went to press.

But I owe so very much to Roy Exum, executive sports editor of the Free Press, who first guided my sportswriting career, then turned me loose in 1985 to cover Tennessee. I could never have undertaken such a task without his understanding and support, and I will, through thick and thin, always consider him a friend.

Finally, I thank God for whatever ability I have. Through Him, all things are possible, as this book, a labor of love, surely proves.

For my parents, Sonny and Margaret Gossett, and my "second mother," Marie Marshall; they always believed in and encouraged me.

— Ward

FOREWORD

I have seen the University of Tennessee as a prospect, a student athlete, as a graduate assistant, as an alumnus away from the beauty of Tennessee, as an assistant coach at UT and now as a fifth-year head coach. I am forever impressed by the love, passion and loyalty so many people feel toward our university. There are so many factors that go into these feelings that it is hard to express them in a short foreword for a book.

I believe that Ward Gossett has done an excellent job presenting these feelings: the traditions, the history and the emotions of what Tennessee football is about, mostly because Ward shares these feelings with all of us who love the university.

There have been hundreds of players over the years who have built the tradition. There are millions who follow it and a few men who have helped build it as coaches. From the mountains of East Tennessee through the rolling hills of Middle Tennessee and the Delta Country of West Tennessee, there is a shared pride in "The Big Orange" that brings Tennesseans together in a spirit of unity.

I look forward to the opportunity to continue building on that tradition, and I appreciate Ward Gossett sharing it with us.

Phillip Fulmer
Summer '96

TABLE OF CONTENTS

The Early Years

VOLUNTEER QUIZ

1. Can you name the last assistant coach to leave UT for a head coaching job?

By the time football made its way onto the Knoxville campus, most teams already had swapped their tights for canvas pants and jackets, the first indoor game — Penn vs. Rutgers, Madison Square Garden — already had been played, tackling below the waist had been legalized and Walter Camp already had begun selecting All-America teams.

When UT played its first football game on Nov. 21, 1891, in Chattanooga, the news of that contest was anything but earth-shattering. As a matter of fact, the game, a 24-0 loss to Sewanee, wasn't reported in the Knoxville Journal until four days after the fact, and it was buried on page 7.

While Sewanee was well on its way to ruling southern football in the early 1900s, the University of Tennessee's fortunes still were very much in the cradle. The team would play its first five seasons, forging a 12-11 record, with a practice field more than a mile's jog from the dormitory and no official head coach.

The Vols' first home in Knoxville was Wait Field, which they used until 1926.

STARTING THE PARADE Tennessee's first victory was a 25-0 shutout of Maryville. The 1892 victory might also have produced the school's first 100-yard rushing game, printed reports crediting C.D. Brown with a 50-yard run and "another long run." In that game, Charles C. Moore was credited not only with kicking Tennessee's first extra point but also its first field goal. But the team finished

the year 2-5, beating the Chattanooga Athletic Club for its second victory.

Shutout losses and wins over Maryville were already becoming commonplace and 1893 was no exception. UT lost its first four games by a combined 250-0 before finishing with victories against Maryville and the Asheville Athletes.

The players of 1893 began setting the stage for great rushing teams that would follow, gaining 333 yards in the 12-6 win over Asheville.

But the next year only two players returned who would confess to having played on that 1893 team. To further muddy the waters, the team's practice facility (across from the main campus entrance) was being graded and improved and was therefore unavailable.

Baseball was the sport of preference in Knoxville at the time and the school's athletic association voted in October of 1894 to abandon football.

GROUNDWORK LAID Though there were no formal teams in 1894 and 1895, UT's club team, spearheaded and captained by William B. Stokely, kept the flickering flames of interest alive with an unbeaten (2-0-2) season. Quarterback for that team and the 1895 team was David Chapman, who later became a driving force in the formation of the Great Smoky Mountains National Park.

Though interest was on the rise after UT defeated the Knoxville YMCA, the Athletic Association again decided to withdraw its support and give the captain and manager the authority to schedule games in 1895. Tennessee wound up playing before 5,000 fans in Bristol (and lost 38-0 to St. Albans), but rebounded with a 40-0 victory over Tennessee Medical College to finish the year 4-2.

The two "non-seasons," though not recognized officially, gave Tennessee its first two winning years (a combined 6-2-2 record) and set the stage for the first unblemished campaign the following year. In 1896, UT went 4-0 with wins over Williamsburg, Chattanooga Athletic Club, Virginia Tech and Central University.

The next year produced a 4-1 record — the only loss being to North Carolina — and the team's first verifiable 100-yard rusher: Strang Nicklin, who had 175 yards vs. Central University of Kentucky. It is the same Nicklin who later served as Bob Neyland's baseball coach at Army.

SOMETHING TO CHEER ABOUT Cheerleaders also entered the UT football scene about this time. R.C. "Red" Matthews, a professor of drawing at the university, had been a cheerleader in high school and college and developed a lively cheering section. Matthews, who eventually became known as "The Root-Leader," even employed gymnastics.

The first undefeated team:
4-0 in 1896
Ends — H.W. Smith, L.L. Bell
Tackles — James A. Baird, Robert R. Baird
Guards — H. White Smith, C.B. Rogan
Center — R.C. Donaldson
Backs — D.C. Chapman, W.M. Newman, Strang Nicklin (captain), Frank Maloney
Subs — Elbert J. Lyman, G.F. Neal, E.T. Warner, M.R. Campbell, Everett Hagy, W.O. Barnes

James A. Baird was captain of the 1897 team, a group that scored 64 points and allowed just 16. Baird played in 1896-97.

And on the field, where their earlier counterparts had been something of a rag-tag bunch, the 1897 team members were dressed in similar outfits: Orange sweaters with large turtlenecks and a white "T" on the chest over a canvas jacket. There were two white bands encircling the neck and the bottom of the sweater, and the outfit was completed with moleskin pants and white and orange stockings. Players furnished their own shoes and nose guards, the latter of which few could afford.

It was in 1897 that Tennessee made what is probably its first real recruiting effort, going after a Nashville youth who had shown a flair for the game. That youngster, who played but one year at Tennessee, was Uncle Charley Moran, who later gained fame as a National League umpire.

THE FIRST COACH After UT went five seasons without a formal coach, former LaFayette standout J.A. Pierce was hired in 1899 by the Athletic Association.

Pierce was hired for one season only. But he produced, winning five games and losing two and closing the year with consecutive shutouts over Kentucky A&M (which became the University of Kentucky), Georgia, Washington & Lee and Kentucky University (which later was renamed Transylvania).

Pierce stayed one more season and posted a 3-2-1 record, extending UT's shutout string to six games (with a win over King and a scoreless tie with Vanderbilt). Tennessee then lost back-to-back games to North Carolina and Auburn before defeating Grant (later renamed the University of Chattanooga and now UT-Chattanooga) and Georgetown.

ABUSE EVEN THEN Yes, even at the turn of the century football players were under attack, prompting the school newspaper to write: "A football player's path is not strewn with roses. He practices daily, rain or shine, exposes his life, limbs and all to keep athletics at U-T among the first in the South. To be abused and criticised [sic] by 'little insignificant cowards' who have no more backbone than a fishing worm takes the life out of the team."

THE FIRST PROFESSIONAL Hired for the 1901 season was George Kelley, the first of two former Princeton players to serve Tennessee as head coach and the first who earned his actual living by coaching. Though Tennessee went 3-3-2, Kelley didn't last the season. Felled by a severe attack of rheumatism, Kelley was forced to leave the team's fortunes to Theo Buckingham, a UT law school student, C.E. Holopete, and to Bill Newman, who had been the star of the previous season's 0-0 tie with Vanderbilt.

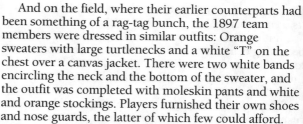

VOLUNTEER QUIZ

2. In its first decade in the Southeastern Conference (1933-42), the Vols suffered but one losing season. Who coached that team?

George Kelley

A RIVALRY IS BORN That 1901 season also saw the first game with Alabama, a game that wasn't completed and ended in a 6-6 tie because of darkness. According to some reports, the game was delayed when Alabama took offense at the referee's offside call and refused to play. The referee gave them five minutes to return to the field and then went to midfield and sat down on the ball. During this time, part of a crowd estimated at 2,500 swarmed onto the playing area.

It was the first time Tennessee had engaged in any trick plays. What the players did was pad the back of one of their teammates, who was then used by another player as a stepping stone-like springboard to clear the line of scrimmage.

And this first game in Birmingham was also the first big payday for Tennessee, which cleared $350 above expenses.

Expenses were a big deal even back then. In 1901, UT professor Charles Ferris, who played at UT (1892) and later served the school as dean of the College of Engineering, proposed the opening of a "book store" with all profits to be used to help maintain the athletic program.

ANOTHER NEW COACH The second of the Princeton men to coach Tennessee, H.F. Fisher, came on board in 1902. He stayed two years, directing UT to a 10-7 record and its first win against Sewanee, a 6-0 shutout.

UT opened the 1902 season with a win over King College, which entered the game with a 2-0 record. Winning two games in three days prior to traveling to Knoxville proved too much for King College, and UT posted a 12-0 shutout.

A major highlight of the season was a 100-yard drop kick (fields were still 110 yards long) by A.H. "Toots" Douglas, who transferred to the Naval Academy and later became an admiral.

Though the Volunteers won their first two games of 1903 (17-0 over Maryville and 38-0 over Carson-Newman), they themselves — 14 men strong and averaging a paltry 153 pounds — were shut out by Vanderbilt, South Carolina, Georgia, Sewanee and Alabama. It was the first time all of Tennessee's games were decided by shutout.

A NICKNAME COMES TO LIFE In their final road game of the 1902 season — in Atlanta versus Georgia Tech — T.B. Green scored a touchdown in the game's final five minutes to give his team a 10-6 victory. But this game is perhaps more noted for what appeared in the following day's Atlanta newspaper.

With the Spanish-American War and Tennessee's reputation for how many men it sent to fight still fresh in

The price of equipment

	1900	1996
Football Pants	$3.00	$45.00
Head Piece/Helmet	$1.35	$125.00
Sweater/Jersey	$1.50	$200.00
Football	$4.00	$60.00

H.F. Fisher

The longest punt by a Vol was 100 yards by A.H. Douglas vs. Clemson in 1902. The field was 110 yards long. Longest on a 100-yard field was by Kent Elmore, 81 yards vs. Vandy in 1988.

many memories, the Atlanta Constitution referred to UT as "the Volunteers" in the following day's edition of the newspaper. It is somewhat surprising that it took so long for someone to pick up on the nickname, which was first used in 1897 for the first Tennessee yearbook.

SAVING GRACE Football at UT was barely better in 1904, a 3-5-1 season that included a 22-0 loss to Vanderbilt, a program that was in its first season under former Michigan standout Dan McGugin. But all was not lost.

On Nov. 24, 1904, in Birmingham, Ala., Tennessee got its first win against Alabama, 5-0. It was in this game that Tennessee ran another of its gadget plays, this one credited to first-year coach S.D. Crawford, one of five coaches in UT history to serve just one season. Running back Sam McAllester was equipped with a harness that featured handles on either side. As he ran toward the line of scrimmage, a halfback on either side would grab hold of a handle and throw him over the line.

S.D. Crawford

BIGGEST WIN Though football continued to struggle at Tennessee, the 1905 season produced the most lopsided victory in the Volunteers' history, a 104-0 win over American University of nearby Harriman. It was a game that took just a little more than 45 minutes to play and one in which Tennessee scored 18 touchdowns for five points each. A man named Parker, who is not listed among UT's lettermen (nor was he listed on the team's roster that year), was credited with four of the scores.

The season had an inauspicious beginning under new coach J.D. Depree, who was forced to quit in mid-season because of illness. Tennessee led Tennessee School for the Deaf, 16-6, and the game actually ended two minutes into the second half when TSD quit after having two players knocked out. Depree, according to one old-timer, actually was forced to play one game for Tennessee. The team was playing its third game in eight days and had but 10 players, so Depree donned a uniform and played fullback.

VOLUNTEER QUIZ

3. Of the 149 men who have served as Tennessee assistant coaches, how many graduated from UT?

COMBAT, ANYONE? It was very much rough-and-tumble in those days. James Riley Montgomery quoted former UT player Benton White, who lettered in 1907 and 1908, in his book "The Volunteer State Forges Its University."

"When you 'made' the team, you were officially known as the best man for that position; hence expected to play every minute of every game. There were no huddles and no time-outs except for injury. When a player was taken out, it was for good.

"Hence an injured player was never removed until at least two buckets of water, liberally sloshed over the fallen warrior, failed to bring him back to life and a desire for further combat," wrote White, who had been expelled from the school in 1903 before being allowed to return in 1907.

But said "combat" brought Tennessee its only victory — and points — of 1906. DePree's illness caused the coaching duties to fall to Piggy Word, a player who had been ruled ineligible for the 1906 season. In a game with American University, one of the American players slugged a Tennessee player. Word, who that day also served as one of the referees, ejected the offending player and the American team refused to continue without him. Word was later arrested by a Harriman police officer and charged with assault, but the American player he supposedly assaulted refused to press charges.

SUPPORT GROWS By the end of the 1906 season, there was enough support for Tennessee to turn its attention toward finding a head coach with promise. Team manager David C. Gaut searched high and low and finally offered the job to S. George Levene, who had been an outstanding player at Penn.

Though Gaut's original offer of $750 for the season was much less than several other schools seeking

4. Other than UT, which college has had the most coaches on Vol football staffs?

The great Walter Camp, maker of All-Americans, endorsed S. George Levene for the job as Tennessee football coach on April 17, 1907.

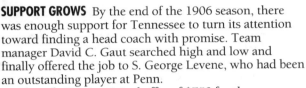

New Haven, April 17,1907

David C. Gaut, Esq.,
University of Tennessee,
Knoxville, Tenn.

Dear Sir:- Your favor of the 9th, is at hand asking me about Mr. Levine's knowledge of the game and capacity for handling his men.

He has followed the game very closely playing a number of years so that he knows the detail of individual positions very thoroughly. I do not know about his capacity for disciplining men because he has been for the most part a player not a coach, but I should think that with his experience he would have no difficulty in this respect.

He is of foreign extraction and it might be at first a little difficulty to understand him but that would not last long nor militate against his ability.

Very truly yours,
Walter Camp

Levene's services, Levene finally took the job for $800 because of a "desire to see the South," according to a letter written to Gaut in late April of 1907.

Levene, in a letter to Gaut dated May 7, 1907, advised Gaut to "have a spring kicking competition open to all who play or may want to play football."

In those instructions to Gaut for what is likely the first spring practice at UT, Levene wrote, "Let each man have five hours at punting, drop kicking and place

NEYLAND STADIUM (SHIELDS-WATKINS FIELD)

Since 1908 the Vols had been playing on Wait Field, site of the Walters Life Sciences Building and a hard-packed pit that left more than one player picking gravel from his knees, elbows and buttocks.

Wait Field was good for the times, but in 1920 a portion of the tightly-packed, ramshackle bleachers gave way under the UT band. The final game at Wait Field was played that year and resulted in a 14-7 win over Kentucky.

Though land had been purchased, the students, faculty and friends who had bought a 7-acre tract with a stadium in mind still owed $22,453. W.S. Shields, president of Knoxville's City National Bank and a new UT trustee, proposed paying off the debt if the university would raise

A look at the North end zone expansion of Neyland Stadium in 1996.

kicking and make careful record of each man's record. This will help me greatly."

Levene, who received an endorsement from the legendary Walter Camp, took UT to 7-2-1 and 7-2 records in 1907 and 1908. It was a grand time for Tennessee fans, who delighted in the first recorded touchdowns via the forward pass — from Lee Wert to Benton White for 70 and 25 yards. Of course, the idea of pass defense in that day was not so much knocking

enough money to prepare and equip the area as an athletic field. The field was subsequently named after Shields and his wife, the former Alice Watkins.

The field was first sodded and catch-basins for field drainage added in 1926. There also was a practice field behind the bleachers.

Over the years many additions have been made but no change had as much impact as the artificial Tartan turf that was installed in 1968. Four years later the Vols played the first night game at the stadium, versus Penn State. The original "rug" was replaced in 1975, in '80 and in '86, and the Vols decided to go back to grass in 1993.

Since 1921, when Shields-Watkins Field was built, the Vols have recorded 65 winning seasons (354 victories and 32 unbeaten home seasons) at what became known in 1962 as Neyland Stadium. Over the years, Volunteer fans have seen 56 All-Americans, 212 players who went on to the NFL and 16 players who went into the College Football Hall of Fame.

CHANGES OVER THE YEARS

Year	Construction	Seats Added	Capacity
1921	17 rows, West stands		3,200
1926	17 rows, East stands	3,600	6,800
1929	42 rows, West stands	11,060	17,860
1937	Section X	1,500	19,360
1938	44 rows, East stands	10,030	29,390
1948	South stands, (horseshoe)	15,000	44,390
1962	Upper deck & press box, West stands	5,837	50,227
1966	North stands	5,895	56,122
1968	Upper deck, East stands	6,307	62,429
1972	Upper deck, Southwest	6,221	68,650
1976	Upper deck, Southeast	9,600	78,250
1980	North stands	10,499	88,749
1987	Skyboxes, West stands	2,361	91,110
1990	Seating adjustment		91,902
1996	Upper deck, North stands	10,583	102,485

S. George Levene

down the ball but rather the intended receiver once the ball was in the air. Also in 1907, J.C. "Fluzie" Loucks scored three touchdowns on onside kicks in a 57-0 blistering of Chattanooga.

Those first two Levene squads were fun-loving types who once saw fit to "borrow" the spittoons from the train on which they traveled home after defeating Georgia Tech on a Saturday and Clemson on the following Monday in 1907.

White described the incident for legendary Knoxville sportswriter Tom Siler. In Siler's book, *Thru the Years with the Volunteers*, White, who jumped from the train to avoid being arrested, admitted that he still had his spittoon.

It should be noted that the Georgia Tech win was contested because of a blocked Tennessee punt that was recovered in the Volunteers' end zone. The official first ruled a Tech touchdown, and then a UT safety. But record books at both schools now list the game as a Georgia Tech win.

By this time the cost of a home game had risen close to $900: $500 for the opposing team, $150 toward Levene's salary, $50 for officials and the rest for field maintenance and miscellaneous expenses.

The team then fell on hard times, going 1-6-2 in 1909, in part because of fraternity politics. If fielding a young and inexperienced team weren't enough, Levene, who was given a room at the Sigma Alpha Epsilon house, was accused of favoritism and he eventually resigned, leaving behind a 15-10-3 record.

ROCKING A REF It was in 1909, after Alabama posted a 10-0 victory, that angry Tennessee fans chased the referee, R.T. Elgin, out of the stadium. Many of the crowd felt Elgin, an Alabama native, had shorted the Vols when he called back a 40-yard run and penalized UT 15 yards. At game's end, he was surrounded by angry supporters. He managed to leap aboard a trolley car, but he was beaned by a rock-throwing sharpshooter and wasn't really safe until he managed to lock himself in his hotel room.

ANOTHER ERA ENDS Tennessee supporters seemed to realize that the catch-as-catch-can era — seven coaches in 11 years — needed to come to a halt. Tennessee needed some stability in the program. So after a one-year stint in 1910 from Andrew Stone, former Indiana standout Z.G. Clevenger was hired as baseball once again entered into football fortunes.

One reason for Stone's quick demise might have been the fact that UT had a total debt of $1,194 from the 1910 season, and students and faculty were asked to pass the

VOLUNTEER QUIZ

5. Which current SEC-member schools have never had a graduate who coached at Tennessee?

hat to pay the bills. The faculty raised $1,000, the students $250.

Clevenger, who supplemented his coaching income at Nebraska Wesleyan by playing summer baseball, wound up playing shortstop in 1910 with Knoxville's Appalachian League team and became friends with Red Matthews, UT's "Root-Leader." Matthews, by now a member of the athletic board, eventually offered the football job to Clevenger.

It was again a rebuilding process, but by this time academic entrance standards had been instituted at UT and a number of students — among them promising football players — were turned away. The team's leading scorer in Clevenger's first season was C.H. Fonde, who had just four touchdowns and one PAT. Fonde was forced out of the season's next-to-last game, against UT Medical School, by an abscess on his kicking foot. In that 1911 group, however, were five "fish," as freshmen were known at the time, who caught Clevenger's eye: Farmer Kelly, Mush Kerr, Russ Lindsay, Tommy Thomason and Goat Carroll.

The 1912 effort was at least back to .500, something the Volunteers hadn't accomplished since the 7-2 season of 1908 under Levene. They started off 3-0, winning by a combined margin of 201-0, but Sewanee was waiting. The early success was rekindling interest and more than 700 fans boarded a train ($2 round trip) for the excursion to Chattanooga to meet the Purple Tigers. Sewanee burst their bubble, 33-6, and UT wound up 4-4.

Four UT head football coaches also coached Vol basketball teams. They were (with years, basketball records): Zora Clevenger (1912-1916; 50-14); John R. Bender (1917, 20-21; 29-15); M.B. Banks (1922-26; 52-33-1); and Bill Britton (1927-35; 80-73). UT football assistants who were head basketball coaches were John Mauer (1939-47; 127-41); Emmett Lowery (1948-59; 169-110); and John Sines (1960-62; 26-45). Also, Sines and John Barnhill served as assistant basketball coaches.

RED MATTHEWS: UT'S NO. 1 FAN

As both fan and cheerleader, R.C. "Red" Matthews will be remembered by Tennessee faithful.

He was, for all practical purposes, the first cheerleader at the University of Tennessee and rallied the fans' support from 1907-1919. He introduced the gymnastic side of cheerleading at UT and was known throughout the South for his series of back flips.

But he knew it was time to give it up in 1919 when UT played the University of the South (Sewanee) in 1919.

"This Sewanee fan came up to me during halftime and said,

'Good God, Grandpa, are you still leading cheers.' Right then I knew it was time to quit," he said.

Matthews, a former engineering professor at UT, was honored in 1967 for his years as Tennessee's biggest fan. He was chosen to serve as grand marshal of the homecoming parade, and the day was made even brighter by the fact that his granddaughter, Leslie, was one of the UT cheerleaders.

Though he gave up active cheerleading in 1919, Matthews served as a member of the UT Athletics Committee for 34 years.

VOLUNTEER QUIZ

6. Over the last decade (1987-96), which state other than Tennessee has produced the most UT scholarship signees?

THE FIRST TITLE The Vols, having added the likes of Morris Vowell, Billy May, Red Rainey, Evan McLean, R.G. Taylor, Frank Sorrells and S.T. Bayer, went 6-3 in 1913.

Among the three losses was a 6-0 defeat by Alabama that was finished in darkness. The Tide won on a pair of Hargrove Vandegraaff field goals, but he paid dearly. Vandegraaff left the game early in the fourth quarter with both ears virtually torn off.

That year, Clevenger awarded 12 letters. Because of a financial "windfall" of $1,000, he also was able to hire what might have been UT's first paid assistant coach, former Michigan standout Miller "Brute" Pontius.

In 1914, Pontius developed a strong and large offensive line that averaged 183 pounds. With a "go-go" backfield of May, Tommy Thomason, Scotty Cameron and Ross Lindsey, UT rolled through its first six opponents, scoring 321 points while giving up just 10.

TENNESSEE TRADITIONS

A football Saturday in Knoxville is a painter's nightmare: So many shades of orange can be found only on an autumn afternoon in East Tennessee — and we're not talking about the bountiful colors of the nearby Smoky Mountains' changing leaves.

From yellow orange to faded orange to burnt orange to neon orange, each in its own way is a Tennessee orange. It might be seen in a punk-rocker's 'do, as a tie, in a sweater, a jacket, a jersey, a shirt or even pants or socks, and most definitely hats — cowboy hats, baseball caps, tams, toboggans, you name it. And a certain UT sports information director, one who shall remain nameless, even had a pair of cowboy boots, one with an inverted "U," the other with an inverted "T."

It is part of the tradition of Tennessee football, a tradition that includes legendary John Ward, the Vol network's play-by-play man, meeting with fans and answering their questions in a live pregame broadcast, fans congregating along the hill for the "Vol Walk" when the team walks from Gibbs Hall to the Stadium, or moving down to the hill across from the bookstore for some pregame spirit-lifting as the school's "Pride of the Southland" band plays its way into the stadium.

But it doesn't end there.

RUNNING THROUGH THE "T" Before the game the band lines up and struts its stuff up and down the field, eventually forming a giant "T." Tennessee players sprint through the "T" and onto the field to rousing applause and general hootin' and hollerin'.

"BIG ORANGE COUNTRY" The term "Big Orange Country" originated as a marketing scheme by former UT basketball coach Ray Mears and it is an idea that eventually encompassed the entire Volunteer athletics program.

UT's success set the stage for its game against Vanderbilt at Nashville, a game that was "broadcast" back to Knoxville's Grand Theatre by telegraph and then announced by megaphone. The hero was Goat Carroll, who had returned to his hometown and caught two touchdown passes from May, kicked a PAT and a 15-yard field goal to score all the Tennessee points in a 16-14 win — the Vols' first against Vanderbilt.

But the season wasn't over. The Vols avenged the 1912 rout by Sewanee with a 14-7 victory and then clinched the Southern Intercollegiate Athletic Association championship by beating Kentucky State, 23-6, in front of a home crowd of 3,500, the largest at UT to that point. One of the team's substitutes that year was C.B. Cates, who went on to become commander of the U.S. Marine Corps.

VOLUNTEER QUIZ

7. Who scored the first touchdown ever for Tennessee?

THE WALKING HORSE At one time, UT football games started with a performance by a Grand Champion Tennessee Walking Horse. The horse entered the field from the South end zone and was ridden around the stadium. However, artificial turf put an end to that and the tradition, to the best of our knowledge, has been revived only once recently, that being for the game against Temple during the 100 Years Celebration.

SMOKEY The Vols' official mascot is a blue tick coon hound that has been part of the athletic setting since 1953.

One of the best stories about the coon was told by Scott Hunter, the former Alabama quarterback. Hunter, it seems, got tired of the dog barking at the Crimson Tide players as they warmed up before the 1968 game and took a kick at the hound. But as the players made their way to the dressing room, Bama coach Bear Bryant walked up to Hunter and said, "Son, we've got enough trouble up here without you trying to kick their dog."

THE "T" The now famous "T" on the Tennessee helmets was introduced in 1964 when Doug Dickey took over as head coach. The helmet had previously been white with an orange stripe down the middle. The only other changes to the helmet were in 1962 — Coach Bowden Wyatt's final year — when he added orange numbers on the sides of the helmets. In 1963, his successor, Jim McDonald, kept the numbers but changed their color to black.

CHECKERBOARD END ZONES These, too, arrived with Dickey in '64 and remained until '68 when artificial turf was installed. The checkerboard end zones returned in '89.

PASSING AS A WEAPON

It was obvious that the forward pass had become part of UT's offensive arsenal when, during the 1914 season, Billy May threw nine touchdown passes, eight of them to Goat Carroll. Those were records that would stand for a while.

But Russ Lindsay, who made the All-Southern team along with Mush Kerr, Carroll and Farmer Kelly, also set a record. Even in the rough-and-tumble, single-platoon days of no-substitution, Lindsay finished at UT having played every minute of all 34 games during his four-year career.

Tennessee's first official homecoming game was 1916 and resulted in a 10-6 UT victory over Vanderbilt.

BANG AND CHANGE

As defending SIAA champion, Tennessee began 1915 with a bang, drubbing Carson-Newman and Cumberland by identical 101-0 scores en route to a 4-1 start. With five touchdowns and 10 PATs, Graham Vowell and Bill McClure set respective single-game scoring records.

But Vanderbilt was up next and the Volunteers sustained their first critical injury when Bennett Jared, a halfback, suffered a spinal injury that left him paralyzed from the waist down. The Vols considered canceling the rest of the season but Jared momentarily improved and his mother encouraged the team to play on. Jared had his appendix removed, then underwent two operations for peritonitis before he died the following summer.

Clevenger, who later returned to Indiana to serve his alma mater for 23 years as athletic director, left Tennessee before the 1916 season, moving to what he thought was a better opportunity and higher-paying job at Kansas State. And in one of the oddest of switches, the Vols hired John Bender, the coach Clevenger was replacing at Kansas State.

John Bender

GATOR-BAIT?

Bender, who had entered coaching in 1904 after his senior season at Nebraska, immediately set up a formal spring practice and also a regular training table. His players responded with an 8-0-1 record. Among the victims was first-time opponent Florida, whom the Vols defeated, 24-0, in Tampa with two touchdowns on interception returns.

The effort even drew the attention of Walter Camp, who placed Graham Vowell on his third-team All-America team. It was the first national recognition for any Tennessee football player.

FUNDING A NEW FIELD

Though there were no official teams in 1917 and 1918 because of World War I, 1917 was the first season for season ticket sales.

Bender returned in 1919 and Tennessee, with former Alabama player Hal Blair among the participants,

finished the year 3-3-3. By this time there was a real need for a new playing facility to replace Wait Field, which had long been a mixture of dirt, clay and gravel.

The site of today's Shields-Watkins Field was originally purchased by University Realty Co., a corporation consisting of alumni, faculty, students and supporters. W.S. Shields, at the time president of City National Bank in Knoxville, proposed to pay off a debt of $22,453 if the university would obtain a matching amount to prepare and equip the area as athletic fields.

UT continued to use Wait for another year, posting a 7-2 record in what would be Bender's last season. He was hired away from UT by Knoxville High, which offered a higher salary.

But the field, in actuality a large ravine that required

The great work day of 1921, when volunteers helped prepare Shields-Watkins Field as the new home for UT football.

FOOTBALL'S SCORING CHANGES

Points scored for the years shown.

Year	TD	PAT	FG	Safety
1884	2	4	5	1
1886	4	2	5	2
1897	5	1	5	2
1904	5	1	4	2
1909	5	1	3	2
1912	6	1	3	2

THE VOLS' SONGS

ALMA MATER
(By Mrs. John Lamar Meek)
(© 1929 by Student Activities Council, UT.)

On a hallowed hill in Tennessee
Like a beacon shining bright
The stately walls of old UT
Rise glorious to the sight.

Refrain:
So here's to you, old Tennessee
Our Alma Mater true
We pledge to love and harmony
Our loyalty to you.

What torches kindled of that flame
Have passed from hand to hand
What hearts cemented in that name
Bid land to stanger land.

Oh, ever as we strive to rise
On life's unresting stream
Dear Alma Mater, may our eyes
Be lifted to that gleam.

FIGHT, VOLS, FIGHT!
(Words by Gwen Sweet. Music by Thornton W.
Allen and Milo Sweet)
(© 1935 by Thorton W. Allen Company, New York)

Fight, Vols fight with all your
    might,
For the Orange and White
Never falter, never yield
As we march on down the field
    (Keep marching!)
Let the Spirit of the Hill
Every Vol with courage fill
Your loyalty means our victory
So fight, Vols, fight!

THE SPIRIT OF THE HILL
(Words and melody by Sam Gooble, arranged by E.
Edwin Crerie)

Here's to old Tennessee
Never we'll sever
We pledge our loyalty
Forever and ever
Backing our football team
Falterning never
Cheer and fight with all of your
    might
For Tennessee.

HERE'S TO OLD TENNESSEE
(Down The Field)

Oh! What a thrill when the boys
    on the hill
Fall in line
We know they'll fight with all
    their might
And then we'll yell, yell and yell
When the Vols take the field.
They're out to win for us again.
Oh! It's Tennessee,
It's the old UT,
It's the Orange and White in the
    field.
So we'll cheer the Volunteers,
As they go through the years
With the Spirit of the Hill.

ROCKY TOP
(By Boudleaux Bryand and Felice Bryant)
(© 1967 by House of Bryant, Hendersonville, Tenn.)

Wish that I was on ol' Rocky Top,
    down in the Tennessee Hills;
Ain't no smog or smoke on Rocky
    Top; Ain't no telephone bills;
Once I had a girl on Rocky Top;
    half bear, the other half cat;
Wild as a mink, but sweet as soda
    pop; I still dream about that.

Refrain:
Rocky Top, you'll always be home
    sweet home to me;
Good Ol' Rocky Top, Rocky Top,
    Tennessee;
Rocky Top, Tennessee.

Once two strangers climbed ol'
    Rocky Top looking for a
    moonshine still;
Strangers ain't come down from
    Rocky Top, reckon they never
    will;
Corn won't grow at all on Rocky
    Top; Dirt's too rocky by far;
That's why all the folks on Rocky
    Top get their corn from a jar.

more than 50,000 yards of dirt to fill in, was a priority. It was on March 16, 1921, that UT student McGregor Smith, later head of Florida Power and Light Company, got Campus Day off the ground. There were more than 2,000 volunteers and they managed to get the cinder track encircling the field virtually prepared thanks to the organization by Smith and his team managers.

The volunteers even got fed that day, a single lunch consisting of two ham sandwiches, a hot dog, a "sweet" sandwich, pickles, apples, doughnuts, a slice of cake, candy, ice cream and buttermilk.

M.Beal Banks

BIG OPPONENT, BIG LOSS UT hired M. Beal Banks away from Drake and he immediately installed a version of the T- formation. But fans were clamoring for a beefed-up schedule and Banks, who took UT to records of 6-2-1 in 1921 and 8-2 in 1922, tried his best to avoid a 1923 contest with national power Army. UT's athletic officials demanded a $5,000 guarantee, a fee they were sure Army would refuse. But West Point officials agreed and UT opened the 1923 season $5,000 richer but with a 41-0 loss to Army. The team never fully recovered, getting wins in the last two games — against Mississippi and Kentucky — to pull out a 5-4-1 record.

THE BIG ORANGE IS BORN M. Beal Banks, whose 1922 team was the first to don the now widely recognized orange jerseys, stuck around two more seasons, but he knew after his team suffered five straight losses to end the 1924 campaign that UT officials were looking for another coach. In 1925, Banks, who was known to change offenses at least twice each season, resigned after leading UT to a 5-2-1 record. He took a job as coach at Knoxville's Central High.

8. Who threw UT's first touchdown pass and who caught it?

The Vols' Own General

Gen. Neyland

Though neither Coach M. Beal Banks nor one of his young assistants, Robert R. Neyland, knew it, 1925 was the end of an unstable era and the beginning of complete regional domination.

When Banks resigned in December 1925, speculation centered on Alabama coach Wallace Wade and Centre coach Charley Moran. But the pick already had been made and that pick, Neyland, was to become the master of Southern football.

NEYLAND THE MEMORY How is he remembered? As a legend. But also as a disciplinarian, a tactician, a mastermind, a teacher, a motivator and the primary influence on hundreds of those who have entered the coaching profession.

This is a man who was part of the U.S. Army chase of Pancho Villa, the infamous Mexican bandit.

They say the man was superstitious: He always wore the same suit to ball games and he wouldn't allow pregame photos.

There are those who say he was eccentric. He did, after all, quite often sit in a chair along the sidelines during games, and once told his players, "I have prepared you for anything you can possibly face."

He was considered, to a point, a "ladies man." He

NEYLAND FACTS

- Born Feb. 17, 1892, in Greenville, Texas
- Son of attorney Robert Reese Neyland, Jr., and Pauline Lewis Neyland
- Married Ada "Peggy" Fitch of Grand Rapids, Mich., on July 16, 1923
- Had two sons, Robert, Jr., (born Feb. 11, 1930) and Lewis (born Dec. 6, 1933)
- Named UT head coach in December 1925 after one year in Knoxville as an assistant coach
- Elected to Football's Hall of Fame in 1956 and was voted Football Writers' Man of the Year in 1954
- Retired as head coach after the 1952 season but remained as athletic director until his death on March 28, 1962, at New Orleans' Ochsner Foundation Hospital, where he'd been undergoing treatment of chronic liver and kidney conditions
- Interred in the National Cemetery of Knoxville, only a few blocks from the place where his life had become one of national renown

used to hold open house for sportswriters after home games. When it came to books, he liked westerns, mysteries and military strategy. He loved to fish, was a master at bridge, and Latin was a hobby. His politics? Neyland often described himself as "far right of right."

He once danced to the Tennessee Waltz in the dressing room to relax his players before a Cotton Bowl game against Texas.

At a banquet in Texas, former Neyland All-American Herman Hickman was quoted as saying, "We (Tennessee) gave you Sam Houston and Davy Crockett. You gave us Gen. Neyland, so the debt's even."

Former Vol captain Ray Graves, who made his coaching mark at Florida, once said, "Anybody who ever played for Neyland had the training to become a coach."

There were many.

But one of the more telling comments about Neyland came from a fellow Army officer, Colonel James Tabb, who served as operations officer under the General in the Far East.

"I have read many contradictory things about him. Some regarded him as a machine and too distant with his men. I was in close touch with him several times daily during planning sessions at Calcutta, and can assure anyone that if he gave the appearance of being distant, it

VOLUNTEER QUIZ

9. Who was the first Vol to gain 100 rushing yards in a game?

ROBERT R. NEYLAND MEMORIAL TROPHY

The Knoxville Quarterback Club gives the Robert R. Neyland Memorial Trophy annually to an outstanding man who has contributed greatly to intercollegiate athletics.

Among coaches who have been presented with the award are Alabama's Wallace Wade, Georgia Tech's Bobby Dodd, Rice's Jess Neely, Mississippi's Johnny Vaught, Oklahoma's Bud Wilkinson, Southern Cal's John McKay, Texas' Darrell Royal, Auburn's Ralph "Shug" Jordan, Arkansas' Frank Broyles, Nebraska's Bob Devaney, Notre Dame's Ara Parseghian, Alabama's Paul "Bear" Bryant, Ohio State's Woody Hayes, Michigan State's Duffy Daugherty, LSU's Charlie McClendon, Georgia's Vince Dooley, Michigan's Bo Schembechler, Florida State's Bobby Bowden and Notre Dame's Dan Devine.

The 1996 winner was Iowa's Hayden Fry.

was simply because of the requirements of his job," Tabb, a Chattanooga resident, told the Chattanooga News-Free Press about his former commanding officer.

"He felt strongly about the welfare of men in his command and spent considerable time in looking out for them. On the surface and in public, however, he minced no words and seemed to be made of steel."

Said Johnny Majors, who later became a Vol head coach himself, "The youngsters we recruit today don't know anything about Neyland; he was long before their time. But the successful program, the first-class facilities, the great fan support can all be traced back to him. He gave us our tradition."

NEYLAND THE STUDENT

By his 20th birthday and his appointment to the U.S. Military Academy, Neyland already had attended Burleson Junior College and also had studied engineering at Texas A&M. He graduated near the top of his class at West Point in 1916, then took graduate courses in mechanical and electrical engineering at the Massachusetts Institute of Technology.

A perfectionist, Neyland had no sympathy for slackers on the field or in the classroom.

"If a country boy like me from a little old jerk-water town in Texas could go to West Point, box, play baseball and football and graduate pretty well up in the ranks, why can't any boy with common sense make decent grades in college?" he once said.

There was no room on his teams for those who wouldn't put forth the classroom effort. "A player who lets himself down in the classroom will, when the chips were down, let you down on the playing field," Neyland said.

NEYLAND THE ATHLETE

Neyland was more than a quality cadet at West Point, and more than once he was referred to as the next Jim Thorpe, the great multi-sport All-American at Carlisle. Neyland was an outstanding football player, Army's heavyweight boxing champion three years straight and an outstanding pitcher for the baseball team.

Though he'd never really pitched until going to Army, Neyland, captain of Army's baseball team in 1916, once reeled off 20 straight wins en route to a 35-5 career record. And he was most proud of the fact that a team on which he participated never lost to Navy.

As a matter of fact, he was beaned in one of those games with the Midshipmen. Neyland, who always batted third even when pitching, was carried off the field and behind the stands, where he was revived. He returned to the game and won. A few days later the Academy superintendent forwarded a letter to him that said: "Please commend that young man for his show of fortitude

VOLUNTEER QUIZ

10. Who was the first Vol to catch passes totaling 100 yards in a game?

VOLUNTEER QUIZ

11. What is the oldest series between UT and a current SEC member?

Robert R. Neyland as a cadet at West Point, where he would captain football, boxing and baseball teams.

against Navy the other day." The letter was signed by Newton D. Baker, Secretary of War. Neyland later wound up turning down contracts from the New York Giants, the Detroit Tigers and the Philadelphia Athletics.

NEYLAND THE SOLDIER His first assignment was with the First Engineers, engaging in levee work on the Rio Grande along the Mexican border. He also spent time at the First Corps Engineering School and the First Army Engineering School in France in 1917 before returning to the States to take charge of training for the Eighth Mounted Engineers and the 15th Calvary Division Engineers at Fort Bliss, Texas. Neyland served as an aide to General Douglas MacArthur in 1921 when MacArthur was Commanding General of the Academy, and also assisted in coaching football, baseball and boxing.

Serving as football coach at Tennessee was actually Neyland's part-time job because he was still an officer in the Army and was very much involved with such Army projects as that at Cove Creek, which was later to become

The University has set aside a memorial area in its Hall of Fame area at Neyland-Thompson Sports Center for those killed through service to their country or while they were a part of the UT athletic program.

VOLUNTEER QUIZ

12. Which non-conference school has UT played the most times?

Norris Dam, the first link in the chain of dams that would become the Tennessee Valley Authority. During that time, Neyland, originally an ROTC instructor at Tennessee, also was stationed in Chattanooga.

Neyland was ordered to Panama in 1935 for his customary three-year hitch of foreign duty. He retired from the army, though, in 1936 as a major. But Neyland was recalled to active duty in 1941 and rose to the rank of brigadier general while serving first in China, then India and charged with the enormous task of supplying all American forces in the China-Burma-India Theatre. Neyland returned from World War II having been awarded the Distinguished Service Medal, the Legion of Merit with Oak Leaf Cluster, Order of the British Empire and Chinese Order of the Cloud and Banner.

NEYLAND THE COACH Herman Hickman, an All-American guard at UT (1929-31) and later coach at Yale, once observed, "If Neyland could score a touchdown against you, he had you beat. If he could score two touchdowns, he had you in a rout.

"His forte was defense, coupled with an air-tight, flawless kicking game. This meant every phase of the kicking game, both returns and coverages. He made a fetish of pass defense and the return of intercepted passes. Only 25 percent of our practices were spent on offense. The practices were short, the lecture periods long. He was a strict disciplinarian."

Neyland's training rules:

1. no tobacco

2. no alcohol

3. no pastries, hot bread, fried or greasy foods

4. no coffee, except at breakfast, and no tea

Because of the grandeur that surrounded his three eras as coach, Neyland's emphasis on defense is often overlooked. But to back up Hickman's observation, consider that of the 173 victories the Vols posted under Neyland, 107 were shutouts. His teams outscored their opponents at a 4-1 ratio, scoring 21.4 points per game while surrendering an average of 5.3. An average Neyland season consisted of eight-plus wins, fewer than two losses.

The man never had a losing season, coming closest in the back-to-back seasons of 1947 (5-5) and 1948 (4-4-2), years in which he actually handicapped himself and his team's chances of winning because he refused to utilize the free substitution rule (basically one team for offense, another for defense) that had been adopted and was being employed by his opposing coaches.

VOLUNTEER QUIZ

13. Who were the first Vols to play in a college all-star game?

Said Bear Bryant, the coaching whiz who succeeded Neyland as Southern football's King of the Hill, "You know what he's going to do, but try and stop it."

Wallace Wade, another of the Alabama coaching legends, said, "He could take his and beat yours, or he could take yours and beat his."

HE HAD FEELINGS Within a day or two of Neyland's death, Austin White, former sports editor of the News-Free

Press in Chattanooga, captured the very essence of this larger-than-life individual.

White, one of the General's friends and occasional antagonists, recalled the 1951 Cotton Bowl to open his farewell to Neyland.

"Pat Shires, trotting off the field, flung his helmet to the ground and slumped dejectedly on the bench. Tears trickled down his cheeks. He had just missed a point-after-touchdown kick that, had it been good, would have projected Tennessee into a 14-to-14 tie with the University of Texas Longhorns. Texas, after yielding seven points to the Vols in the first quarter, had run up 14 in the second period and had dominated the game until UT's desperate, last-ditch rally.

"With five minutes to play, Gen. Neyland turned his back on the field, strode over to Shires, slapped him on the back and barked, 'Don't worry about that, son. We didn't come out here to tie.'

"Prophetic or not, the General's consoling words brought the Tennessee bench to its feet. And ultimately, Texas to its knees."

White continued: "Neyland was not a person you could take or leave. Either you loved him or you vigorously opposed him. There was no compromise. Yet, his friends and his foes had one common bond — each respecting him all the way.

"The General's military bearing, piercing eyes that bored through you from underneath coal-black eyebrows, and his rather brusque manner of speaking sometimes alienated people who were never accorded the privilege of knowing the true Bob Neyland.

"Here was a man who, once he laid down the armor of aloofness that shielded him from a prying, curious world, could sit and reminisce for hours. He had his favorites, of

Gen. Neyland with his 1952 coaching staff. The group, from left: Harvey Robinson, Farmer Johnson, Ike Peel, Chan Caldwell, Neyland, Al Hust, Ralph Chancey, Burr West and legendary trainer Mickey O'Brien. All but Neyland and O'Brien played for the Volunteers.

VOLUNTEER QUIZ

14. Who was the first Vol to play in the NFL?

Neyland's teams: recorded 107 total shutouts; averaged 8.5 wins; averaged 21.36 points per game; gave up 5.3 points per game; had an average victory margin of 16 points per game

course, among the hundreds of stout-headed young men who had cut such a swashbuckling gridiron path for him but he rarely ranked one man above another."

And Neyland, White was fond of telling, never lumped his players into one mold. "Each boy is an individual," White quoted Neyland as saying. "You might pat one on the back and get more out of another with a figurative kick on the rump — but the first thing a successful coach must do is to acquaint himself with the individual."

At a testimonial dinner in August of 1953, Neyland said, "I have tried to teach my men to accept defeat as a steppingstone to victory, to accept victory without gloating and to accept defeat without bitterness."

THE FIRSTS Neyland is generally regarded as the first coach in the South to use telephone hookups from press box to field. But Neyland's first phone line ran from the bench to the top floor of Morrell Hall. It was in 1927. Neyland also was the first coach to have teams play in the four "major" bowl games: Rose, Cotton, Sugar and Orange. He was in the first group of inductees in the Orange Bowl Hall of Fame. He also introduced "kapok" pads for uniforms, and his teams were the first to utilize "tear-away" jerseys.

He was one of the first nationally to study game film of opponents and later to film his own practices for later study. Though some laughed when his backs first came out in low-quarter shoes rather than the traditional high-tops, other coaches were quick to join him. He also is credited as the first coach in the South to take his team to an off-campus site the night before a game, and he was the first to cover his football field when inclement weather threatened.

THE GAME MAXIMS There were, to Neyland's way of thinking, football's version of the Ten Commandments. "No matter how much the game changes, his basic teachings endure," said Ray Graves, a former player.

The maxims included:

"The team that makes the fewest mistakes will win."

"Play for and make the breaks and when one comes your way — SCORE."

"If at first the game — or breaks — go against you, don't let up ... Put on more steam."

"Protect our kickers, our quarterback, our lead and our ball game."

"Cover, block, cut and slice, pursue and gang tackle ... For this is the WINNING EDGE."

"Press the kicking game. Here is where the breaks are made."

"Carry the fight to our opponent and keep it there for 60 minutes."

Over the years he added others, his personal notebooks reportedly holding as many as 38 such maxims that even

VOLUNTEER QUIZ

15. Who did the Vols beat for their first SEC win?

today carry weight in Big Orange locker rooms.

"They're part of my Tennessee heritage," said Phillip Fulmer, a former Vol who is now coaching UT. "It just wouldn't seem right to take the field without them."

DUTIES OF A COACH Neyland had a personal set of rules that outlined the framework of a successful coach, many of which were surely drawn from his military experiences.

Neyland felt a head coach should remain a little aloof from his players and, though to a lesser degree, his assistant coaches. He felt a head coach had to possess the ability to remain cool and calm in games, that a head coach worth his salt was often the only one who could see the entire picture.

But Neyland once wrote, "Football is composed of nothing but accidents; the great art is to profit from such accidents. This is the mark of genius."

While Neyland was often thought to be aloof, former Vol Bob Woodruff, who wound up his career as Tennessee's athletic director, never thought of the General in such a fashion.

"Neyland, as a coach, looked for answers. When he found them, he stuck with them more than any coach I have known. His staff meetings were liberal. Ideas and all details of the day's coaching assignments were carefully gone over. His attention to detail and consistency of performance by his team had more influence on college football than any other coach," Woodruff once wrote in a tribute to Neyland.

"I think General Neyland, more than any other man, helped to put Southern football at the top of the heap during his illustrious coaching career," Woodruff added. "Neyland-coached teams always went on the field with one thought in mind, TO WIN. He was conservative — his teams played for the breaks — and they did a remarkable job of carrying out his teaching of never giving the other side an easy touchdown.

"Intelligence, teamwork, loyalty, military training all played their part in and characterized Neyland-coached teams."

HE BROUGHT OUT THE BEST They called him "The Bull" behind his back, and it's true that his players sometimes didn't know how to take him.

Respect him, yes, but former Neyland quarterback Bobby Dodd told the '75 Tennessee team, "I didn't love Coach Neyland. He didn't love me. But, brother, I respected him. He knew football. He was a genius. The opportunity to play under Neyland has affected my entire life."

One of Dodd's greatest coaching thrills came in 1949 when his Georgia Tech team bested Neyland's Vols 30-

Sideline Generals Neyland Produced

Name (Final UT Season), Team(s) coached

Bill Barnes (1939), UCLA; John Barnhill (1927), Tennessee, Arkansas; Quinn Decker (1930), Centre, The Citadel; Phil Dickens (1936), Wofford, Wyoming, Indiana; Bobby Dodd (1930), Georgia Tech; Hooper Eblen (1935), Tennessee Tech; Beattie Feathers (1933), N.C. State; Ray Graves (1941), Florida; Ralph Hatley (1934), Memphis State; Herman Hickman (1931), Yale; Allyn McKeen (1927), Mississippi State; Gene McEver (1931), North Carolina; Bill Meek (1942), Kansas St., Houston, SMU; Jim Myers (1946), Iowa State, Texas A&M; Harvey Robinson (1932), Tennessee; Clayton Stapleton (1947), Iowa State; Murray Warmath (1934), Mississippi State, Minnesota; DeWitt Weaver (1936), Texas Tech; Bob Woodruff (1938), Baylor, Florida; Bowden Wyatt (1938), Wyoming, Arkansas, Tennessee

16. Which team was the opponent in UT's first night game at Neyland Stadium?

13. After the season, he gave his lettermen watches with the score of the game engraved on the back.

When Amos (Skeet) Horner, a Vol fullback in 1929, received an invitation to a 1953 testimonial dinner for Neyland, he immediately went on a strict diet. When asked by his wife why, Horner responded, "I'm 30 pounds over my playing weight. I'm not going to let Coach see me like this."

And then there was the story former Vol Bob Woodruff loved to tell about Murray Warmath, another ex-Vol. The two were watching a Tennessee bowl practice when they spied Neyland coming their way. Warmath had just lit a cigar, which he promptly tossed away.

"Why do that?" Woodruff said. "He's not your boss anymore."

PROFILE: BOBBY DODD (1928-30)

Where did Bobby Dodd contribute the most: Tennessee as a player or Georgia Tech where he coached for 45 years? The answer probably depends on which side of the Tennessee-Georgia border one lives.

Tennessee fans, where Dodd is concerned, are most thankful for Peabody College.

Peabody?

About the only college coach to express an interest in Dodd, a Georgia native, was Vanderbilt's Dan McGugin. Most schools were more interested in Dodd's best friend, a muscular youngster named Paul Hug. But McGugin, so Dodd later explained, wanted Dodd to enroll at Peabody for a year (to bolster his academic standing) and then transfer to Vanderbilt.

Dodd and Hug, who wanted to play together, considered enrolling at Mercer University. They were in a dilemma and wound up at the home of Dodd's brother, who called Capt. Robert Neyland at Tennessee.

As the story goes, Neyland wasn't real happy about Dodd taking Hug, whom he coveted, to Vanderbilt and his terse reply was "Tell 'em to be here in 24 hours and I'll take 'em both."

Hug was an All-Southern end, Dodd, an All-American quarterback. Dodd was a whale of an athlete, earning three letters each in football and basketball, two in baseball and one in track.

Though Neyland and Dodd didn't always see eye-to-eye, UT's coaching legend was rather lavish — at least for Neyland — in his praise of the quarterback who directed Tennessee teams to a 27-1-2 record (1928-30), the only losing coming at the hands of Alabama (18-6) in 1930.

"He had as much poise as any player I ever saw, and he was a genius at calling the one single play that would fit the time of game, position on the field and the score. He unerringly played his hunches," Neyland later said.

Dodd went from Tennessee to Georgia Tech where he served as the Yellow Jackets' coach and/or athletic director for 45 years.

By now a General (U.S. Army, retired), Robert R. Neyland watches from the sidelines with All-American Hank Lauricella.

"I know that," Warmath responded, "but I'm not sure he knows it."

After he gave up the head coaching job, though, Neyland once said, "I might get closer to the players — relax some of my strongest rules on discipline."

HIS PRINCIPLES Neyland always told his team, "Never underestimate an opponent."

But there were other ideals that became very much a part of Tennessee football, both during Neyland's tenure and thereafter:

"One good blocker is worth three ball carriers.

"The kicking game rules.

"Seventy-five percent of football is above the neck.

"No good blocker or tackler was ever left off a Tennessee team.

"No offensive play should be used in a game until it has been rehearsed 500 times.

"There are more ways to score on defense (pass interception. blocked kick, fumble recovery, kick return) than on offense (run, pass, kick.)"

FIRST SPEECH On his first day as UT's head coach — Labor Day, 1926 — Neyland greeted the 25 football candidates. "Men," he said, "we will practice two and one-half hours each day. That's all. Each practice will be organized. We will know what we want to accomplish each day, and we will work full speed. Any questions? Let's go."

And go they did.

The Vols kicked but one field goal in the national championship season of 1951. It came against Tennessee Tech on a first-down play and was kicked by Oaka Williams, a little-used sophomore end from Bluefield, W.Va., who is not listed among the Vol lettermen. Neyland's teams only kicked 14 field goals during his entire head coaching tenure.

The Glory Begins

There was plenty of work to be done before General Robert R. Neyland greeted his first team in 1926. But Neyland had a firsthand look at the situation in 1925, as an assistant to M. Beal Banks. Neyland and Bunny Oaks, another assistant, had taken over when Banks fell ill.

Though only $55.85 remained in the budget from 1925, it was Neyland's hope to upgrade the assistant coaches, the playing field, the equipment and to expand seating capacity at Shields-Watkins Field to 6,800.

He accomplished more than simply upgrading Tennessee's facilities.

Neyland Stadium as it looked in 1935 when it was known only as Shields-Watkins Field. It received the Neyland name in 1962.

TENNESSEE TRIUMVIRATE It is a nickname, along with the "Three Musketeers," pegged on Neyland and the first two assistants he hired, two former Army teammates: Paul B. Parker and William H. Britton.

Parker, a former Army tackle, coached the line and

Robert R. Neyland, by now a U.S. Army major, is flanked by his first two assistants (both former Army teammates) — Paul B. Parker (left) and William H. Britton.

often served as Neyland's disciplinarian. Britton, who played end at Army, coached receivers and backs, but perhaps more importantly served Neyland as the soother of ruffled feathers and the recruiter.

THE START After spending three weeks on conditioning in the fall of 1926, Neyland put his troops on the field and UT posted a 13-0 victory against Carson-Newman. It was Allyn McKeen, who went on to coach at Mississippi State, who scored the first touchdown of the Neyland era, but it was Jimmy Elmore, scoring on a 95-yard run, who got the glory of that first victory.

Later in the year, Elmore would run for more than 200 yards in a 34-0 win against North Carolina.

The Vols went on to post an 8-1 record (losing only to Vanderbilt, 20-3) behind the likes of Elmore, McKee, Roy Witt, John Barnhill, Farmer Johnson and Dick "First

VOLUNTEER QUIZ

17. Who holds the record for the longest kickoff return in UT history?

CHARTING NEYLAND'S CAREER

1st win vs. Carson-Newman (13-0), Sept. 25, 1926
10th win vs. North Carolina (26-0), Oct. 1, 1927
20th win vs. Alabama (15-13), Oct. 20, 1928
25th win vs. Florida (13-12), Dec. 8, 1928
50th win vs. Carson-Newman (31-0), Nov. 7, 1931
75th win vs. Kentucky (7-6), Nov. 26, 1936
100th win vs. N.C. State (13-0), Sept. 29, 1939
125th win vs. Mississippi (18-14), Nov. 9, 1946
150th win vs. North Carolina (16-0), Nov. 4, 1950
Final win (173rd) vs. Vandy (46-0), Nov. 29, 1952

Down" Dodson. Barnhill and Johnson would later become UT assistants and Barnhill would spend four seasons as UT's head coach while Neyland was serving in Burma during World War II.

Though he reached All-American status at Tennessee under Gen. Neyland, Bobby Dodd made an even larger mark as a head coach at Georgia Tech.

Herman Hickman, the All-American guard who played at Tennessee from 1929-31, was at one time a professional wrestler. That was long before he became coach at Yale.

CHANGING AT HALFTIME Neyland's team seemed to have grown not only physically but also in confidence, and the Vols rolled to a 6-0 start in 1927. But against Sewanee, which already was losing its grip as Southern football's king, the Vols found themselves down at halftime, primarily because three players had not dressed for the game because Neyland thought UT could win easily. They changed into their football togs at halftime, went into the game and UT won going away.

TIDE CHALLENGED After two years of serious construction, Neyland was ready for Tennessee to move onward and upward. He chose Alabama, under Wallace Wade, as the next power that the Volunteers would challenge.

Wade had taken Alabama to back-to-back Rose Bowl wins in 1925 and '26. Neyland, who would later gain a reputation for avoiding gamesmanship, walked up to Wade and told him the game would likely be a rout. He asked Wade to cut the time of the third and fourth quarters, which Wade agreed to do if the score merited.

But Gene McEver, the "Wild Bull," ran back the opening kickoff 98 yards, and Tennessee won 15-13 — ending the debate on which echelon the Volunteers belonged.

It was the birth of the "Flaming Sophomores," a group led by McEver, UT's first All-American; Bobby Dodd, who later went on to coaching greatness at Georgia Tech; Quinn Decker, the strong blocking back; and Buddy Hackman, the "Hack" in the famed "Hack & Mack'" duo with McEver. That group went undefeated through '27, '28 and '29, posting a 26-0-3 record (tying Vandy 7-7 in 1927, Kentucky 0-0 in 1928 and Kentucky 6-6 in 1929). The streak reached 30 games without a loss before Bama, in Tuscaloosa, posted an 18-6 triumph in 1930.

TWO TIMES 100 It was during the 57-0 victory against Transylvania in 1927 that Tennessee had its first recorded set of backs to rush for 100 or more yards. Vincent Tudor, with individual touchdown runs of 93 and 73 yards, finished with 198 yards and Jimmy Elmore added 114. The Vols almost had three in the game — Dodson, who rushed for four touchdowns, finished with 98 yards.

BULLISH Besides the "Wild Bull," Gene McEver was also referred to as the "Black Knight of Bristol." He had

PROFILE: GENE M^cEVER (1928-31)

He might have been the best thing to hit the University of Tennessee football team since sliced bread.

"The Wild Bull," they called him; "The Black Knight of Bristol."

He was the scourge of the South, perhaps the greatest football player ever under Gen. Robert R. Neyland. He set oodles of scoring records and one year led all of college football. His "dipsy-do" move, as he often called it, left more than one defender waving in the wind.

But Gene McEver was ever so close to being a Deacon. He was on the campus at Wake Forest when he changed his mind.

In an interview with Marvin West of the *Knoxville News-Sentinel*, McEver told how he got from Bristol to Wake Forest to the University of Tennessee.

"All those boys always thought I got paid more than they did," said McEver, who had often joked previously about getting $75 a month. "One of the Tennessee coaches came over to the Wake Forest-North Carolina game. I bumped into him. I found out later that's why he came.

"The coach had a $1,000 check in his hand. I took it. That was 1928. A thousand dollars was a lot of money."

Though there were many outstanding afternoons for McEver, the one he remembers most fondly is the Alabama game in October 1928 in Tuscaloosa. It was at that game that McEver ran back the opening kickoff 98 yards for a touchdown and Tennessee beat the touted Crimson Tide team, 15-13.

It was also a game, McEver told West, in which Neyland showed his expertise at pushing the buttons of his players.

"We got to the motel, I don't remember the name, and Neyland locked us in our rooms. He told us to think football, to think about beating Alabama. He let us out for dinner and then locked us in our rooms again. When it was time to play, he just let us out. That's how you beat Alabama."

McEver sat out the 1930 season with a knee injury sustained while playing baseball, but he returned in '31 with a heavy steel brace and, sharing the spotlight with Beattie Feathers, led Tennessee to a 9-0-1 record.

McEver was the first Tennessee player to be named to an All-America team, and he was the first Volunteer inducted into the College Football Hall of Fame (1954).

Gene McEver, "The Black Knight of Bristol," was originally headed to Wake Forest. He was on the campus there when he changed his mind and decided to attend Tennessee.

superb seasons in 1928 and 1929, rolling up four 100-yard efforts in '28 despite being a marked man. He opened '29 by returning the season's first kickoff 90 yards and subsequently turned in three-touchdown efforts against Centre, Washington & Lee and Auburn; a four-touchdown effort against Ole Miss; and a five-score afternoon against South Carolina. The "other" part of the celebrated "Hack & Mack" duo, Buddy Hackman, had a 205-yard rushing effort in the 54-0 shutout of South Carolina.

Buddy Hackman teamed with Gene McEver to form the "Hack & Mack" duo in 1928-30.

IN DODD WE TRUST Gene McEver sat out 1930 with a knee injury, opening the door for Bobby Dodd, whose first touchdown came on a 43-yard pass to Buddy Hackman. It was Dodd's only touchdown that year, but he did score on eight point-after attempts and fans came to cheer "In Dodd We Trust" in years to come.

THE FIRST TANDEM Tennessee has boasted some good backs over the years. One of the first tandems was the 1931 backfield featuring Gene McEver and Beattie Feathers, who scored 103 points between them. For those who keep up with such things, Feathers' first 100-yard game as a Vol was a 141-yard effort against Mississippi.

Beattie Feathers was voted the SEC's first Player of the Year (1933) and was inducted into the College Football Hall of Fame in 1955. As a Chicago Bear and teammate of the famous Bronko Nagurski, Feathers (in his rookie season) became the first NFL player to rush for 1,000 yards. He served as head coach at N.C. State from 1944-51.

PROFILE: BEATTIE FEATHERS (1931-33)

The two-sport antics of Deion Sanders would've been like old hat to Beattie Feathers, an All-American at Tennessee in 1933 and a 1955 inductee for the College Football Hall of Fame.

Feathers, who endeared himself to UT fans in the early '30s, was a powerful, even punishing runner who averaged a touchdown per game in his 33 contests in the orange and white. He was Player of the Year in 1933, the first year of operation for the Southeastern Conference.

But Feathers, who played four years with the Chicago Bears, also played professional baseball, although an arm injury cut short his stay with the Cincinnati Reds.

He continued to play pro football in the fall and baseball in the spring and summer (with the Knoxville Smokies).

Though his 198 points remain a Top 10 figure among Vol scorers, Feathers wrote himself into the NFL record books in a way that will never be forgotten. He was the first 1,000-yard rusher in NFL history, and he averaged 9.9 yards per carry in one of his six pro seasons.

Feathers coached at Appalachian State, North Carolina State, Texas Tech and Wake Forest, taking N.C. State to the Gator Bowl against Oklahoma.

He died March 10, 1977, in Winston-Salem, N.C.

HITTING THE SKIDS Well, they didn't exactly hit the skids, but the Vols, who hadn't lost three games in a season since that abysmal 3-5 season of 1924, were 7-3 in 1933 and 8-2 in 1934 as the nation sought to pull itself from the throes of the Depression.

When Neyland was called back to active duty in 1935, Bill Britton took over for a year and the Volunteers suffered their first losing season in more than a decade, finishing 4-5 with shutout losses against Alabama and Kentucky and a 13-7 defeat by Vanderbilt.

RECONSTRUCTION Though Neyland, by the standards he had set, struggled in 1936 and '37 (the Vols were a combined 12-5-3), he was merely setting the table for another incredible run that included three straight years of double-digit victories.

In 1938, the Vols went 11-0 and were named national champions by Litkenhouse and Dunkel. They went 10-1 in '39 and took the SEC championship. In '40, UT went 10-1 while winning its third straight conference crown and receiving national champion proclamations from Dunkel and Williamson services.

Seniors on the 1938 team included Joe Little, Bowden Wyatt, Cheek Duncan and Bob Woodruff. There were two juniors, George Cafego and Jimmy Rike, and a large

Bill Britton, originally brought to Tennessee as a football assistant by Neyland, also served as the Vols' head basketball coach from 1927-35 and as the football team's interim head coach in 1935.

Departing for the 1939 Orange Bowl after a 10-0 season in 1938 are, from left, Abe Shires, Bob Suffridge, Bowden Wyatt, George Cafego and Babe Wood.

VOLUNTEER QUIZ

18. Who holds the record for the longest punt return in UT history?

group of sophomores that included Bob Andridge, Jimmy Coleman, Ed Molinski, Bob Suffridge, Ed Cifers, Abe Shires and Bob Foxx. The team surrendered 16 points all season, Wyatt and Suffridge made All-America teams and Cafego was about to help put the Orange Bowl on the map by taking his Vols to Miami to play Oklahoma.

Tennessee thumped Oklahoma, 17-0, with Cafego setting the stage by knocking Oklahoma All-American end Waddy Young for a flip early in the game.

But before UT played the game, several of the Vols went deep-sea fishing, a day legendary trainer Mickey O'Brien never forgot. Seems Boyd Clay got rather sick on the way out and begged O'Brien for help. But Foxx made sure O'Brien knew how Clay felt, eating a can of sardines under O'Brien's nose and causing him to join Clay at the rail.

The 1939 season was the year of Johnny Butler's snaking 56-yard touchdown run against Alabama, a run described and re-described as one of the most outstanding plays in college football annals. It also was the year of the first Rose Bowl trip, one that resulted in a 14-0 loss to Southern Cal but also provided UT with a $100,000 payout.

It should be noted that this second group of "flaming sophomores" was a most spirited, unbridled group —

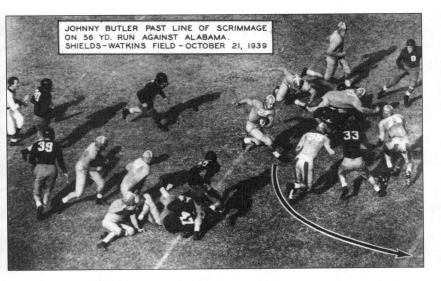

JOHNNY BUTLER PAST LINE OF SCRIMMAGE ON 56 YD. RUN AGAINST ALABAMA. SHIELDS-WATKINS FIELD - OCTOBER 21, 1939

one that Neyland had to rein in hard on more than one occasion. Leonard Coffman took off for home one weekend without permission and Neyland asked him how far it was. The youngster got a lap for each of the 72 miles from his home in Greeneville, Tenn.

Neyland was called back to active duty when war broke out in 1941.

Johnny Butler's 56-yard run against Alabama is still considered one of the finest broken-field efforts in UT history.

ANOTHER MASTER During Neyland's World War II service, the Vols called upon one of his former players, John Barnhill, to take the Tennessee reins. All he did was post the best winning percentage by a UT football coach (.846) and a four-year record of 32-5-2.

Three of the five losses and one of the ties came against Alabama. Another defeat came against Duke and another to Southern California in the 1994 Rose Bowl. The second tie came in the '45 season-opener at South Carolina.

When Neyland returned prior to the 1946 season, Barnhill went to Arkansas as head coach, posting a record of 54-22-5.

RAZORBACK TIES Later serving as the Razorbacks' athletic director, John Barnhill is credited with establishing the Tennessee-Arkansas connection. Barnhill hired former Vol Bowden Wyatt away from Wyoming in 1953. Wyatt was hired away from Barnhill and Arkansas in '55, so Barnhill hired Frank Broyles off the Georgia Tech staff of former Vol Bobby Dodd.

Broyles then hired former Florida quarterback Doug Dickey at Arkansas, and he was then replaced by ex-Vol

George "Bad News" Cafego starred for the Vols in 1937-39 and he served UT for 29 years as an assistant coach, working under former teammate Bowden Wyatt, Jim McDonald, Doug Dickey, Bill Battle and Johnny Majors.

John Barnhill, who played for Neyland from 1925-27, filled in for Neyland from 1941-45. It was a four-year term on the field because the Vols fielded no team in '43. He posted a record of 32-5-2 and the best winning percentage (.846) by a Vol football coach.

Al Rotella played at UT in 1942 and 1946-47, later coaching on both the collegiate and high school levels. His son, Jamie, played for the Vols from 1970-72, serving as captain his senior season.

Johnny Majors. Dickey, of course, then moved to UT as head coach (1964-69) and Majors coached the Vols from 1977-92. But it doesn't end there — former Arkansas head coach Ken Hatfield played at Fayetteville when Majors and Dickey were there as assistants and later served as an assistant on Dickey staffs at both Tennessee and Florida.

"Barney seldom went into detail about anything," Broyles later wrote in a tribute to Barnhill. "He could get his point across with a couple of old Tennessee sayings and start you thinking in the right direction."

THE MAN IS BACK Neyland returned from World War II in time for the 1946 season. As he had in 1936, Neyland immediately began setting the table for another long run, although by now rule makers had instituted liberal substitution rules that allowed for offensive and defensive squads and OK'd the T-formation.

These new rules were burrs under the saddle of Neyland, who had fought off all suggestions of change when he was a member of the national rules committee before the war.

The 1946 team went 9-2, winning the SEC championship behind a flock of boys just home from the war — Al Rotella, Al Russas, Jim Powell, Dick Huffman, Ray Drost, Bud Hubbell, Mark Major and

Denver Crawford. UT finished the year with an 8-0 loss to Rice in the Orange Bowl.

The Vols struggled in '47 and '48 with records of 5-5 and 4-4-2 (the closest he ever came to losing seasons as the UT coach). Opposing coaches reveled in the "downfall" and critics questioned Neyland's refusal to scrap the single-wing in favor of the "T".

A major victory for Neyland came in 1947, however, as Tennessee fought off Bobby Dodd's Georgia Tech team 13-6 in Atlanta. Though Dodd finally got his win over his old mentor the following season, Tennessee had regrouped enough under the "ol' man" to put together Neyland's 15th winning season.

But by now he'd had time to reload and accept the fact that two-platoon football was a way of life in collegiate circles.

STUBBORN BUT SMART Though Neyland wouldn't exactly give in to two-platoon football in a conventional sense — offensive and defensive units — he went to two-platoon units, as in first unit for one quarter and second unit for the second quarter.

And he made it work, beating his critics at their own game. UT reeled off a 29-4-1 record from 1950-52 after going 7-2-1 in '49.

In 1950 the team posted an 11-1 record and gained a

A football and basketball player at UT, Doug Atkins was an All-SEC and All-America pick at defensive end and tackle. He is in both the College and Professional Football Halls of Fame.

Jim Haslam was an outstanding tackle for Neyland and served the General as team captain in 1952. Haslam is now a member of UT's board of trustees.

national championship ranking from the Dunkel Ratings.

And then came 1951 — the SEC and consensus national championship season.

In assessing the group's chances, Neyland wrote, "Our 1951 team will be far below the average in weight, much smaller than most teams we will meet.

"Last year's team went far beyond expectations, and the big factors were spirit and incentive. Having gone through a successful season last year and having played in the Cotton Bowl and won, that fine edge of ambition is certain to be dulled."

Neyland pointed out the losses of halfbacks Bud Sherrill and Jimmy Hill, safety W.C. Cooper, defensive end Bud Sherrod and tackle Ray Smith.

"Sophomores and freshmen will have to fill those critical spots," he said. "The very achievement of our success last season will make the 1951 season immeasurably more difficult. Last year's team was the underdog in key games against Duke, Alabama, and Texas in the Cotton Bowl. That position always carries with it a certain definite psychological advantage."

So he went to working his magic.

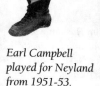

Earl Campbell played for Neyland from 1951-53.

Hank Lauricella set records from 1949-51 that stood for decades, and his 7.9 per-rush average in 1951 still stands as the best single-season standard.

CONSERVATIVE? Because Neyland was considered a conservative, it's ironic that the magic of the 1951 season began with a pass. The Vols' first score came on a 17-yard pass from Hank Lauricella to Vince Kaseta, followed by a Bert Rechichar extra point.

The Vols scored again in the first quarter after Gene Moeller, who serves UT today as assistant athletic director for operations, fell on a punt that had been blocked by All-American Ted Daffer. Andy Kozar, now Dr. Andy Kozar and a member of the UT faculty, then scored on a 2-yard run. Rechichar's second PAT was the end of the scoring as the Vols returned to their more conservative mode for the final three quarters of a 14-0 win over Mississippi State.

Another shutout (26-0 against Duke) followed, and then Chattanooga fell, 42-13, behind Kozar, Lauricella, Vic Kolenik, Jimmy Wade and Herky Payne, who led UT in scoring for the year with 15 touchdowns.

It set the stage for the Birmingham battle with Alabama, where UT rallied from a 7-0 deficit for a 27-13 victory behind Rechichar, Dick Ernsberger and Lauricella, who threw a first-half scoring pass to Rechichar and then scored on a 35-yard run early in the fourth quarter.

PROFILE: HANK LAURICELLA (1949-51)

He never caught a pass for the University of Tennessee, but it's the one offensive category at which Hank Lauricella never excelled. Had he not been throwing the ball, chances are that Lauricella, a unanimous All-America choice and Southeastern Conference MVP in 1951, would've caught a bunch.

In his three years Tennessee went 28-4-1, tying for the conference championship and winning the national championship in 1951. And his 7.9 yards-per-carry average in '51 still stands as a single-season record.

It was on New Year's Day of 1948 that Lauricella had his first contact with Gen. Robert Neyland, who was in town for the Sugar Bowl. After a visit to Knoxville, Lauricella fell in love with UT and the hills of East Tennessee and signed with the Volunteers.

There were others who could run better and others who could pass better, but none who could do both as well as the 5-foot-10, 165-pounder, who ran for 1,463 yards and 13 touchdowns and passed for 1,105 yards and 16 touchdowns during his three varsity years. He also punted, averaging 36.5 yards, and averaged 20.1 yards on kickoff returns and 11.6 yards on punt returns.

Lauricella, a Louisiana native, served in the state legislature for 17 years and in the Louisiana state senate for several more terms.

A runner-up in 1951 Heisman balloting, Lauricella was elected to the College Football Hall of Fame in 1981.

On a roll, Tennessee put together back-to-back shutouts over Tennessee Tech (68-0) and North Carolina (27-0) before allowing a pair of scores in a 60-14 victory over Washington & Lee. The Vols, by the time W&L scored in the second period, were up 35-0.

They were ahead 25-14 at Ole Miss the following week before burying the Rebels with a 21-point fourth-quarter splurge. Payne scored three touchdowns, Kozar two.

The team followed with a 28-0 whitewashing of Kentucky, its fifth shutout of the year, then nailed down a 35-27 win against Vanderbilt when Kozar scored with five seconds left in the game.

A consensus two-time All-American defensive lineman, Ted Daffer starred in Neyland's six-man front in 1949-51.

Good, Bad & Ugly

VOLUNTEER QUIZ

19. Who holds the UT record for most interceptions in a game?

Harvey Robinson never wanted the Tennessee coaching job. He thought that when Gen. Robert Neyland asked him to take over the team for the 1952 Cotton Bowl game against Texas that Neyland, who'd been sick during much of the '52 season, would resume control in '53.

It wasn't to be. After a split vote among athletic board members came out in Robinson's favor, the Neyland student was officially named UT's coach in February of 1953.

"I didn't ask for the job. I didn't want to be head coach. I accepted because the General asked me to do so," Robinson later told Knoxville sportswriter Ed Harris.

But Robinson's hands were tied in that he was never allowed to select his assistant coaches or institute his own ideas. Also, NCAA rules had reverted to single-platoon football — at the suggestion of an NCAA committee headed by Neyland — so Robinson was saddled with teaching one-way players the ins and outs of the other side of the ball.

UT football fell rather quickly on hard times. Robinson's '53 team went 6-4-1, the worst effort by a UT

Harvey Robinson, who succeeded Neyland and spent two years as Tennessee's coach, played for Neyland's varsity teams in 1931-32.

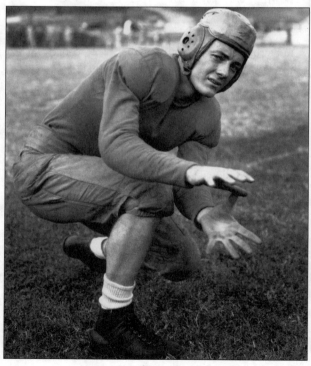

squad since 1948. His '54 team went 4-6, the first losing record in Knoxville since Bill Britton filled in for Neyland in 1935.

PAYBACKS Oddly, it was an old teammate who greeted Robinson in his first game as the Vol skipper in 1953. Murray Warmath, a member of Neyland's staff just two years before, had moved to Mississippi State and appeared to have a pretty fair team — headed by Jackie Parker, a youngster who'd played high school ball at Young High in Knoxville.

Warmath wanted to win, sure, but not nearly as much as Parker, who'd been overlooked by UT recruiters. Later an All-American for the Bulldogs, Parker passed for one touchdown, scored two more, kicked two extra points and made six tackles.

Mississippi State won, 26-0, and UT fell to 0-2 after a 21-7 loss to Duke — the first back-to-back losses since defeats from North Carolina and Mississippi in '47. Chattanooga was next, and Robinson got his first victory when Tommy Priest carried the ball twice and scored two touchdowns in a 40-7 victory.

The team had promise and showed it by beating the odds and gaining a tie with highly-touted Alabama the next week. The Vols almost pulled out a victory late when Bama quarterback Bart Starr was sacked inside his own 1-yard line.

The Vols moved back to .500 the next week by making another future NFL star, Louisville's Johnny Unitas, miserable in a 59-6 thrashing. They followed up by dropping North Carolina and then pulling out a win against Florida on a 20-yard field goal by Pat Shires. But the team lost its final two games, to Kentucky (Paul Bryant's first win over Tennessee) and to Houston.

The '54 season was worse — the worst in 30 years — and it ended on a very low note: A 26-0 shutout at the hands of Vanderbilt.

BACK HOME There might have been differences between Robinson and Neyland, in his first years solely as UT's athletic director, but they were never made public. Though Neyland would later tell friends Robinson's dismissal after the 1954 season was "The toughest thing I ever had to do. In fact I didn't know how to do it." Robinson learned of his firing only after picking up a copy of *The Knoxville Journal*.

Neyland also dismissed Robinson's entire staff, many of whom had coached under Neyland. But Robinson went to Florida as an assistant to Woodruff and returned to Knoxville six years later to work as an assistant under the man who replaced him as head coach.

Ray Martin holds the record for long returns with a pass interception. He ran 100 yards with a theft against Louisville in 1953. The longest non-scoring interception return in UT history was 74 yards by Eddie Brown against Kansas in 1973.

Former Vol player and coach Bowden Wyatt once had a chance to become an actor. While attending the Vols' Rose Bowl game against Southern Cal, Wyatt was interviewed by several Hollywood moguls.

Bowden Wyatt (right) takes part in Sugar Bowl pregame festivities after directing Tennessee to a 10-0 regular-season finish. It was the first two bowl games a Vol team coached by Wyatt would reach.

JOB ALREADY FILLED Though it has never been substantiated, many UT football-following veterans believe that Neyland had already talked to ex-Vol Bowden Wyatt about "coming home."

Wyatt had won the Skyline Conference championship at Wyoming, then the Southwest Conference championship after being hired by another former Vol, John Barnhill, at Arkansas. The time was right.

PROFILE: GEORGE CAFEGO

There are at least two ways that Tennessee fans should remember George Cafego.

Yes, he was an oustanding tailback for Neyland from 1938-39, but Cafego also was a key member of the staffs of five Tennessee coaches, including that of Johnny Majors, whom he had coached in the mid-'50s.

Cafego, a native of Whipple, W.Va., was a two-time All-American and a star and leader on the '38 team that brawled its way past Oklahoma in the 1939 Orange Bowl. He also played on the '39 team that went through the regular season unbeaten and unscored upon before losing to

Southern Cal in the 1940 Rose Bowl.

Cafego first began coaching at Furman, but he decided to join Bowden Wyatt at Wyoming and then Arkansas before "coming home" with Wyatt in 1955. He remained at UT until his retirement in the mid-'80s, but by that time he had worked under Wyatt, Jim McDonald, Doug Dickey, Bill Battle and Majors and had cast his shadow on UT's kicking game for years.

A member of the West Virginia and Tennessee Sports Halls of Fame, Cafego was inducted into the College Hall in 1969.

Johnny Majors (left) was runner-up in the 1956 Heisman Trophy balloting. A favorite target of Johnny Majors — and they made a splendid passing combination — was Buddy Cruze (right).

UP, UP AND DOWN Respectability returned immediately, with Coach Bowden Wyatt capitalizing on the talents of a skinny (5-foot-10, 162 pounds), triple-threat tailback by the name of John "Drum" Majors. The Vols went 6-3-1 as Majors — rushing for 657 yards, passing for 476 and averaging more than 48 yards per punt — was named the league's MVP. He had help, of course. Tommy Bronson, recognized along with Andy Kozar as one of the Vols' all-time top fullbacks, was there as was Majors' favorite passing target, Buddy Cruze.

But Wyatt's only real shining season came in 1956. Majors, the team's alternate captain, finished runner-up to Paul Hornung in Heisman Trophy balloting as Tennessee claimed Wyatt's only SEC championship with

Johnny Majors prepares to turn the corner in the Vols' 13-7 Sugar Bowl loss to Baylor — Tennessee's only loss of the 1956 season.

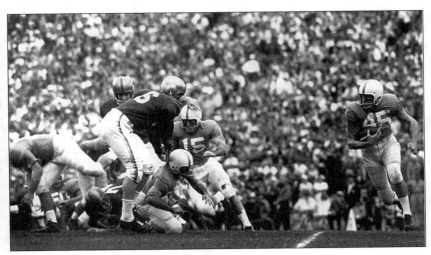

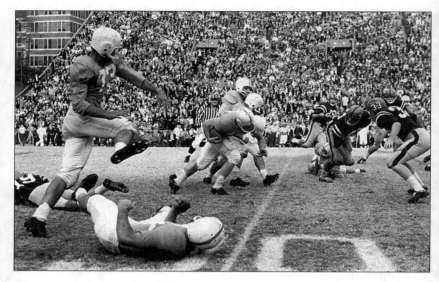

Glenn Glass takes off for some of his 958 yards total offense. He led the Vols in rushing in '59 and in passing in '60.

A near-scratch golfer, Bowden Wyatt loved the game and played at every opportunity during his head-coaching days at Wyoming and Arkansas. But heeding the advice of Robert Neyland, a man he loved dearly and respected deeply, Wyatt gave up the game when he returned to Tennessee in 1955. "because the General believes it consumes too much time and opens the door to criticism."

a 10-0 regular-season run that included early victories against Auburn, Alabama, Maryland, North Carolina, and then the monumental win over Georgia Tech before the closing sweep of Mississippi, Kentucky and Vanderbilt.

The team made it to the Sugar Bowl, losing to Baylor, 13-7, and followed up with an 8-3 record in 1957. The '57 squad was co-captained by Bill Johnson, now a member of UT's athletic board, and Bill Anderson, who became the sidekick for John Ward on the Vols' radio network.

But in the five ensuing seasons, Tennessee slid and won no more than six games in any of the five years.

Historians wonder if Wyatt hadn't been force-fed more than he could chew. When he returned to Tennessee as football coach, Wyatt also assumed most of Neyland's athletic director's duties. He won national Coach of the Year honors in '56, but he continued all of his chores plus traveling often to New Orleans to visit Neyland, who by then was critically ill.

There were highlights — the accomplishments of the '56 team, the '57 team's 3-0 Gator Bowl win over Bryant's Texas A&M team, the '59 team's upset win over LSU — and there were lowlights — the 10-0 loss to Florida State and the 14-6 setback against Chattanooga in 1958.

Neyland died in March of '62 and Wyatt carried on, but his heart might not have been in it. UT went 4-6 that season and Wyatt was allowed a year's leave of absence after reportedly slugging a fellow coach and "helping" a sportswriter into a swimming pool at the SEC's spring meetings in '63. Wyatt, by this time, already had been in a hospital in Virginia.

Wyatt never returned to coach at UT and never

returned to head coaching, although he did spend two seasons (1963-64) as an assistant at Oklahoma State.

Harris, who authored several books on Tennessee football, summed it up best when he wrote, "It is likely they buried the coaching spirits of Neyland and Wyatt in the single (grave of Neyland) at National Cemetery."

CHANGING OF THE GUARD

It wasn't until June 20, 1963, that Bowden Wyatt was officially "granted" the leave of absence, but UT President Dr. Andy Holt already had received a letter signed by more than a dozen UT players naming Jim McDonald as their choice if Wyatt were to be replaced.

Bob Woodruff, another Neyland disciple who was hired as athletic director in 1963, was another candidate.

But the athletic board had made it clear that athletic director and football coach should be separate jobs filled by different persons. So McDonald, a former Ohio State standout who had been with Wyatt at UT since '55, took the football job for 1963.

Jim McDonald unveiled the T-formation at Tennessee, though sparingly, in the Vols' 49-7 win against Chattanooga.

After Tennessee went 5-5 in 1963 — losing along the way 35-0 to a Bama team led by Joe Namath and shutting out Kentucky and Vanderbilt in the final two games to reach .500 — Woodruff went searching for another head coach. McDonald remained a member of the UT family as an assistant athletic director until 1981.

The choice, a Neyland disciple by way of Woodruff's coaching tenure at Florida, was Douglas Adair Dickey.

And Tennessee, which had finally introduced the T-formation (though briefly) under McDonald, was on the doorstep of another golden era.

Tennessee running back Mallon Faircloth led the Vols in rushing and passing in 1963, gaining 509 yards through the air and 652 on the ground.

Gator Returns Success

Doug Dickey had a Tennessee coaching record of 46-15-4.

In one of his first moves as UT head coach, Doug Dickey tried his best to get in touch with Vince Dooley about an assistant's job. But at the same time, Georgia Athletic Director Joel Eaves was also looking for Dooley, and found him first. Dooley went on to serve as Georgia's head coach for 25 years (1964-88).

Recruiting had suffered under Bowden Wyatt, specifically when Steve Sloan and Steve Spurrier, two highly-sought, in-state quarterback prospects, spurned the idea of a single-wing offense at UT for Alabama and Florida, respectively.

It was, therefore, the first duty of Doug Dickey to get the athletes back to Knoxville, and to employ an offense that would be attractive to high school talent.

PRESSURE ON WOODRUFF UT folks had grown used to winning, to ruling the roost rather than bumming a spot on an also-ran's perch, so the pressure was on new Athletic Director Bob Woodruff. The Volunteer fans had not enjoyed a Neyland-esque season since Bowden Wyatt took Tennessee to 10-1 and 8-3 campaigns in 1956 and 1957. As a matter of fact, UT had put together a six-year record (under Wyatt and Jim McDonald) of 30-25-3, a winning percentage (.543) well below Neyland's career standard of .829.

The house, so to speak, was divided on the direction Tennessee would take. Among serious contenders for the job was ex-Vol Murray Warmath, who had not exactly set the Big 10 on its ear at Minnesota. Roy Striegel finally stepped into the breech that had developed among his fellow athletic board members and suggested that Woodruff, a former Vol with head coach experience, find the university a coach.

At this point in Tennessee's football history, the intensity of the rivalry with Florida had not yet begun to simmer, much less boil over. There was, therefore, really no problem with ex-Gator head coach Woodruff, who had returned to Knoxville in '63 as athletic director, hiring someone other than a UT man as the Vols' head coach.

Woodruff, in recalling the reasons he went after Doug Dickey, said, "I knew Doug as a man of unusual intelligence, and you can't overestimate the value of brains. He was a self-made athlete who made himself into a football quarterback, basketball player and baseball pitcher."

The Neyland connection was there, Woodruff having played for the General and then later coaching Dickey at Florida.

And, of course, Dickey was hired away from Arkansas, which was coached by Frank Broyles, who had coached under Woodruff at Baylor but also had played quarterback at Georgia Tech for Bobby Dodd, another Neyland disciple.

Dickey, who spent six years at Arkansas, was the first of numerous Broyles assistants who Broyles recommended for head-coaching positions.

THE ATTRACTION When he was offered the job at Tennessee — Dickey was initially interviewed by UT trustee Col. Tom Elam — the young Arkansas assistant saw a program that had gone awry but not so far that it couldn't be repaired.

PROFILE: BOB JOHNSON (1965-67)

The first high school player Doug Dickey went to see after he became UT's head coach was Bob Johnson, and today Dickey calls Johnson his favorite player.

"If you drew up a football player on a blackboard, you'd probably come up with someone very much like Bob Johnson," Dickey said. "He was commanding physically, he was dignified as a leader and he was a quality student."

Bob Johnson combined brawn — he was 6-4 and weighed 240 pounds — with brains. He was an All-American and a member of the Academic All-America team and was recognized by the National Football Foundation as a scholar-athlete.

"Bob was always the first on the field and the last to leave," assistant coach Ray Trail wrote in the 1969 UT media guide. "He was blessed with an exceptionally quick mind and read defenses as well as any lineman I have known. He could anticipate exactly what was going to happen after the snap of the ball. His presence virtually gave us a coach on the field."

Johnson, from Cleveland, Tenn., was the first of three brothers to play center at the University of Tennessee, and with the exception of two years, the Vols' center position was filled by one of them for 11 seasons. Bob played 1965-67, Tom 1970-72 and Paul 1973-75.

Bob went on to become captain of the Cincinnati Bengals — he was the first player the Bengals selected in the '68 NFL draft — and is now a member of the National Football Foundation's College Football Hall of Fame. His No. 54 jersey was retired by the Bengals in 1978.

All-American center Bob Johnson was the first player ever drafted by the Cincinnati Bengals.

VOLUNTEER QUIZ

20. Who did UT play in its first televised game and where?

In his first game as UT's quarterback (against Mississippi State, 1964), Art Galiffa called the ancient Statue of Liberty play, allowing Hal Wantland to score on a 14-yard run.

"I looked at Tennessee as a place that had gotten out of sync with its traditions. It had a tradition of great winning success," Dickey said. "You know, I played (for Florida) in '52. They had a national championship team here in '51. Neyland had been here.

"Times had become bad. I know Wyatt had some problem years. I knew he'd had some success but that personal problems were probably affecting the program, and the program was not that far off to get it going again.

"This was a place that could recapture its esteem. That had a lot of magic to me."

Then, too, there was the attraction of serving as head coach under a man who had been his college coach. "I knew Coach Woodruff was here. I knew him, trusted him. I thought he had good judgment about the way things should be run. With his prowess and the long-time tradition, I thought I could do it again in a more modern way."

FIRST WAS WORST His initial season was the only losing season Dickey endured at Tennessee, turning in a 4-5-1 record that began with a 10-6 victory against Chattanooga. That 1964 team won three of its first four, losing only to Auburn, 3-0. The Vols got to 4-2-1 before losing their last three, two by shutout to Ole Miss and Vanderbilt.

IT WAS TRANSITION The single-wing formation and Tennessee football were synonymous for all those many years, and it might have been the move away from the single-wing to the T-formation that caused the problems.

"The transition (from the single-wing) was going to be an opportunity rather than a problem," Dickey recalled. "This was an opportunity if one applied his working principles and had the right kind of folks around him."

WHY THE "T"? Recruiting, purely and simply. The Vols couldn't even get the top athletes in their own state to stay at home, much less top athletes in surrounding states, without switching to the T-formation.

The single-wing, though quite effective, was not an exciting type of offense and many prospective players already were coming out of high school programs that had specialized in the T-formation.

"Players didn't want to play in the single-wing. The 'T' was easier on mixing running and passing plays and the ratio, which now is probably 50-50, was about 2-to-1. Option plays were threatening defenses. We needed an option package, and it allowed for versatility in recruiting," Dickey said.

What Dickey was looking for in recruiting were

VOLUNTEER QUIZ

21. What team gained the fewest yards ever against UT?

quality athletes more than just position players.

"If you had a Bobby Scott, you could throw more, but if you had a Charlie Fulton, you maybe did a little more running," Dickey said. "We recruited a lot of athletes who played all over the field. The quality of the athlete and the speed of the team came up.

"You just couldn't recruit enough speed on the single-wing level."

THAT FIRST YEAR Jim McDonald, Dickey's predecessor, and Athletic Director Bob Woodruff had undertaken a state-wide campaign to bolster declining support in the program. But the idea, while good, needed something on which to grow. It was a return to winning, obviously, which would come with the new offensive philosophies.

The Vols bolted to a 3-1 start, the three wins coming by a total of seven points and the shutout loss to Auburn on a field goal.

Those who felt good about UT's 3-1 beginning felt even better about the Volunteers' returning to glory after a loss to Alabama the next week. The Crimson Tide was on a national championship run, alternating quarterbacks Joe Namath and Steve Sloan, but the Tide was forced to reach down deep to pull out a 19-8 victory.

The next week, the Vols got a break thanks to the television networks. UT was scheduled to play LSU at rowdy Tiger Stadium in a night contest. Anybody who

Defensive end Jim McDonald lost his starting job when he missed much of the 1966 season with the mumps.

This defensive stand against LSU, which allowed UT to tie the Tigers, was an early return on the stout defensive units that Doug Dickey turned out.

Ron Widby was an outstanding punter and still ranks third on UT's all-time list with a career average of 42.3 yards.

has ever been to Baton Rouge on a football Saturday night knows the crowd is capable of making life miserable for visiting opponents.

But NBC wanted the game as a regional telecast, so the time was changed to the afternoon. Though it was a tremendous goal-line stand that halted LSU as UT pulled out a 3-3 tie, it also was the kicking game that kept the Vols in this one on a sunny Louisiana afternoon.

Ron Widby, who also made a name for himself in collegiate basketball and baseball circles, punted five times for a 52-yard average against LSU. Fred Martin, the difference earlier in the year at Mississippi State, kicked a field goal as the two teams played to a 3-3 deadlock.

But the game, UT's seventh television appearance, isn't remembered so much for the efforts from Widby and Martin, although the Vols picked up just 75 yards and six first downs.

No, it's remembered for the goal-line stand led by All-American Steve DeLong, who went on to win the Outland Trophy — awarded annually to the nation's top lineman.

The drive started at the UT 15-yard line and ended when the Vols repelled Tiger running back Rusty Schwab less than a foot from the Tennessee goal on a fourth-down attempt.

But UT fell upon hard times after an upset win over Georgia Tech the following week, losing to Ole Miss, Kentucky and Vandy. Though they had looked for offensive balance, the Vols threw only two touchdown passes — one each from Art Galiffa and David Leake, the latter a former walk-on who was named SEC Player of

David Leake led UT from a 14-3 deficit to a 22-14 win over Georgia Tech.

the Week for his fourth-quarter heroics in the win over Georgia Tech.

Hal Wantland, the third Vol to throw passes that year, was also the Vols' leading receiver (21 catches for 284 yards) and scorer (32 points). And the UT coaching braintrust began to shift from the T-formation to the I-formation.

THE STAGE SET Though his first effort left UT a victory shy of .500, Dickey had shown his platform to fans and followers, to opposing coaches and — most importantly — to promising high school athletes like Richmond Flowers, the two-sport specialist who would an integral part of the football offense and the Vols' blossoming track program.

Hal Wantland led the Vols in scoring in 1964.

BUCKLING DOWN Charlie Fulton, often referred to as a "knuckleball" runner by Dickey because of his darting style, opened the 1965 season in grand fashion. On his first pass attempt, he connected with Hal Wantland on a 22-yard touchdown, helping UT to a 21-0 victory against Army.

UT had not bested Shug Jordan's Auburn team since 1960 and many fans believed this was the year. But Auburn, thanks to two interceptions by defensive tackle Jack Thornton, rallied from a 13-6 deficit to a 13-13 tie despite two touchdown runs by Fulton.

Though Fulton tossed a touchdown strike to David Leake, the ex-quarterback, it was finally Walter Chadwick's day and the tailback scored twice to lock up a win over South Carolina and set the stage for a showdown with Alabama, which was in the process of making a national championship run.

Walter Chadwick had a running style all his own.

SETTING THE TONE The turning point in UT's game against Alabama might have come in the first half when Doug Archibald, a senior linebacker from Sarasota, Fla., blocked an Alabama field goal try. UT drew first blood by going 69 yards, the final 10 producing the touchdown on determined runs by fullback Stan Mitchell.

Alabama, which had run off four straight wins over UT, tied the score at 7-7 on the last play of the first half on a 1-yard keeper by quarterback Steve Sloan, the high school standout from Cleveland, Tenn., who had spurned the Vols primarily because of the single-wing offense.

With a 2-0-2 record, UT went on a tear in Dickey's second season, reeling off wins over Houston and Georgia Tech, losing to Ole Miss, but closing out with victories over Kentucky, Vanderbilt and UCLA.

Doug Archibald emerged as a force.

COACHES LOST The 1965 season was hardly under way

Bob Jones

Bill Majors

Charles Rash

when three of the Vol assistants — Bob Jones, Bill Majors and Charles Rash — died in an automobile-train wreck. They were on their way to work Monday morning after a 7-7 tie with Alabama.

"You just don't play for coaches, you learn to love and respect them," said Hal Wantland, the team's captain.

It was much to overcome, but Tennessee was bound for the Bluebonnet Bowl.

"SWAMP RAT" ARRIVES Tennessee was looking at a 6-1-2 record in '65. A berth in the Bluebonnet Bowl had been secured, but one final regular-season contest remained: Rose Bowl-bound UCLA in Memphis.

It was one of those games Dickey points to as significant during his tenure as the Vols' head coach. It was an offensive shootout that ended with UT on top, 37-34.

Bob Petrella's interception iced the 1965 victory against UCLA.

"It was one of the most exciting games I've ever been a part of … 37-34 in 1965 was something they played in the WAC (Western Athletic Conference). We played 17-14 games down here (in the South)," Dickey said. "But in this game all of a sudden, the ball's going up and down the field and we had enough ability to be in the mix. It taught me that you better be able to throw the ball."

Throw they did. The lead swapped hands six times when the Vol offense, led by Dewey Warren, the "Swamp Rat," trotted back onto the field with 3 ½ minutes to play. Warren, who set a number of single-game records that stood for a while in this game, scored the game-winner from one yard out and Bob Petrella then intercepted a Gary Beban pass at the UT 6-yard line to sew up the win.

ROAD TO RECOVERY There was to be one more victory, another notch in Dickey's gun, another step up the ladder to national notoriety. The Bluebonnet Bowl was UT's first bowl appearance since '57 and the Vols made the most of it. Sure, they stuffed on shrimp at the San Jacinto Inn in Houston and they visited the Astrodome for a concert by the Supremes, but they left Houston with a 27-6 victory

The defensive and offensive MVPs for Tennessee in the '65 Bluebonnet Bowl — linebacker Frank Emanuel (second from left) and quarterback Dewey Warren (right) are shown in a postgame celebration with UT President Dr. Andy Holt (left) and Tennessee Governor Frank Clement.

over Tulsa and UT's best record (8-1-2) since Bowden Wyatt's 10-1 SEC championship team of '56.

Though he had split time with Charlie Fulton much of the year, Dewey Warren was now the quarterback, finishing the season by completing 55.7 percent of his passes for 588 yards. The defense, led by All-American Frank Emanuel, intercepted 17 passes that season, four each by Bob Petrella and Harold Stancell. Hal Wantland won the Jacobs Award as the SEC's best blocker, Dickey was named SEC Coach of the Year and the team finished seventh in both national polls.

MORE TRAGEDY Linebacker Tom Fisher was likely headed for an All-America season and tackle John Crumbacher and guard Gerald Woods were being counted on heavily as UT began preparations for spring practice in 1966. Fisher and Crumbacher were killed and Woods was badly injured in an automobile accident near Benton, Tenn., while returning to Knoxville for spring practice.

JINX ENDS The frustration of its inability to beat Auburn finally ended with the opener of 1966 as Tennessee went airborne behind Dewey Warren and Austin Denney, who was on the receiving end of two Warren touchdown passes. But Johnny Mills pulled in 11 passes that afternoon for a new single-game record, and Art Galiffa, taking over for Warren, threw another touchdown pass as UT rolled, 28-0, for its first win in six tries against the Tigers.

Warren threw for 233 yards in the win over Rice and Mills, one of seven players who caught passes in the Vols' '66 home opener, got his first collegiate touchdown catch. But Georgia Tech solved the passing mystery and dumped the Vols, 6-3, on national television, and then Alabama rallied for an 11-10 win the following week in Knoxville. It was one of the few gaffes that this relatively

Austin Denney

It was quite a passing combination — Johnny Mills (left), who caught a school-record 11 passes against Auburn, and Dewey Warren.

VOLUNTEER QUIZ

22. Against what team has UT rushed for the most yards?

young UT coaching staff committed. For whatever reason, the Vols elected to try and score a touchdown as time ran out rather than let kicker Gary Wright boot a straight-on kick for the win. Yes, UT eventually tried a field goal – from the right hash mark – that sailed wide in the game's waning moments.

Tennessee rebounded to beat South Carolina on a Warren-to-Richmond Flowers pass late in the game. Then the Vols routed Army, 38-7, with defensive end Nick Showalter, a converted quarterback from Kingsport, deflecting a pass and running 43 yards for a touchdown; and then Chattanooga, 28-10, before losing to Ole Miss for the eighth straight year. UT closed out with wins over Kentucky and Vanderbilt.

ANOTHER HIGHLIGHT When Dickey spoke of games he relished, one mentioned was the 1966 Gator Bowl game: The Big Orange vs. the Orangemen of Syracuse.

Syracuse was loaded to the gills with talent, led by two future NFL stars — Floyd Little and Larry Csonka. By the time either scored (and both did), Tennessee had run up an 18-0 halftime lead on Dewey Warren passes to Austin Denney and Richmond Flowers and a Gary

Wright field goal. The Vols won 18-12.

"It was kinda like the win after the '95 season over Ohio State; a couple of sneaky plays and we held 'em on a couple of crucial downs. We sort of reached a peak of performance in the program on that given day that I think of as a special moment," Dickey said.

BOLD MOVE It was going to happen sooner or later and Dickey decided sooner was better, so he found good black athletes and began recruiting them.

"I'd been here about three years and it was obvious to me that we were seeing a pretty good mix of the black athletes in Tennessee high schools and along came Albert Davis at Alcoa," Dickey said. "He appeared to be the most renowned athlete in East Tennessee, obviously a Division I prospect.

"But we didn't want just one, we wanted two or three to break the color barrier at that time. We looked around and found what we considered to be an outstanding athlete and citizen in Lester McClain. We signed both of 'em. It appeared to us to be the normal process because of the integration in high schools."

Lester McClain was the first black to play at Tennessee and in the Southeastern Conference.

Davis failed to qualify academically, but McClain did.

"Lester was a great individual to get into the mix, and we really never had any problems because of the type of person that Lester was. He was a decent student and a good, solid football player who made fine contributions to

The "Swamp Rat," quarterback Dewey Warren, takes off behind All-American center Bob Johnson.

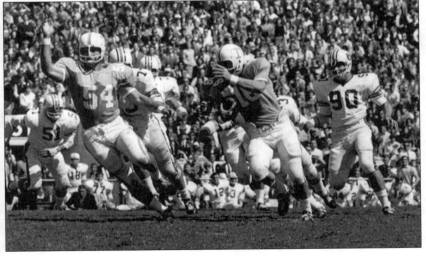

our teams of '68, '69 and '70. The transition really was without much incident at all and it was a very positive job by Lester with all of that," Dickey recalled.

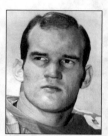

Charles Rosenfelder was part of the talent Doug Dickey had assembled for 1967.

AN SEC TITLE Dickey had the Vols on the right track. Two bowl games in back-to-back seasons, his second and third years at the helm. But what about an SEC championship?

The first of two SEC crowns was to come in 1967 (along with a national championship awarded by the Litkenhous ratings). Dickey's recruiting efforts were paying off. Some of the standouts: center Bob Johnson, quarterback Dewey Warren, tackle John Boynton, ends Nick Showalter and and Neal McMeans, sophomore linebackers Jack Reynolds and Steve Kiner, receivers Richmond Flowers and Ken DeLong, guard Charles Rosenfelder, tailbacks Charlie Fulton and Walter Chadwick, and defensive backs Jimmy Weatherford, Mike Jones, Jimmy Glover and Bill Baker.

RIGHT ROAD? They flunked the first test of 1967, however, losing at UCLA, 20-16. Still, Dickey and his staff had two weeks to get ready for the SEC opener with Auburn. But no one could have foreseen a knee injury to Dewey Warren, who was being touted as a candidate for All-America and Heisman Trophy honors.

Into the breach stepped the ever-versatile Charlie Fulton, who teamed with Walter Chadwick and Richard

PROFILE: PAUL NAUMOFF (1964-66)

When he came to the University of Tennessee, they called him "Butch." When he left four years later, they were calling him "Mister."

UT had lost two great All-Americans after the 1965 season, Frank Emanuel through graduation and Tom Fisher in an automobile accident, and spring practice hadn't yielded any great shakes in the University of Tennessee's vaunted 5-3 Monster defense.

So Paul Naumoff volunteered for an experiment that he felt would help the UT football team but one that could have meant sacrificing some personal goals. Naumoff had established a reputation as the best

defensive end in the SEC and stood a good chance to be an All-America pick at that position in 1966.

But he went to coaches and volunteered to move from defensive end to linebacker. Coach Doug Dickey balked at the idea of moving Naumoff, who had established credentials as a starter. But the switch finally took place and Naumoff worked like a charm because of his quickness and tracking strength.

He gained All-America honors as a linebacker and then helped UT to its eighth win of the '66 season, an 18-12 victory over Syracuse. Most of the UT staff felt a highlight of the

Pickens to run over and through Auburn in a 27-13 win. But during the very next game, Fulton was forced to the sidelines by broken ribs, leaving the quarterback duties in the hands of virtually untested junior backup Bubba Wyche, who responded admirably as the Vols subdued Georgia Tech, 24-13.

ROCKY ROAD Next up was Alabama. The Vols' chances, with quarterbacks Dewey Warren and Charlie Fulton on the sidelines, weren't so good. But Bubba Wyche performed admirably — although the winning score came on Walter Chadwick's first pass as a Vol, an 11-yard toss to Ken DeLong. The highlight of the game, though, had to be the performance of Albert Dorsey, who'd missed spring drills. Three times Dorsey, who was named national back of the week, turned away Ken Stabler-led Bama with interceptions, the last of which he returned 31 yards for a game-clinching score.

Karl Kremser was a high school high-jumper, going as high at 6-10 1/2 before accepting a football scholarship with the Big Orange.

With Warren returning, UT skipped past LSU on a Karl Kremser field goal, then rocked Tampa and Tulane before ending an eight-game losing skid to Ole Miss. The Vols beat Kentucky and then locked up the conference title with a 41-14 drubbing of Vanderbilt as each of the quarterbacks — Warren, Fulton and Wyche – directed scoring drives.

A second-half rally fell short as UT lost to Oklahoma, 26-24, in its postseason trip to the Orange Bowl.

game was Naumoff's classic tackle of Larry Csonka, the 255-pound Syracuse fullback who went on to fame with the Miami Dolphins.

It's all record, of course, but Naumoff, a native of Columbus, Ohio, came to Tennessee as a receiver. While he wasn't sold on Woody Hayes' "three yards and a cloud of dust" offense, neither was he sold on the idea of going south of the Mason-Dixon line.

But Jim McDonald, who'd wind up being his first coach, offered to fly Naumoff down to Knoxville and Naumoff, who'd never been on a plane previously, fell in love with the area, the campus, and the program.

Still, he spent his first two seasons as a split end, catching a 30-yard pass that set up the Vols' only touchdown in a 10-6 win over Chattanooga in the season-opener of Dickey's first year.

Yet Dickey and his first coordinator, Vince Gibson, wanted to experiment. They wanted the best athletes, the guys with a lot of speed, on defense. So Naumoff moved to the other side of the ball.

He wound up playing three different positions in three years, made all-conference twice and took All-American honors his senior season. He then spent 12 seasons with the NFL's Detroit Lions.

Lester McClain, with two pivotal catches against UCLA in 1970, began emerging as a star against Georgia Tech in 1968.

DOUG'S RUG The first artificial playing surface, which became known as "Doug's Rug," was installed in the spring and summer of 1968. It was made by the 3M Corporation and was called Tartan Turf.

But after a season-opening tie, UT didn't trip on the new carpet.

UT had to rally for a 17-17 tie in that first game, with the tying two-point conversion (a pass from Bubba Wyche to Ken DeLong) actually coming after time had expired on the stadium clock.

UT then ripped through Rice 52-0 with sophomore Bobby Scott getting into the game for his Vol debut. Scott passed for 170 yards and two touchdowns. Lester McClain emerged as a Vol star the following week with two sensational catches on tosses from Wyche in a win over Georgia Tech.

And then came Alabama in Knoxville. Richmond Flowers, the Alabama transplant, scored UT's only touchdown, Karl Kremser kicked a 54-yard field goal and Jimmy Weatherford blocked a late field goal as the Vols held off the Scott Hunter-led Crimson Tide 10-9.

UT finished the regular season 8-1-1 to set up a Cotton Bowl date with Texas, which manhandled Tennessee 36-13.

Of that particular game, Flowers later said, "Of the losses we had while I was at Tennessee, there was only one I felt we could not have reversed if we had played again. That was the one to Texas in the Cotton Bowl. We could have played 10 more games, and they would have beaten us 10 more times."

WHAT GOES AROUND ... For years Southeastern Conference writers had gathered in Birmingham, loaded up on a plane and winged their way across the South from campus to campus to write football previews. The contingent swooped down on Knoxville and, after standout linebacker Steve Kiner had said he figured Alabama and Georgia were the teams to beat, a writer asked of Kiner, "How about Ole Miss? They look like they have the horses this year." Kiner replied, "They played more like mules up here last year."

The Big Orange had crushed Ole Miss 31-0 in 1968, setting a single-game record by intercepting Rebels quarterback Archie Manning seven times. But more than anything else — when asked about the '69 season – veteran Tennessee fans will grimace and reply, "Oh yeah, Kiner and the Mules."

The Vols skated through the first seven games —

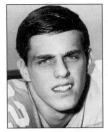

Richmond Flowers, a football and track star at UT, was one of the stars during the Doug Dickey era.

PROFILE: STEVE KINER (1967-69)

Though he is most remembered for an off-the-wall comment about Ole Miss, a comment that led to what now is referred to as "the Jackson Massacre," Steven Albert Kiner to this day is regarded as one of the best linebackers ever to wear the orange and white.

Youngsters playing defense in a backyard football game in the late '60s most often wanted to be Kiner or his also-talented linebacking buddy, Jack Reynolds.

Kiner, a former high school quarterback at Hillsborough High in Tampa, Fla., was the Southeastern Conference Sophomore of the Year in '67 and led a defense that took the Vols to a 26-6-1 record in his three seasons.

He led the team in tackles in '68 and again in '69, earning All-America honors both years. And during that time even Alabama Coach Bear Bryant paid homage, calling Kiner the best SEC linebacker to play in the '60s.

When asked to consider what made All-American players, former UT assistant coach Ray Trail wrote in a UT media guide, "Steve Kiner is an example of a dedicated athlete. Our defensive coaches were amazed continuously at his tremendous drive. It manifested itself in practice, during games and in the film room where he studied religiously the moves of other great linebackers."

Drafted by the Dallas Cowboys in 1970, Kiner played in the NFL for nine seasons with Dallas, the New England Patriots, the Washington Redskins and the Houston Oilers.

including a 41-14 win over Alabama in one of Dickey's most satisfying wins — but the eighth game? Well, what goes around comes around.

The week of this particular game, the Vols, ranked third nationally by now, voted to accept an Orange Bowl date with Notre Dame. But in Oxford, Miss., a mule named "Mr. Kiner" showed up all over the Ole Miss campus, an airplane dropped leaflets on the Ole Miss campus, one saying "Archie Who? — Archie Mud, that's who. At least that's what his name will be come Saturday." Another had pictures of Kiner and linebacker mate Jack Reynolds and the third had "Wreck the Rebels" with a signature that was supposedly Dickey's.

Though UT supporters streamed to Jackson, Miss., with large "Archie Who?" lapel pins, it just wasn't to be. The Rebels rolled to a 21-0 first-quarter lead and won, 38-0.

PROFILE: CHUCK ROHE

He's now executive director of the Florida Citrus Bowl, which has most recently matched the runners-up in the Big Ten and the Southeastern Conference.

But Chuck Rohe first was track coach at the University of Tennessee, a guy who doubled as Doug Dickey's recruiting coordinator (though there was really no such thing at the time) and, most notably, the first to really mix the speed of a track star with the helmeted, hard-hitting world of football.

Dickey wanted speed; Rohe showed him how to get it. Though a couple of years ahead of Dickey in their Knoxville arrivals, Rohe was a man who knew how to get things done and it was suggested that Rohe serve on Dickey's staff.

First and foremost, though, he was a highly successful track coach, a coach who saw the benefit of speed — like Dickey.

"Chuck had the track-football player relationship — sprinters, hurdlers and even some high-jumpers who could do some things in football. We packaged that thinking into our recruiting," Dickey recalled.

The thinking brought a number of two-sport athletes to UT, including lineman Chip Kell, kicker Karl Kremser, receiver Stan Trott and — perhaps the most famous of Rohe's products — wide receiver/tailback Richmond Flowers.

But Rohe's efforts didn't end with the recruitment of such players. Though he'd never coached a lick of football, Rohe set up an off-season conditioning program that stressed running and speed as much as strength training. Players began to get quicker starts. Their 40-yard dash times were reduced by two-tenths of a second and more.

And all of a sudden other schools were sending coaches to look over the Vols' off-season program, and UT was on the verge of becoming "Wide Receiver U."

HOMEWARD-BOUND Though the Vols would finish the regular season 9-1, the loss to Ole Miss had ruined their chances for a major bowl. Somehow, the Vols and Florida's Gators were matched in the Gator Bowl. And by then there were strong rumors that Dickey was leaving for Florida, his alma mater, to take over as head coach. It was a bloodletting that Florida won, 14-13, but the game itself was overshadowed by the repeated stories that Dickey was headed to Gainesville. He was.

"The Florida people had contacted me and asked if I'd be interested and the timing was very poor because of the Gator Bowl game," Dickey recalled. But the lure of home was too much for Dickey, who'd rung up a 46-15-4 record in Knoxville.

"We had won two championships at Tennessee. I was comfortable that I could coach a championship team. But Florida was my place. My mother was there, my father-in-law in Daytona Beach. The attraction to go home was extremely strong. It appeared to me to be a valid place to be. I felt we could recruit instate significantly. Although I'd been gone 15 years, there were still a lot of personal contacts."

Though he didn't make it happen, Dickey saw back in 1969 what could transpire at Florida.

"I think I had the right idea but I was probably 10 years ahead of time … that it would succeed. Obviously Steve (Spurrier) has done it. It wasn't me but Steve that did it. I was a little bit before my time.

"Though Coach (Bear) Bryant and Coach (Adolph) Rupp later told me I'd made a career mistake, I'd probably do it again. The decision was a whole lot more personal than professional," said Dickey, who came back to Tennessee as athletic director, replacing his old coach (Bob Woodruff) in 1985.

But Dickey's departure for Gainesville opened the door for, of all things, an Alabama man in Knoxville.

23. Against what team has UT passed for the most yards?

24. Who was the combination on the longest pass in UT history?

Battle On Their Hands

It wasn't to be, but as fans checked in for the 1969 Gator Bowl game versus Florida — Coach Doug Dickey's swan song — the word was strong that Jimmy Dunn, Dickey's offensive coordinator and basically his assistant head coach, had the UT job wrapped up.

Though Dunn got an endorsement from Dickey, there were factions within the UT family pulling for defensive coordinator Doug Knotts.

But as it had when replacing Jim McDonald, the athletic board put the selection in hands they'd learned to trust — Athletic Director Bob Woodruff. In a press release, Woodruff, intent on maintaining as much continuity as possible, said the top three candidates would be Dunn, Knotts and 28-year-old Bill Battle, who'd been on the staff as the team's ends coach since 1966.

On Saturday, Jan. 3, 1970, Woodruff announced that Battle would be Tennessee's 18th football coach.

Though Battle had played for the legendary Bear Bryant at Alabama and had coached under Oklahoma's Bud Wilkinson and Army's Paul Dietzel, not to mention three seasons under Dickey at Tennessee, there were those who wondered about Battle's youthful inexperience.

And there was one question on every Vol fan's mind: Did the winnin' go with Dickey and the departed seniors such as linebackers Steve Kiner and Jack Reynolds?

There also were two gigantic hurdles facing the

Bill Battle, seated center, is flanked by his coaching staff in 1971. Members of that staff were Lon Herzbrun, Gary Wyant, Ray Trail, Rex Dockery, Conan (Connie) Smith, Bob Davis, Jerry Elliott, Jim Wright, Sid Hatfield, George Cafego, Dewey Warren and Clifton Stewart.

Bill Battle always worked to sell the Tennessee program.

youngster: Alabama and his old coach and Florida with Dickey at the helm.

But before Tennessee faced either, Battle had questions to answer.

1970: A SWEET SEASON

Some fans breathed a sigh of relief when the Volunteers opened the Battle era with a resounding victory over SMU, which had come into the game with one of the nation's more touted senior quarterbacks in Chuck Hixson. By now, Battle had moved Bobby Majors from wingback to the defensive secondary and the Vols, with two interceptions, kept Hixson from at least one touchdown pass in a game for the first time since his sophomore year. Too, the rushing defense — keyed by Bill Emendorfer — held the Mustangs to minus 12 yards.

HOLD ON The SEC-opener was next and the Vols were facing another great quarterback in eventual Heisman Trophy-winner Pat Sullivan at Auburn. The Vols' Bobby Scott, who was to have so many outstanding days, was the Tigers' primary target. The Tigers picked off a pass at their own 36-yard line late in the second period and turned it into a five-play touchdown drive. But also in that five-minute span until halftime, Auburn had a 40-yard pass play for a score, an interception return for a touchdown, a third interception, a fumble recovery and a safety. Auburn won, 36-23.

PROBLEMS SOLVED Auburn remained a thorn in UT's side but those woes were closeted and Tennessee strung

Before the 1970 UT-Florida game, a song entitled "Tricky Dickey" was written by Don Canham, a Loudon Banker. But a member of Florida's team retaliated with "Bad Billy Battle, You Mean and Nasty Boy." Both added to the early fires for what has become one of the nation's nastiest football feuds.

Bobby Majors didn't just play defense; he punted and returned punts.

together 10 victories overall in '70, the first year the NCAA allowed 11 regular-season games.

Though tailback Don McLeary, now the coach at UT-Martin, sat out most of the next game, UT thundered past Army with Bobby Scott throwing one touchdown before retiring for the day. The quarterback duties were then handed off to untested sophomore Dennis Chadwick, who proceeded to throw three touchdown passes in the 48-3 rout.

One of the Vols' most productive all-time runners, Crossville native Curt Watson (left), went on to fly with the Blue Angels, the U.S. Navy's precision flying team.

Tim Priest (middle), who got three of UT's eight interceptions against Alabama in 1970, was an academic All-American.

All-American Chip Kell (right) was named national lineman of the week against Kentucky in '70.

With a 13-0 lead in a driving rain storm during the second half of the Auburn game, Bill Battle reached into his UT coaching history books and ordered a kick on first down from punter Neil Clabo.

DEFENSE, DEFENSE With running back Curt Watson slowed by a knee bruise, the Vols turned to defense in a 17-6 win over previously unbeaten Georgia Tech (4-0) and Bobby Majors was named United Press International (UPI) National Defensive Player of the Week. That same defense intercepted eight passes the next week in a 24-0 win over Alabama, and this time Tim Priest, who picked off three of those passes, took the UPI honor.

DICKEY'S RETURN Florida — with Doug Dickey in his inaugural year as Gators coach — was next and the Vol players placed special emphasis on this game. They wanted it. For the third week in a row a Vol won Defensive Player of the Week honors, this time linebacker Jackie Walker. But the day belonged to Bobby Scott, who was often overshadowed nationally by the likes of UF quarterback John Reaves. Scott blistered the Gators for 385 yards on 21 completions, including two touchdown passes to Joe Thompson, on the way to a 38-7 victory. Though coaching at another school, Dickey received a standing ovation as he left Shields-Watkins Field at the game's conclusion.

SCOTT CAN RUN Both Curt Watson and Don McLeary sat out much of the next game but the usually pass-happy Bobby Scott had runs of 52 and 47 yards as Tennessee forged a 27-6 halftime lead and backup runner Steve Wold added 92 yards as the Vols crushed Wake Forest, 41-7.

George Hunt's 31-yard field goal lifted the Vols over stubborn South Carolina and quarterback Tommy Suggs,

20-18, and then Tim Priest and Bobby Majors got two interceptions each and David Allen one as UT assured itself of a single-season theft record in a 45-0 win over Kentucky. All-American guard Chip Kell was named Associated Press (AP) national lineman of the week as UT backs ran for 360 yards.

A THEFT RECORD Bobby Majors had two interceptions. Tim Priest snagged one. But it was a pickoff by Danny Jeffries, the team's 35th of the year, that set an SEC interception record as UT rolled past Vanderbilt 24-6.

Last on the regular-season slate was a rematch with UCLA. The Vols scored last — on a 19-yard run by Curt Watson — to capture a seesaw battle with the Bruins, 28-17.

Nine players picked off passes during the year for UT: Majors had 10, Priest 9, Jackie Walker 5, Conrad Graham 3, David Allen 3, Jamie Rotella 2, Jeffries 2, and Ray Nettles and Bill McGlothlin 1 each.

Chip Kell and Walker were All-America picks, and Walker was named UPI's Defensive Player of the Year. Watson, center Mike Bevans, Majors, Priest, Walker and Kell were named all-SEC; Priest was an academic All-America pick and offensive lineman Don Denbo was named as a scholar-athlete by the National Hall of Fame.

Danny Jeffries' interception against Vanderbilt allowed UT to set an SEC record.

HOW SWEET IT IS Though a senior, Bobby Scott wasn't done. He wanted to go out with a flourish and did so against Air Force in the Sugar Bowl, as UT quarterbacks riddled the Falcons for 306 passing yards. It was UT's first bowl victory in four tries. The defense picked off four passes from Air Force quarterback Bob Parker while holding his running backs to minus 12 yards rushing.

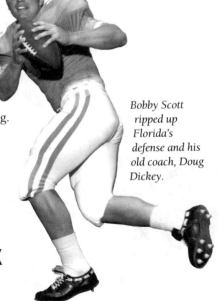

Bobby Scott ripped up Florida's defense and his old coach, Doug Dickey.

SIGNS OF FUTURE The 1970 season was great for UT, one that left most celebrating, but the writing for Battle's demise might have been on the wall as early as 1970: The freshman team went winless, losing to Kentucky, Vandy, Notre Dame, Bama and Georgia Tech.

1971: BOUNCING BACK

The Vols were written off and their season adjudged a losing one in 1971 almost before they got started.

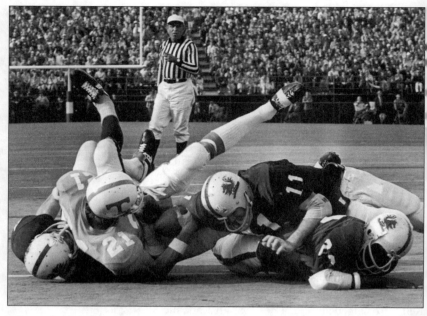

Dennis Chadwick wasn't always the most graceful of quarterbacks.

UT drilled Cal-Santa Barbara, 48-6, but over the next four games the Vols dropped a heart-breaker to Auburn (10-9) and Pat Sullivan, and then got blistered by rejuvenated Alabama (32-15) after losing four fumbles and throwing four interceptions. In between, though, UT broke out white jerseys for the first time since the 1969 Cotton Bowl and beat Florida, 20-13. They won at home the next week against Georgia Tech.

The win at Gainesville came late on a 99-yard march and the winning score came on a touchdown pass from Phil Pierce, the third Vol quarterback in as many games, to Stan Trott. The Georgia Tech victory saw Curt Watson move past Beattie Feathers for first place on the Vols' career rushing chart.

Three missing teeth didn't slow Eddie Brown.

POST-ALABAMA The Vols refused to roll over in 1971 as they won six straight games. During those games, UT fans saw the emergence of senior Jim Maxwell at quarterback against Mississippi State, Gordon Turnage's 71-yard interception return against Tulsa, scoring interception returns by Eddie Brown and Danny Jeffries against South Carolina, an intercepted pitchout and return by Carl Johnson against Kentucky and on Majors Day as the Vols whipped Penn State, 31-11. Bobby Majors returned a pair of punts for 82 yards and a touchdown versus Penn State.

UT rallied for Battle's second bowl win, snuffing out the hopes of Arkansas quarterback Joe Ferguson and

Razorback fans, 14-13.

As he looked back on the season, which ended 10-2 despite the demoralizing losses to Auburn and Bama, Battle said, "You just have to be proud of a team that can come back and achieve this kind of season after a couple of losses that hurt as much as the Auburn and Alabama losses did. We managed to win some games in which we didn't play particularly well just because our players hung in there and kept working the full four quarters."

PAYING ATTENTION Battle had obviously kept an eye on the freshman team during 1971. The young Vols went 4-1, but as was to be proven the next three seasons, it would always be easier to win with a quarterback named Condredge Holloway.

THE ARTFUL DODGER Condredge Holloway was a cool customer, one stolen out of Huntsville, Ala., away from the Crimson Tide and the Tigers. He also was the first black quarterback in the SEC, a fact that would come home to roost more than once — the latest being the Vols' 1995-96 signing of Tee Martin, another black quarterback from Alabama.

Though he played well, mixing UT's run-pass game as well as it had been mixed since the departure of Bobby Scott, Holloway didn't figure in the scoring of the season-opener, a 34-3 swamping of Georgia Tech on national television. No, running back Bill Rudder and backup quarterback Gary Valbuena threw the scoring passes. The game, though, belonged to senior linebacker Jamie Rotella, whose dad had played at UT three decades earlier. Rotella was named national lineman of the week.

In the first night game at Neyland Stadium, Haskel Stanback scored three touchdowns en route to national back of the week honors as UT defeated Penn State 28-21. But after a 3-0 start, UT lost two (Auburn and Alabama) of its next three. Surprisingly, Stanback, who would break Hank Lauricella's long-standing single-season rushing record later in the year, won his second national back of the week honor against Bama after rushing for 133 yards in the 17-10 loss.

FIRST PAT RECORD There was much hoopla in Knoxville in 1994 when John Becksvoort set the NCAA record for consecutive PATs without a miss, but he wasn't the first. Ricky Townsend, the barefoot, soccer-style kicker from Dalton, Ga., established a similar record in 1972.

To get back to the nine-win mark, UT reeled off wins over Hawaii, Georgia, Ole Miss, Kentucky and Vanderbilt and made it 10-2 with a 24-17 win over LSU in the Astro Bluebonnet Bowl. The game's offensive MVP

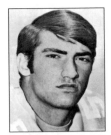

Carl Johnson was defensive MVP of the Astro Bluebonnet Bowl win over LSU.

Haskel Stanback broke Hank Lauricella's long-standing single-season rushing record.

Conrad Graham, who played at UT from 1970-72, has the all-time fumble recovery record (8).

In 1972 the first night game was played at Neyland Stadium (a 28-21 win over Penn State). The cost of powering the lights was figured at $67.90 per hour.

award went to Condredge Holloway, who also was named the SEC's sophomore of the year. Defensive MVP honor went to Carl Johnson, whose eldest son, Greg, was a senior linebacker in 1996 and whose second son, Neil, signed with the Vols in February of 1996.

1973: MISSED OPPORTUNITIES

As much as he had loved the 1971 team for its refusal to roll over, Battle just couldn't get over the hump in 1973.

For the first time in 27 years, both UT and Alabama went into their game unbeaten — UT ranked 10th nationally, Bama second. With ABC-TV cameras tracking the action, the Crimson Tide finally put UT down to stay and won 42-21 with a fourth-quarter surge.

The Vols opened 5-0 but went 3-4 the rest of the way — including a 28-19 loss to Texas Tech in the Gator Bowl.

PROFILE: CONDREDGE HOLLOWAY (1972-74)

It wasn't so much that he was black — the first black quarterback in the Southeastern Conference — and it wasn't so much what he did.

It was how he did it.

Condredge Holloway was one of the most elusive players ever to pull on pads and cleats. He was a smaller, but perhaps more mobile, version of Archie Manning, who led Ole Miss to such lofty heights in the late '60s, and a forerunner of Alabama's David Palmer, who stood so many SEC teams on their ear as they reached for him and rarely came away with much more than sweat.

A more literate writer took to calling Holloway, who made his way to Knoxville from Huntsville, Ala., "The Artful Dodger" after the imp of a fleet-footed young rascal in the musical "Oliver." Others later referred to him as "The Huntsville Houdini" for his crafty way of leading Vol rallies.

Holloway, at one point in UT's football history the Vols' career total

Condredge Holloway was also called the Huntsville Houdini.

offense leader, was first "Mr. Elusive" and then "Mr. Comeback" during his playing days in Knoxville. He still ranks among the school's top five total offense leaders and the program's top 10 passing leaders. He is still part of the duo (along with Tommy West) that holds the mark for the longest non-scoring passing play (81 yards vs. Vandy in '74).

In his career, Holloway ran for 966 yards and passed for another 3,102 for a total of 4,068. It has been bettered now only four times: by Jimmy Streater (1976-79) and by UT's last three quarterbacks prior to Peyton Manning, a group that includes Jeff Francis (1985-88),

The season opened with Condredge Holloway leading the Vols back for a win over Duke and getting national back of the week honors. Then, UT endured a record 347-yard passing performance by Kingsley Fink to beat Army. An unsung linebacker, Hank Walter, single-handedly wrecked Auburn the next week as he racked up 20 tackles, recovered a fumble and scored on a pass interception en route to national player of the week honors.

Despite having three teeth knocked out, senior safety and team captain Eddie Brown returned an interception 74 yards, recovered a fumble, returned a punt 48 yards and put the primary hit on Kansas quarterback David Jaynes on a late two-point conversion try as the Volunteers held on 28-27. Then it was Holloway again, tossing a touchdown pass to Bill Rudder and running for another score against Georgia Tech to set up the battle of unbeatens in Birmingham.

All-time total tackles leader Andy Spiva (1973-76) was killed in a car accident after joining the NFL Atlanta Falcons. Spiva caused more fumbles (14) than any player in UT history.

Heath Shuler (1991-93) and the school's all-time leader, Andy Kelly (1988-91).

After completing his UT career, Holloway spent more than a decade as a star quarterback in the Canadian Football League. He can still be seen as part of the broadcast team when the Volunteers have pay-per-view games via Host Communications.

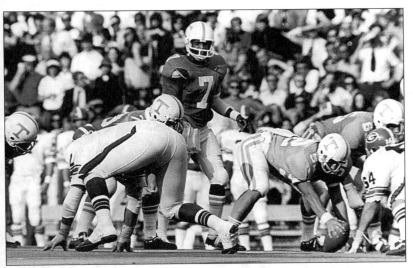

Condredge Holloway bypassed Bobby Scott to become UT's all-time yardage leader in a 34-6 win over Memphis State on Nov. 9, 1974.

Tommy West, now head coach at Clemson, was a high school fullback who converted to tight end. He was on the receiving end of UT's all-time longest non-scoring pass play. It was an 81-yard hookup with quarterback Condredge Holloway.

In post-Bama games, Stanley Morgan caught 201 yards worth of passes in a rout of TCU, but Georgia won a seesaw affair on a late Andy Johnson run and the Vols then suffered back-to-back losses for the first time in Battle's head-coaching career by falling to Ole Miss.

They slid past Kentucky and Vandy to set up the Gator Bowl trip.

SLIP-SLIDING AWAY Maybe it was a failure to recruit as well as he had as an assistant on Doug Dickey's staff. Maybe it was changes in the coaching staff from his first couple of years as head coach. Regardless, Tennessee's winning style of football was slipping. The Vols had to beat Maryland in the Liberty Bowl to salvage a 7-3-2 finish in '74, and it took a trip to Honolulu and a 28-6 victory over Hawaii in 1975 to get to 7-5.

But in '76, UT slipped back to the six-win mark, something it hadn't seen since Dickey's 4-5-1 first-year effort back in 1964.

For whatever reason, the Battle touch was no longer mystical. As quickly as he'd been accepted, Battle was disowned.

As a matter of fact, a moving van was dispatched by parties unknown to the Battle household during the '76 season, "For Sale" signs were placed in his front yard and someone even sent an exterminator to his office.

That isn't to say there weren't some outstanding individual performances over those years.

Condredge Holloway broke six tackles — on a 20-yard scoring run — in a 20-14 win over Georgia Tech. In that same 1973 game, by the way, UT's consecutive PAT string, which had reached 105, was broken when Ricky Townsend misfired. That particular streak was put

Bill Battle, UT Chancellor Dr. Jack Reese and linebacker Ronnie McCartney celebrate UT's 500th victory, a 1975 win over Kentucky.

PROFILE: LARRY SEIVERS (1974-76)

If Tennessee is fortunate enough to have a sure-handed receiver on the field and that receiver stays around for any length of time, chances are he'll be compared to Larry Seivers.

At one time UT's single-season and career pass-catching leader, Seivers was one of the Golden Boys of the Bill Battle era.

He scored but eight career touchdowns in his time on The Hill, but Seivers finished a three-year stint in Knoxville with 117 catches for 1,924 yards, still good enough to be among the top five all-time ahead of such greats as Carl Pickens, Craig Faulkner, Anthony Hancock, Alvin Harper, Richmond Flowers and Willie Gault.

And his single-season high of 51 catches in 1976 remained an all-time best until 1984, when Tim McGee pulled in 54 catches.

A two-time consensus All-America pick, Seivers almost was passed over by UT recruiters. He was the last of three players signed off the '72 Clinton (Tenn.) team and even when they signed him, coaches saw him more as a youngster who'd grow into a tight end than an all-conference split end. It's been said that in third-and-long, Seivers was most always the target because he had a knack for making the play in life-and-death times on a football field.

When he looked back at the young men who'd played for him, Battle told *The Big Orange* author Russ Bebb, "If you drew a picture of a true All-American, you'd be drawing Larry Seivers … the right size, timing; unselfish; a rare player loved by teammates and coaches. I never saw a great one as humble as Larry. And he'd do anything for the team."

---

together by George Hunt (60) and Townsend.

Linebacker Art Reynolds was credited with 21 solo tackles and three assists in a 16-14 win over Kentucky the same year, and Townsend's field goal brought UT back from a tie to a win over Vandy. And, of course, these were the years of Larry Seivers and Stanley Morgan, who was moved to tailback in a '74 win over Tulsa, and running backs Mike Gayles and Terry Moore.

A winning season in 1976 was in jeopardy until Hubert Simpson scored a third-quarter touchdown against in-state rival Vanderbilt.

But by then Battle was history, having announced his resignation the previous Monday — Nov. 22, 1976.

It was probably the best thing for Battle, who, though he had several coaching offers, went into the business world and became a millionaire. Among those offers — as a head coach — were Miami, which had decided to upgrade its program (and everybody knows what happened there), Purdue and Army.

Stanley Morgan led the SEC in scoring in 1974 with 14 touchdowns. He still ranks among the Vols' Top 10 rushers, with 1,952 yards.

Johnny Marches Home

Johnny Majors.

There were those who politicked for Johnny Majors, then in his early years at Iowa State, when Doug Dickey opted to return to Florida. It was a sizable contingent in 1969, a contingent that had grown immensely as Bill Battle's reign dropped off.

So it was no surprise, really, when UT Athletic Director Bob Woodruff announced on Friday, Dec. 3, 1976, that Majors would indeed be coming home.

By then Majors had moved from Iowa State to Pittsburgh and was on the verge of putting the finishing touches on another rebuilding job with a national championship-clinching victory over Georgia in the Sugar Bowl.

A press conference was called in Knoxville for the early afternoon of Saturday, Dec. 4, for Majors to acquaint himself with the Knoxville media. Fifteen minutes before the start of the press conference, more than 100 media representatives were seated and waiting for one of the school's favorite sons, a man whose mere hiring rejuvenated lagging season ticket sales.

It was that enthusiasm that Majors, whose family had given so much to the University including the life of his elder brother, Bill, and the talents of younger brother, Bobby, perhaps feared more than anything. Yes, he considered himself a good program-builder and had accomplished the feat twice already. But as he would say and repeat to any Vol fan within earshot, "I'm a hard worker, not a miracle worker."

Always in the middle of things in practice in the early years, Johnny Majors has a turn at quarterback.

The sign that had been on the wall in the Battle era — a drop-off in the talent pool — was so very apparent to Majors. When criticized for his honesty about the talent, Majors responded, "I'm not down on our players. They're ours and they're all we've got. I just believe in telling people what I think, how it is, not what they want to hear."

That philosophy — telling people what he thought — would later lead to his demise as the modern-day equivalent of Davy Crockett and Andrew Jackson.

But such troubles were well into the future. In Majors' first year home, UT's spring game drew a crowd of 26,000.

"I thought it was most realistic for the people to see this game. These were the Tennessee football players, and the fans saw I wasn't shooting smoke screens. We don't have a lot of first-line quality and we're woefully thin in the backup areas," Majors said.

He wasn't blowing smoke, but there was no doubt in which direction he wanted to go. "We've been track champions, we've been basketball champions, and we've been swimming champions. But we haven't been champions in football in the past few years. And we have to get Tennessee back where it should be — and to me that's on top."

VOLUNTEER QUIZ

25. Who holds the record for most tackles in a season at UT?

Johnny Majors (left) with his famous father, Shirley (center), and brother, Bill.

Craig Colquitt averaged 45 yards per punt.

Jimmy Noonan led the Vols in tackles in Johnny Majors' first year.

Kicker Alan Duncan came to UT from Kenya.

LOSING YEAR The enthusiasm continued although UT lost its first game under Majors and finished the year 4-7, the first losing season in a dozen years for the Volunteers. That season included a 14-12 loss to Auburn after UT failed to score from the Auburn 1-yard line to open the fourth quarter and a 24-10 setback to Alabama, UT's seventh straight loss to the Crimson Tide.

There were highlights: Kelsey Finch's 99-yard touchdown run against Florida, the emergence of punter Craig Colquitt and the arrival of quarterback Jimmy Streater. Colquitt averaged 45 yards on 66 punts, and Jimmy Noonan, the squatty nose man from Dyersburg, led the team in tackles (104) and total hits (150).

RECRUITING HARD Picking up a battle cry that was later to become a state advertising ploy, Majors and his assistants hit the recruiting trail on the run with Johnny pleading to each and every recruit: "Follow me to Tennessee."

It was quite a group, including such players as running back James Berry, defensive back Terry Daniels, wide receiver Anthony Hancock, fullback Mike Miller and linemen Lee Otis Burton, Mike Cofer and Lee North.

A BETTER LOOK It still wasn't winning but it wasn't losing, either. UT went 5-5-1 in 1978. This time the Vols lost their season-opener to UCLA 13-0, and lost three straight SEC games (Auburn, Alabama, Mississippi State) before finally getting untracked in November with a modest three-game win streak included in a 4-1 roll.

GOING NATIONAL By this time, Tennessee had moved from regional to a more national recruiting scope and had players from 15 states plus Kenya (kicker Alan Duncan) and South Africa (Severin Anderson, a 6-5, 235-pound freshman middle guard).

HAPPY DAYS For the first time, Majors got off to a quick start in 1979, directing Tennessee to a 3-0 beginning before falling to Mississippi State. Included, finally, was a smashing 35-17 win over Auburn but also another loss to Bama (27-17) and then an unexpected setback to Rutgers for a 4-3 start.

But if you can't beat somebody in the conference, then beating Notre Dame might be the next best thing and Tennessee delivered on Nov. 10 with a 40-18 thrashing of the favored Irish.

Anthony Hancock had six receptions in the season-opening win over Boston College, which had lost all 11 games the previous season, but UT scored all its touchdowns on runs — two for James Berry and one each for Jimmy Streater and Hubert Simpson.

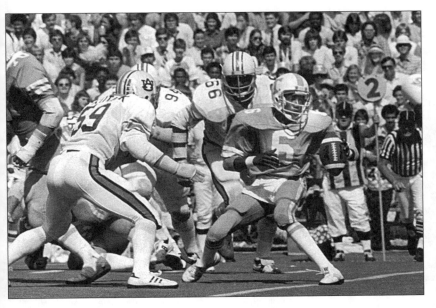

It was just the opposite the next week, though, with Streater getting more than 200 yards of total offense and Hancock, Reggie Harper and Willie Gault pulling in touchdown catches in a 51-18 win over Utah. UT got the upper hand early against Auburn when Gary Moore returned the opening kickoff 98 yards for a touchdown, but the Vols' appearance in the Top 20 was short-lived after a 28-9 loss to Mississippi State.

Streater passed Condredge Holloway as Tennessee's all-time total offense leader in a 31-0 win over Georgia Tech, but then top-ranked Alabama dropped the Volunteers, 27-17, after rallying from a 17-7 halftime deficit. And on the heels of that disappointment came a 13-7 loss to Rutgers.

And, finally, Notre Dame. Simpson, from Athens, Tenn., moved into the starting lineup and gave UT fans a sparkling performance in a duel with the Irish's Vagas Ferguson. Simpson, running from fullback, rushed for 117 yards and four scores as UT amassed 441 yards of total offense. However, it was a goal-line stand anchored by linebackers Craig Puki and Chris Bolton near the end of the second period that Majors would later point to as a turning point in the game.

The Vols moved back into the Top 20, but again it was a short stay as they fell to Ole Miss, 44-20. However, wins over Kentucky and Vanderbilt assured UT of a spot in the Bluebonnet Bowl, the first postseason trip for a Majors-coached team. The Vols lost that one, 27-22, despite scoring 16 fourth-quarter points.

Quarterback Jimmy Streater passed Condredge Holloway's all-time total offense mark.

Hubert Simpson's finest day produced four touchdowns against Notre Dame.

VOLUNTEER QUIZ

26. Which former UT coaches have gone on to become head coaches in the NFL?

Also a track star, Willie Gault left a lasting impression on UT's football program.

GETTING BETTER? Majors finally had some of his own prospects stepping up and 1980 was full of promise with such talent as Anthony Hancock, Lee North, safety Bill Bates, Hubert Simpson, Jimmy Noonan, Reggie Harper, offensive tackle Tim Irwin, defensive tackle Brad White and defensive end Brian Ingram.

But before the season started, Majors made a decision that would have future importance. He brought former Vol offensive guard Phillip Fulmer back to the program by hiring him to coach UT's offensive line.

"I am," Majors said, "delighted to add to the staff a native Tennessean and former Volunteer player."

The Vols were facing what Majors called UT's toughest schedule — the likes of Georgia, Southern Cal, Washington State, Auburn, Georgia Tech, Alabama, Pittsburgh and Virginia — and this time there would be no bowl game.

In the opener, Georgia Coach Vince Dooley unveiled an untested freshman by the name of Herschel Walker, who ran for two second-half touchdowns in leading the Bulldogs to a 16-15 upset.

It was close but no cigar the next week, too, with UT coming up short against Southern Cal.

But the Vols then rebounded with three weeks of wins — including a 42-0 shutout of Auburn — to enter the Bama game at 3-2. It was a ballyhooed, anticipated contest as always. UT didn't pick up a first down until the game was midway through the third period and wound up rushing for just 22 yards on 33 attempts. Alabama went on to a 27-0 shutout in the first of four straight Volunteer losses to the Tide.

But then there were Kentucky and Vanderbilt — good ol' Kentucky and Vanderbilt — with which to close out the season, and Tennessee finished upbeat, whipping the two by a combined score of 96-27. A highlight was Willie Gault's 95-yard kickoff return in Nashville, the third time in 1980 he accomplished the feat.

VOLUNTEER QUIZ

27. Who holds the UT record for most field goals?

STILL, THEY SLIPPED ... The dropoff from the previous year's bowl appearance left UT at 5-6 in '80, just when it appeared that Majors was ready to turn the corner.

But it was nothing compared to the opening of '81: Georgia? The Vols lost 44-0 as Herschel Walker, already an All-American, picked up 161 yards in UT's worst-ever SEC defeat. Southern Cal? The Vols lost 43-7 as Marcus Allen ran for 210 yards and four touchdowns.

... AND THEN REBOUNDED Majors had, by then, had enough. He promoted freshman Alan Cockrell to the starting quarterback position and Cockrell guided the Vols to a 21-0 halftime lead over Colorado State en route to a 42-0 UT rout. Cockrell, however, was lost for the season on the first series the next week against Auburn, and Steve Alatorre returned in time to take UT to a 10-7 win over the Wishbone-running Tigers, who fumbled away a snap at the UT 4-yard line as time ran out.

Alatorre fumbled in his own end zone to give Georgia Tech the lead the following week, but then he countered with a 42-yard scoring strike to Anthony Hancock as the Vols moved a game above .500 at 3-2. Reggie White made his first notable appearance of 1981, garnering Southeastern Defensive Player of the Week honors.

Again, though, Bama was next up on the schedule. It was the Vols' first taste of Top 10 competition since the debacle against Southern Cal, and they fell behind 28-0 by halftime and were routed 38-19.

Steve Alatorre removed the goat's horns against Georgia Tech.

SILVER LINING For the first time since 1974, UT rebounded from a Bama loss to win the next week, this time defeating Memphis State 28-9. Then Fuad Reveiz, signed by UT only a few days before fall practice began, kicked a 28-yard field goal with nine seconds left in a win over Wichita State.

Regaining their stride nicely, the Volunteers

Now an NFL legend, defensive tackle Reggie White was second on the team in tackles in 1981.

celebrated as Willie Gault set a UT career combined yardage record in a 28-20 win over Ole Miss and quarterback John Fourcade. However, Kentucky caught UT napping and overcame a 10-point Vol lead for a 21-10 win, and then upstart Vandy gave them fits — Whit Taylor passing for 464 yards — before falling, 38-34.

The regular-season performance of '81 was enough to get UT into a bowl game — the final Garden State Bowl at East Rutherford, N.J. UT responded with a 28-21 win as Steve Alatorre, named the game's outstanding player, completed 24 of 42 passes for 315 yards. Anthony Hancock caught 11 of those passes, while Gault made another long kickoff return.

Though a defensive tackle, Reggie White was second on the UT team in tackles (to linebacker Lemont Holt Jeffers) with 95 total stops.

SLIPPING AGAIN It seemed to be, in retrospect, a hallmark of Majors' early years at Tennessee — two steps forward, one step back. And in 1982, UT dropped to 6-5-1 after the previous season's 8-4 campaign.

HALLELUJAH? There was, however, a saving grace. Alabama, finally, would fall.

Neyland Stadium was rocking. The press box, perched high atop the west stands, was literally swaying as if gripped by a huge heavenly fist.

It was a so-so beginning to the season, UT giving no indication of what was to come on the "Third Saturday in

Johnny Majors ran off four straight wins (1982-85) against Alabama, the 1982 win snapping an 11-game losing streak.

October" in 1982 by waffling to a 2-2-1 start. How much of a chance was there, after all? UT had lost 11 in a row to the Tide, and the Tide — ranked second nationally — was coming off a big win over Top 10 rival Penn State.

The Vols were down 21-13 at the half when lightning struck: Three UT scores in the third period to none for Alabama. The points came on two Fuad Reveiz field goals, a 39-yard pass from Alan Cockrell to Terry Miller and Cockrell's conversion pass to Kenny Jones. But UT wasn't done. Tailback Chuck Coleman, who ran for 139 yards, scored UT's final touchdown with 7:21 left and Jones got another two-point conversion pass from Cockrell. The game wasn't decided until Mike Terry intercepted a Bama pass in his own end zone with 17 seconds left in the game.

TOO MUCH PROSPERITY The week-after-Bama opponent, this time Georgia Tech, was ready, willing and able and UT fell, 31-21. Fuad Reveiz entered the SEC record books on a five-field-goal performance the following week, and Doug Furnas and Chuck Coleman sliced up Ole Miss the next game. A 28-7 victory against Kentucky nailed down a Peach Bowl bid, but then UT once again lost its footing, dropping a 28-21 decision to Vanderbilt.

VOLUNTEER QUIZ

28. Who holds the UT record for most points scored?

Fuad Reveiz set an SEC record with five field goals in one game.

Reggie White is still the all-time sack leader at UT.

The Peach Bowl outcome wasn't much better, with UT falling to Iowa, 28-22. But Coleman averaged 9.4 yards per carry (a UT bowl record), picking up 103 yards on 11 totes; Alan Cockrell was tabbed Tennessee's outstanding player after passing for 221 yards; and punter Jimmy Colquitt outdueled the man who edged him for the national punting title, Iowa's Reggie Roby.

1983: A GOOD ONE

If 1982 was a down year — UT went 6-5-1 — then Majors' coaching pattern called for a good year in '83. And it was.

UT went through the regular season with eight wins and captured a berth in the Citrus Bowl opposite Maryland. Between the season-opening loss to Pittsburgh and the bowl game was a whole lot of fun.

The best single-game punting average by a Vol is 53 yards. Jimmy Colquitt did it twice: 1983 vs. Auburn, 1982 vs. LSU.

Alan Cockrell, who couldn't buy a handful of completions against the Panthers, did manage to throw a 53-yard touchdown pass to Clyde Duncan, and Johnny Williams blocked a kick and a punt — both leading to Vol scores against New Mexico. It was in that game that Reggie White, the mammoth tackle from Chattanooga, established a new career sack record.

Auburn swamped the Vols and a lot of fans were thinking, "Here we go again." But a 45-6 rout of the Citadel cleared the air, and UT then moved to 3-2 to set another stage for the annual test with Alabama.

TRIED AND TRUE Majors, who had forged a national championship drive at Pitt around running back Tony Dorsett, was once again turning to a talented back in 1983. This one didn't disappoint either. Johnnie Jones raced 66 yards to ice a 41-34 Vol victory against Alabama, UT's second straight over the Crimson Tide

Johnnie Jones was the first Vol to rack up 1,000 yards rushing in one season. He was UT's all-time rushing leader for a decade, then "Little Man" Stewart surpassed his total in 1994.

and its first in Birmingham since 1969. Alan Cockrell stepped up big, too, and his 292 yards and three touchdown throws were more than enough to see him named Southeast back of the week.

The defense, though it surrendered 34 points, came up with some huge fourth-quarter stands led by Reggie White and held the Tide out of the end zone during the final 21 minutes.

Cockrell was named back of the week again the next week after tossing touchdown strikes to Clyde Duncan and Lenny Taylor, and Jones ran for 128 yards in the Vols' win over Georgia Tech.

It was then the defense's turn, although Jones ran for 234 yards to rewrite single-game records belonging to Stanley Morgan (201 yards) and Hubert Simpson (35 carries). The defense held Rutgers to 83 rushing yards and intercepted two passes.

Ole Miss knocked UT for a loop on Homecoming, but Jones turned in his fifth 100-yard game of the season (only the second Vol to accomplish that feat) and White recovered a fumble in the second half that led to a score as UT blanked Kentucky.

Jones then smashed a flock of records as UT beat Vandy 34-24. Among the standards that fell, Jones ran for 248 yards and became the first Vol runner ever to

VOLUNTEER QUIZ

29. Who is the highest-scoring kicker in a single season at UT?

reach the 1,000-yard mark in a season. Jones finished the year with 1,116 yards.

The Vols rallied with a pair of fourth-quarter touchdowns — both runs by Jones — to defeat Maryland in the Citrus Bowl, and it marked UT's best record since 1972.

Alan Cockrell left a year early to pursue pro baseball.

DECEPTION? It looked once again like UT had turned the corner and was ready to advance consistently from mediocrity. But Majors was cautious. Alan Cockrell had decided to forgo his senior season for pro baseball and Reggie White was in pro ball, having signed with the Memphis Showboats of the United States Football League.

"Alan made a great contribution to Tennessee, and the loss of Reggie White, well, it's inestimable. He provided humor, leadership and morale," Majors said.

Still there was reason for optimism: Linebackers Alvin Toles and Carl Zander, Fuad Reveiz, Johnnie Jones, sophomore defensive back Charles Davis, punter Jimmy Colquitt and senior guard Bill Mayo, who'd been a starter since the first game his freshman season.

BET-HEDGING "I can't put my finger on it. I still can't say what I think we are capable of doing as a team. I'm still not satisfied that we accomplished all our objectives in spring practice," Majors responded when asked of Tennessee's title hopes in 1984.

There was, however, an ace up his sleeve. Though the quarterback position was a question mark, Randy Sanders had graduated high school early to come in for spring drills.

But already there was a lanky kid named Tony Robinson, a youngster who was destined for almost two years of greatness.

"Tony has a lot of talent, but there is more to playing quarterback than having talent. You don't see anybody better at throwing long passes, but I'm interested in seeing how he improves on the intermediate and short patterns," Majors said.

Also on campus — and he would play an integral part in UT football lore the next season — was Daryl Dickey, son of the former Vols head coach.

Then, too, there was a budding young receiver named Tim McGee, and Majors had uncharacteristic plans to go to the airways a lot more.

VOLUNTEER QUIZ

30. Who kicked the longest field goal in school history?

DEFENSIVE WOES The offense was all it was cracked up to be. The Vols scored fewer than 20 points only twice — in a 29-10 loss to Auburn and a 17-12 loss to Kentucky. But the defense was questionably porous, allowing at its best nine points to Memphis State but giving up an

Quarterback Tony Robinson bested Alabama twice, but his UT career ended with an injury in the 1985 win over the Tide.

average of 23.9 points in the other 10 games.

Tony Robinson was fine in his debut (completing 13 of 16 passes) and Johnnie Jones ran for 203 yards as UT beat Washington State, 34-27, for its first season-opening victory since 1979. Jones then gained 197 yards as UT outscored Utah, 27-21. But the Vols' Top 20 appearance was fleeting: Army rallied for a 24-24 tie; Auburn, with national title aspirations, blistered UT, 29-10; and Florida won a shootout 43-30 despite Robinson's record-setting 371-yard passing performance.

But again Majors, his team having struggled to a 2-2-1 record, silenced his critics by turning back Alabama. Robinson, running the option, faked a pitch to Jones and capped an 18-point fourth-quarter spree as UT won, 28-27. The game wasn't actually decided until a Tommy Sims interception allowed UT to escape the SEC cellar.

Still, the Volunteers continued to struggle. Jeff Smith came up with a key catch for 31 yards on fourth down,

VOLUNTEER QUIZ

31. What linebacker intercepted an option pitch and scored a touchdown in the Kickoff Classic win over Iowa in 1987?

Tim McGee surpassed Larry Seivers as the single-season receiving leader with a 10-catch afternoon against Vanderbilt.

which allowed Fuad Reveiz' game-winning field goal against Georgia Tech.

There were back-to-back wins over Memphis State and Ole Miss before Kentucky, denying Robinson the long-ball tosses for which he was becoming famous, posted a 17-12 triumph.

With a Sun Bowl bid in their pockets, the Vols rolled over Vandy. Robinson broke Jimmy Streater's single-season total offense record, Tim McGee moved past Larry Seivers as the best single-season receiver, and Jones, with 119 yards on the day and 1,290 on the season, nailed down his second-straight SEC rushing title.

VOLUNTEER QUIZ

32. Name the only three Vols to make All-SEC three times?

PANUSKA SHINES This particular Sun Bowl was a rematch of the previous season's Citrus Bowl, won by UT. Despite a 100-yard kickoff return by Pete Panuska, Maryland turned in a phenomenal second half, scoring all its points en route to a 28-27 decision that left the Vols with a 13-14 bowl record.

1985: ORANGE CRUSH

In 1985 another former Volunteer had come home. Majors, the wolves growling at his door, hired former Neyland player Ken Donahue, naming him defensive coordinator and defensive line coach after Bill Shaw left for Tulane.

It was the beginning of a very special season, an unexpected Tennessee title year in the SEC, which by now had allied itself with and promised its champion to the New Orleans-based Sugar Bowl.

It was a unique year, a season of "stick-to-it-tiveness" as Majors used to say.

On a warm and sunny Knoxville afternoon, the Vols allowed UCLA to score 16 fourth-quarter points and leave with a 26-all tie.

Auburn, with the great Bo Jackson, was next. Despite three interceptions, Tony Robinson completed 17 passes for 259 yards and four touchdowns. Jackson, crunched early on by linebackers Dale Jones and Darrin Miller, was never really a part of the Tiger attack.

Another Reveiz, Carlos, a transfer from UT-Chattanooga, kicked a 52-yard field goal in a close win over Wake Forest, but Tennessee fell the next week to Florida, 17-10, despite sacking quarterback Kerwin Bell five times.

DOWNS AND UPS Once again Alabama loomed on the horizon.

It is a game that Tony Robinson most likely will remember for the rest of his life, as he suffered a horrible knee injury on the Bama goal line in what would be his final collegiate performance.

But as much of a downward turn as it was for Robinson, the Bama game — one play in particular —

Dale Jones, now an assistant coach at Appalachian State, launched an All-America campaign with one spectacular play against Alabama.

Carlos Reveiz found great success against Georgia Tech in '85. He had kicks of 55 and 51 yards, the latter being the game-winner.

launched linebacker Dale Jones on the All-America trail. Clinging precariously to a 16-14 lead, Tennessee was being assaulted by tailback Bobby Humphrey and then by the arm of Mike Shula. But on one particular fourth-quarter play, Jones went crashing through the Tide line. He tipped Shula's pass high in the air, then lunged to intercept it. And UT held on to win.

Unsung senior Daryl Dickey, written off and forgotten by most, stepped up the next game to fill Robinson's shoes, but it was a defensive struggle against Georgia Tech. Carlos Reveiz, with the final seconds ticking off, launched a game-tying, 51-yard field goal. It was his second long bomb of the night, the first being a 55-yarder.

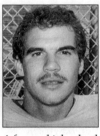

A former high school quarterback, Chris White gained national prominence as a safety.

DEFENSE A WATCHWORD After giving up 26, 20 and 29 points in the first three games of the 1985 season, UT's defenders began to respond quickly to Ken Donahue's preaching and fans all of a sudden were just as much in love with the ex-Vol as they'd been with Majors when he returned.

Over the final seven regular-season games, UT surrendered an average of 8.28 points per game and registered shutouts of Rutgers, Kentucky and Vanderbilt. The Vols were led by the likes of safeties Chris White, who intercepted nine passes, and Charles Davis, now assistant athletic director at Stanford; tackles Richard Cooper, who went on to a lengthy career as an offensive lineman for the New Orleans Saints, and Mark Hovanic; and linebackers Dale Jones, Darrin Miller and Kelly Ziegler.

Daryl Dickey took over when Tony Robinson was injured against Alabama and took UT the rest of the way, including a program-boosting Sugar Bowl win over Miami.

HOW SWEET IT IS The Vols were up 6-0 on Kentucky at the half when Daryl Dickey made one of the more phenomenal plays in a phenomenal season. Scrambling for his life, literally in the arms of a Wildcat defender, Dickey somehow flipped a pass to Tim McGee, who completed the play 37 yards downfield for a touchdown.

The Vols exploded, going on to win, 42-0, and they approached the Vandy game with the knowledge that a win would lock up a Sugar Bowl appearance since Florida had been locked out of the title chase because of NCAA sanctions.

Vandy never had a chance. Dickey finished the game without an interception to maintain a 106-pass string without a theft and finished the season having completed 64.9 percent of his passes. The end zones were littered with tiny sugar cubes tossed from the stands. The Volunteers, 8-1-2, were headed for New Orleans.

HURRICANE BREWING The 1985 season was a tremendous victory for Majors. But standing in the Vols' way were

the Hurricanes of Miami coached by Jimmy Johnson, who had been an assistant to Majors at Iowa State. Even then, Johnson — who would later take the Dallas Cowboys back to the top of the NFL — was a brash, if not arrogant, individual, and it was an attitude willingly employed by his team and Hurricane fans.

The Vols were underdogs, decided underdogs — by as many as 17 points — and Miami and its fans left open wounds with their verbal jabs and then poured salt in 'em. It wasn't such a good idea, even on Bourbon Street where raucous, rowdy behavior was the norm.

Tennessee players had been forewarned: behave or be home. So they stored up the numerous memories of being verbally shellacked and saved each and every one for game day.

Miami scored first on a medium-range pass from Vinny Testaverde to Michael Irvin. And then Ken Donahue's defensive game plan and all those stored-up emotions came flowing out of the Vols like a surging Tennessee river storming over its banks.

Testaverde, sacked twice by Dale Jones and twice by Mark Hovanic, was intercepted four times. Reggie White got one of those interceptions and 10 tackles. Daryl Dickey was picked as the game's MVP and Jeff Powell, filling in for an injured Keith Davis, had a 60-yard touchdown run.

When the dust had settled the Vols had scored 35 points, the most ever by a UT team in a postseason game at that time, and limited talented Miami to just seven.

Mark Hovanic had two sacks and two tackles for loss in the Vols' upset of Miami in New Orleans.

VOLUNTEER QUIZ

33. Who was the first Vol to win the Jacobs Award, given annually to the SEC's best blocker?

More Good Ol' Days

The 1985 season — ending in an Orange Bowl victory against Miami — only whetted appetites hungry for dominance in the Southeastern Conference. On the trip from New Orleans, during which one must pass through Birmingham, a bus traveled with a sign draped on either side: "Pardon us, Alabama and Auburn, while we run through you one more time."

AN EXTENSION Coach Johnny Majors, aware of the pre-'85 rumblings of discontent, confided one day: "I guess we shut 'em up this year, huh?"

There was an opportunity to leave; Pittsburgh, which he'd taken to a national championship, wanted him back. Majors instead used the offer as a bargaining chip for a six-year contract with an annual salary of more than $250,000.

Too, Majors had been hounding Athletic Director Bob Woodruff to upgrade facilities, which had not seen a serious facelift in almost two decades. Out of their discussions (but under the direction of Doug Dickey, who had by then been hired as Woodruff's replacement) came a completely refurbished Gibbs Hall, the athletic dormitory, and Neyland-Thompson Sports Center, which houses the coaches' offices, the weight room, the training room, UT's football Hall of Fame and a 70-yard indoor practice facility.

Tailback Keith Davis was slowed by a knee injury but refused to have surgery and the knee healed by itself.

GUINNESS RECORD Enthusiasm was at an all-time high. It was so high that the spring game, with a little promoting, drew a crowd of 73,801.

UGLY HORIZON UT had found a silver lining behind a dark cloud in 1985, but there was another dark cloud behind that silver lining.

Just a week or so after the Vols' astonishing victory over Miami, Tony Robinson and former teammate Kenneth (B.B.) Cooper (1981-84) were arrested on felony cocaine charges, accused of selling cocaine to an undercover Knoxville officer. Robinson was convicted, spent 90 days in a workhouse, was released, then returned to jail for violating his work release agreement. Then after gaining probation, Robinson was once again returned to jail after failing to report to his probation officer.

But it was just the tip of the iceberg. The two Knoxville newspapers, the Journal and the News-Sentinel, began a spirited competition with UT athletics as the primary focus.

There had been rumblings that Robinson had been using a booster's car, and when Robinson was arrested, a credit card belonging to that booster was in Robinson's possession. An in-house investigation was ordered by UT President Dr. Edward Boling. UT was placed on a year's probation (without sanctions); Majors received a formal reprimand.

To make a long story short, UT players — some of whom who'd been selling their complimentary tickets — boycotted the media at the first 1986 game. They did so with 10 of their teammates suspended.

34. Name the only Vol ever to win the Outland Trophy, which recognizes the nation's best interior lineman.

1986: STUMBLING THROUGH

UT won the '86 season-opener, rolling over New Mexico, 35-21, as Keith Davis scored on touchdown

PROFILE: DALE JONES (1983-86)

As a senior at Bradley Central High in Cleveland, Tenn., Marvin Dale Jones wasn't big enough to land a major-college scholarship. Oh, there were those like Tennessee recruiter Phillip Fulmer who were interested, but most every recruiter told Jones he should look at smaller schools or perhaps attend a prep school for a year or two.

Jones had no interest in other schools. He wanted to play for Tennessee, so he spent a fall at Tennessee Military Institute, where he worked hard on the weights and stuffed his face every chance he got to put on the weight the Vols felt was necessary.

And from TMI, Jones sprang into the UT picture.

A hard-working, hard-hitting linebacker, Jones keyed the Vols' stunning 38-20 upset of then top-ranked Auburn in '85 when he and teammate Darrin Miller knocked prized Tiger running back Bo Jackson out of the game. Jackson was sidelined with a deep thigh bruise when Jones' helmet had hit with the ferocious intent of breaking a leg.

But it was the '85 Alabama game when he pulled off one of the most spectacular plays in UT history, a play that preserved a 16-14 Tennessee win over the Crimson Tide and propelled the Volunteers into the Sugar Bowl.

His team was nursing a two-point lead and had lost its starting quarterback (Tony Robinson) to a knee injury. With Alabama trying to mount a drive, Jones crashed through the line from his outside linebacker post. The Bama quarterback, Mike Shula, was fading back to pass. Jones leaped and knocked the pass high into the air. Staggering to maintain his balance, Jones leaped once more and intercepted the pass, thus preserving UT's win.

Jones left a defensive coordinator's post at Georgia Military Academy in the spring of 1996 to join the staff at Appalachian State as linebackers coach.

Upon graduation, Charles Davis (left) went to work for the Southeastern Conference, then the U.S. Olympic committee and then Stanford, where he currently serves as an assistant athletic director.

William Howard (middle) set an NCAA record for consecutive carries with 16 against Ole Miss.

Randy Sanders (right), now a member of UT's coaching staff, is a likely head coaching candidate for the future.

Though it was only once, UT wore orange shoes. It was against Alabama in 1986 when UT lost 56-28. The shoes, boxed up and shelved after the loss, eventually made their way to the U.S.S.R., after UT received an equipment request from a group of Russians interested in starting an American football team.

runs of 46 and 41 yards and Charles Davis returned an interception 55 yards for a touchdown.

But while UT was whipping New Mexico, Mississippi State was whacking Syracuse and it was Mississippi State the Vols had to face next.

Jeff Francis, the apparent winner over Randy Sanders in the quarterback derby, went down early with a shoulder injury and UT's seven-game win streak was in jeopardy. It was one of the highlights of State quarterback Don Smith's career as he threw for a pair of touchdowns and then ran 62 yards for another.

Tailbacks Davis and Charles Wilson missed the game, leaving the running load to junior fullback William Howard, who carried 34 times for 184 yards.

UT had a chance to pull it out but Sanders, who since has often said he wonders what would've happened had he completed it, overthrew 5-foot-8 wide receiver Terrence Cleveland in the end zone as time ran out.

It got no better the next week as Brent Fullwood ran for 207 yards in a 34-8 Auburn victory. The only Vol highlight, really, was a fourth-quarter, 60-yard scoring pass from Sanders to junior college transfer Anthony Miller.

Howard scored three touchdowns in a win over Texas-El Paso, but Army blocked a Bob Garmon punt and returned it for a win to drop UT to 2-3 with Alabama on the horizon.

The struggling Vols, victimized perhaps by problems within the coaching staff, got buried by Bama. They were outscored 56-28 in a game Alabama led 42-14 at the half. For the second time of the season, a back gained more than 200 yards against UT. This time it was Bobby Humphrey with 217 yards. The final score reflected the most points surrendered by a Tennessee team since the Vols surrendered 60 to North Carolina way back in 1893.

The Vols dipped to 2-5 with a 14-13 loss to Georgia Tech, but moved back into the win column with a 33-3 trouncing of Memphis State and finally reached .500 with victories over Ole Miss and Kentucky.

A Liberty Bowl bid was extended after the win over Kentucky, in which UT defenders sacked Wildcat quarterback Bill Ransdell eight times. UT locked up a

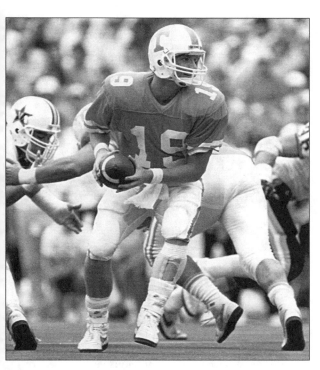

Jeff Francis was UT's all-time leading passer until he was displaced by Andy Kelly.

winning season with a 35-20 win over Vanderbilt.

Francis was named the bowl's MVP after completing 22 of 31 passes for 243 yards and three touchdowns as UT defeated Minnesota, 21-14. Dale Jones, getting nine tackles, two assists, a fumble recovery and two tackles for loss, was named the outstanding defensive player, and Joey Clinkscales, who'd become a favorite target for Francis, was the game's outstanding offensive player.

1987: COUNTING

They were building on a five-game win streak — hoping to, anyway — and had been selected to begin the 1987 season against Iowa in the Kickoff Classic at East Rutherford, N.J.

A new star was born that day: Knoxville native Reggie Cobb, who ran 25 times for 138 yards. But the hero had to be senior outside linebacker Darrin Miller, a burly New Jersey native who intercepted an Iowa pitchout and returned it 96 yards for a second-quarter touchdown.

The clinching points didn't come until just three seconds were left on the clock, with a 20-yard field goal by walk-on (soon-to-be-scholarshipped) kicker Phil Reich, and UT won 23-22. Middle linebacker Kelly Ziegler, now a physical therapist, overcame the plate and

A very competitive player, linebacker Kelly Ziegler played much of his career with a plate and screws in his ankle.

In his first game, Reggie Cobb ran for 138 yards in the Kickoff Classic.

It's been said that a sun dial was used to time the 96-yard run made by Darrin Miller in the Kickoff Classic.

Mike Whitehead was an unsung defensive lineman who was used mostly in special defensive situations.

screws in his ankle to turn in a 16-tackle performance.

The Vols shelled Colorado State, 49-3, and won their SEC-opener, 38-10, against Mississippi State before a 20-all tie with Auburn. Then they moved to 4-0-1 on a 38-12 pasting of California to set up an anticipated battle with Alabama, which was coming off an upset loss to Memphis State.

Jeff Francis, as he had the previous year, passed for more than 300 yards, but UT was held to 51 rushing yards and Bama coasted to a 41-22 win to end UT's unbeaten streak at 9-0-1.

UT busted Georgia Tech, 29-15, with members of the 1967 team, which finished No. 2 in the nation, watching. But Francis sustained a first-quarter ankle injury that came more into play the next week as UT fell to Boston College, 20-18, with Francis on the bench.

Again, though, UT recovered, with freshman Sterling Henton making his debut as the Vols' starting quarterback against Louisville. The Vols won, 41-10, with Keith Davis, who'd been slowed by knee injury, scoring two touchdowns and gaining 73 yards on the day and Cobb adding a 127-yard rushing performance.

Francis was still on the bench the next week and Henton directed a 55-13 dismantling of Ole Miss on homecoming. With 94,237 fans on hand, UT broke the team total offense record with 368 yards rushing and 210 passing.

Ahead 24-20 at Lexington, UT turned to unsung defensive lineman Mike Whitehead, who stopped Kentucky runner Mark Higgs inside the Tennessee 1-yard line late in the final period. The Vols' Bob Garmon, standing at the edge of his own end zone, then killed most of the few remaining ticks of the scoreboard clock by meandering around in the end zone before stepping out of bounds. It gave Kentucky a safety, but also allowed the Vols a free kick from their own 20-yard line, which sewed up the win.

But excitement in 1987 came from the most unexpected places, including Vanderbilt, which broke on top for a 28-3 lead before UT's first touchdown, a 10-yard pass from Francis to Terrence Cleveland. UT took a 35-28 lead by scoring on five straight possessions in the second and third periods, but it took a 47-yard field goal by Reich to provide the winning edge in a 38-36 shootout. Cobb, who tied Herschel Walker and Jackie

PROFILE: JEFF FRANCIS (1985-88)

He was a gawky, skinny-looking youngster when he arrived on the Tennessee campus from Mount Prospect, Ill., a Chicago suburb. But he was intelligent, something for which offensive coordinator Walt Harris

Jeff Francis is currently No. 2 on Tennessee's list of all-time career total offense leaders, with 5,900 yards.

had looked for almost as much as the talent.

There were those who questioned that talent, but quarterback Jeff Francis, who eventually spent a couple of years in the National Football League, wound up scrambling to the top of the Vols' passing lists. He broke or tied 12 school records and also set the SEC standard for completion percentage in a career at 62 percent.

"Jeff is as fine a young man as I've ever been around," said Vol Coach Johnny Majors. "He's so unselfish, so team-oriented. So many young people are after instant gratification. You couldn't have an athlete who will make a sounder decision, one that is best for the football team."

Francis, who won the starting quarterback's job over current Vol assistant coach Randy Sanders, had four 300-yard passing games in his career — two in 1986, one in 1987 and one in 1988 — and directed UT to a Liberty Bowl victory over Minnesota in '86 and a Peach Bowl victory over Indiana following the 9-2-1 regular-season effort of '87.

Punter Bob Garmon (left) once preserved a UT victory by dancing out of the end zone against Kentucky.

Phil Reich's (middle) 47-yard field goal was the difference against Vanderbilt.

Keith DeLong (right) was a first-round draft pick by the 49ers.

Parker for the SEC single-single scoring record (20 touchdowns) finished the year with 1,197 yards and became only the second Vol to rush for 1,000 yards in a season (joining Johnnie Jones). Vol linebacker Keith DeLong, who'd later play for the San Francisco 49ers, had a tremendous performance against the 'Dores, with a 19-tackle effort.

EVERYTHING'S PEACHY Majors was one victory from his first 10-win season as the Vol skipper and UT's first since Battle's 1972 team reached double-digits with a win over LSU in the Astro Bluebonnet Bowl.

The Vols, as they had four times previously during the season, rallied in the final period of the Peach Bowl. Again it was Reggie Cobb and Jeff Francis behind a bruising offensive line, with Cobb scoring the game-winner on Indiana. The final score: 27-22.

CORNER TURNED? The foundation was in place for the Vols, who were one of the early favorites to win the Southeastern Conference in 1988. Haywood Harris, the affable UT sports information director who has been known to turn a colorful phrase more than once, unknowingly pegged the season when he wrote in the Vols' media guide:

Because linemen were having a tough time hearing his snap count and audibles due to crowd noise, quarterback Jeff Francis spent several sessions with a speech therapist in 1987 learning to use his diaphragm more in speaking.

"The prospect of playing four Southeastern Conference games by mid-October has underscored the need for coach Johnny Majors to have the Tennessee Vols in fine fettle when they burst out of the starting blocks for the 1988 season.

"By the time the leaves have turned deep orange in the nearby Smoky Mountains, UT will either have some impressive scalps on its belt or will have been bloodied by some of the biggest ogres in college football."

The ogres won.

The Volunteers, who had such high hopes after the 1987 season, might well have seen too much of their own press clippings. They opened the season with six straight losses, a time during which assistant coach Ken Donahue — the hero of the miraculous 1985 season — was asked if the play of his defense was causing him

Defensive coordinator Ken Donahue, the hero of 1985, was dismissed in 1988.

nightmares. Donahue, in his best country drawl, responded: "No, when you don't get any sleep you don't have nightmares."

UT lost at Georgia, then at home against Duke and LSU before falling at Auburn. The Vols returned home again to lose to Washington State and Alabama.

To say the least, Majors was beside himself. But Majors, always the feisty one, talked of his team "closing ranks." A friend and supporter sent him a quotation which he and his team took to heart: "Tough times never last, tough people do."

PRECARIOUS PERCH Though searching high and low for positives, a lot was getting overlooked. Stunts like that of Nashville disc jockey Duncan Stewart were getting more positive publicity than UT.

Stewart climbed high atop a billboard platform and vowed not to come down until UT won a game.

He remained for two weeks until a strong wind brought him down from his perch. He slipped, managed to grab a rung on a ladder along the catwalk and saved himself from a 30-foot fall. Nevertheless, he was "grounded" after receiving treatment at a local hospital for a leg injury.

SIX STRAIGHT Overlooked in the loss to Georgia, which just lined up and ran right at the Vols, was quarterback Jeff Francis displacing Alan Cockrell as Tennessee's all-time passing yardage leader.

In '86, UT re-retired the only numbers ever retired by the Vols'. Those four numbers — 32, 49, 61 and 62 — were originally retired in '46 but were returned to active status during the '50s, a time of increased squads. The numbers were retired originally in memory of fullback Bill Nowling (32), guard Rudy Klarer (49), center Willis Tucker (61) and fullback Clyde "Ig" Fuson (62). All four players were killed during World War II. The last players to wear those numbers were Charles Wilson (32), Kelly Ziegler (49), Nick Zecchino (62) and Mike West (61).

Thomas Woods was UT's single-season receiving leader until 1995 when he was displaced by Joey Kent.

Anthony Morgan, later drafted by the Chicago Bears, set a single-game kick return record (143 yards) against LSU.

A good receiver, Alvin Harper also is remembered as a team player and a vicious blocker.

But it was something of same song, new chapter. Though the Bulldogs threw only 10 passes, completing seven for 25 yards, Georgia backs Rodney Hampton and Tim Worley ran for a combined 340 yards, more than offsetting the 354 for which Francis threw.

UT out-coached itself in spending the next week's practice on run defense. Duke's Anthony Dilwig and Clarkston Hines saw to that. Dilwig threw for 311 yards and Hines caught eight passes good for 145 yards and two touchdowns. It more than offset UT receiver Thomas "TD" Woods' first 100-yard game (128). The Duke coach? Steve Spurrier, who now haunts the Vols from Gainesville.

LSU combined the run and pass to perfection behind Tommy Hodson and Eddie Fuller, and the Tigers' defense was near stone-wall as LSU got its first win in Knoxville in 11 visits.

Auburn led only 10-6 at the half, but this time the Vol offense faltered, allowing 21 points off turnovers as the Tigers blitzed UT, 38-6. Keith DeLong had 10 tackles and Anthony Morgan set a single-game UT record with 143 yards on kick returns.

Washington State had been scheduled as a breather. Although it was in this game that Alvin Harper set a single-game reception record with 12 catches and Francis took over the No. 1 spot on the all-time attempts list, the Cougars ripped UT, 52-24.

CHANGING THE GUARD The boo-birds were out in force. Majors was under fire and there were rumors that he would either be canned or resign. He promised change.

What some couldn't understand was how Majors could part ways with Ken Donahue, the hard-working hero of 1985. But he did, bumping Doug Mathews into the position.

For the second-straight season, Alabama was coming off a loss when it met UT in 1989. The Tide roared out to a 14-0 lead and held a 14-9 halftime advantage but had to have a 55-yard, fourth-quarter run from Murray Hill to win the game. UT's Keith DeLong continued to shine, chalking up 19 unassisted tackles, a pass interception, a sack and a tackle for loss.

Yet the change in coaches at the beginning of the season might have been a jump-start for UT, which was about to soothe some ruffled feathers by closing out the year with a more suitable streak.

"CHECK, CHECK, CHECK" Though a winning season was out of the question, Majors rededicated himself to the task. There was no job too large or too small to get a piece of his time.

He went on a tear on the practice field, too, and players and coaches alike quivered when they'd hear him trigger his bullhorn from high atop his platform. They knew when he keyed the bullhorn's trigger what was coming.

"Check, check, check," Majors would shriek, asking that something be run again. And if it wasn't to his liking, the Hall-of-Famer would come tearing down the platform steps to set it right. An assistant or two were occasionally overheard pleading with their players: "Get it right, get it right. None of us wants him over here."

Granted, the second half of the schedule was nowhere near the rough-and-tumble grind of the first, but Majors wasn't going to quit and wasn't about to let his team quit either.

So the Vols righted the ship, reeling off victories over Memphis State, Boston College, Ole Miss, Kentucky and Vanderbilt. But only two opponents failed to score in double digits against the Vols — Boston College and Vanderbilt.

The losses of '86 and the debacle of '88, however, spurred folks on. UT's recruiting picked back up, and the foundation was laid again.

Doug Mathews, right, was promoted to defensive coordinator when Johnny Majors dismissed Ken Donahue.

1989: SILENCING CRITICS

Majors had done it before, sweeping to a league championship in 1985. He'd silenced his critics again with a 10-win season in '87. And he was about to do it once more.

Though the record-setting Jeff Francis had graduated, UT swept to an 11-win year in 1989, losing only to — who else? — Alabama. It was the first 11-victory season

Eric Still led a vicious blocking effort against UCLA.

The Cobb-Webb: Reggie Cobb (above) and Chuck Webb (below).

at UT in 19 seasons.

Yet it opened precariously, the Volunteers holding on in a close 17-14 win over Colorado State, a team that was to have been a patsy. The next week they were flying to Pasadena to tackle UCLA and few were giving 'em much of a chance at all.

But the Vols' Phillip Fulmer, by now assistant head coach and offensive coordinator, had what would become a bruising offensive line led by guard Eric Still. Most people believed UT would fail in its effort to run the ball in California. How wrong they were.

THE "COBB-WEBB" UT rushed for 247 yards and rolled over UCLA, 24-6, for the Vols' first win against the Bruins since 1970. Reggie Cobb gained 78 yards and Chuck Webb, rolling up the highest rushing total by a freshman since Cobb gained 140 against Vandy in 1987, finished the night with 134 yards.

Duke fell, 28-6, before Auburn came calling. Cobb rolled up 225 yards and Webb another 93. With ESPN televising the homecoming game nationally, Cobb-Webb gained 189 yards and Darryl Hardy and Shazzon Bradley racked up 14 and 11 tackles, respectively, as UT beat Georgia, 17-14, for the first time since '72.

PROFILE: ANDY KELLY (1988-91)

Andy Kelly

They called him "Mammaw," a nickname he picked up in junior high and a nickname that was most appropriate for those of us who watched him run 40-yard dashes in spring time trials.

"I was running one day and one of my coaches told me his mammaw ran faster than I did," Kelly admitted.

In an era filled with strong-armed quarterbacks, Andy Kelly was more of a touchdown-maker, that coach on the field that offensive coordinators love. His arm wasn't the strongest, and he certainly wasn't a breakaway threat. He just won: two SEC championships and a pair of victories in three New Year's Day bowl games.

Kelly, for all his reported shortcomings, directed UT to a

A SHOCK Reggie Cobb, who'd been suspended from the team and then reinstated in the summer of '89 for what Majors called a "violation of team rules," was dismissed from the team after the UCLA game, reportedly for testing positive for marijuana. The Cobb-Webb was Cobb-less.

WHOOPEE! Some call it a shovel pass, some call it a Utah pass, some call it a whoopee pass. Regardless, Alabama made whoopee with the toss in 1989 and nailed UT, 47-30, as Siran Stacy came off the Bama bench to run for 125 yards. He also caught nine passes for 158 yards and scored three touchdowns, offsetting a 100-yard effort by Chuck Webb, a 15-tackle effort by Darryl Hardy and the off-the-bench performance by quarterback Andy Kelly, who threw a pair of touchdown passes.

VOLUNTEER QUIZ

35. There are 16 former Vols in the National Football Foundation's College Hall of Fame. Who is the latest such honoree?

NEW NAME His performance against the Crimson Tide (15 for 28, 226 yards) gave Andy Kelly the opening he needed to move past Sterling Henton and into the starting quarterback's role.

Kelly settled in rather nicely, outdueling LSU's Tommy Hodson on the next Saturday in Baton Rouge. Tennessee won, 45-39, but more importantly, the Volunteers were no 26-5-2 record as a starter and climbed to the top of the Vols' all-time passing charts. En route to throwing for 6,397 yards and 36 touchdowns, the native of Evensville, Tenn., completed 60.8 percent of his passes.

Over his two-plus years as a starter, Kelly directed some major wins, including a 45-39 shootout victory over touted LSU quarterback Tommy Hodson in Kelly's first varsity start. He also led UT in a 30-16 win over UCLA and heralded quarterback Tommy "Machine" Gunn.

But no regular-season victory in UT history was bigger than that amazing comeback in 1991 at South Bend, Ind., when the Volunteers rallied to beat Notre Dame, 35-34. Rebounding from a first-quarter interception that was returned for a touchdown, Kelly completed 24 of 38 passes for 259 yards and three touchdowns. On that day, he took over as UT's all-time leader in career passing attempts, passing yardage and touchdown passes.

"You can say what you want. Andy Kelly just wins," offered Phillip Fulmer, who was the Vols' offensive coordinator at the time.

And even when he lost, Kelly was good at what he did.

The year before, Notre Dame was in Knoxville and rallied to beat the Vols, 34-29. But Kelly was at his best that blustery November night, completing 35 of a school-record 60 pass attempts for 399 yards, the best single-game passing performance in Vol football history.

Andy Kelly (right) replaced Sterling Henton as the starting quarterback against LSU.

longer relying solely on Chuck Webb, who gained 132 yards. No, Kelly completed 11 of 17 passes for 180 yards although he didn't have a single touchdown pass.

The game's turning point, though, came with just seconds left before halftime. The Tigers had just taken a 17-14 lead on a David Browndyke field goal and appeared to be headed for the locker room on an emotional high. There was, however, time for a kickoff, which was gathered in by freshman Carl Pickens at his own 7-yard line. He went the distance and UT went on to take its sixth victory of the season.

RELUCTANT DEFENDER By this time, Carl Pickens was playing offense, defense and special teams — wide receiver, safety and kick returner.

The Vols nailed Akron, 52-9, as Chuck Webb ran for 162 yards. Most significant, though, was fullback Greg Amsler's scoring pass to Vince Moore. It was the first such (halfback) pass for a touchdown since Frank Foxx found Billy Arbo in the 1978 Duke game. Thomas Woods caught only two passes, but they covered 112 yards.

Then it was back to SEC play for the final three-game swing: 33-21 over Ole Miss as Webb ran for 294 yards, 31-10 over Kentucky as Pickens got his third interception in as many games, and 17-10 over Vanderbilt on a 4-yard pass from Andy Kelly to Pickens and a 1-yard run by Tony Thompson, who had a career-

VOLUNTEER QUIZ

36. Who was the first Vol to be honored as SEC Player of the Year?

high 128 yards.

The effort against Ole Miss made Webb only the third Vol to reach the 1,000-yard rushing plateau. Along the way that year, he answered some questions.

"I knew he was pretty good," recalled Kelly, "but I

PROFILE: JACK SELLS

He is a former Volunteer, as both player and assistant coach, but Jack Sells' name will likely live former in infamy regarding Tennessee football history.

Sells, a Cookeville native who walked on and earned a scholarship, spent a couple of seasons at UT as a graduate assistant, then worked a year at Middle Tennessee State and Kent before coming home to coach tight ends. Already he was known as an outstanding recruiter.

But Sells broke some rules in recruiting several players and was suspended with pay, then fired. Coupled with an investigation into UT's summer camp — the NCAA had received an anonymous note saying it was "invitation only" — the Vols wound up with a serious in-house investigation.

Coach Johnny Majors hired no one to replace Sells, and while other schools were still enjoying the 90-scholarship limit Majors cut his total grants to 85, a rule that was to go into effect in a couple of years anyway. The Volunteers wound up with two years of non-sanction probation.

If the Sells saga ended there, most would look back and say, "OK, he made a mistake, but he did sign Chuck Webb."

But Sells wasn't through with Tennessee. One of his former UT coaching buddies, defensive backfield coach Ron Zook, was at Florida and Sells took it upon himself to fax play diagrams with notes pertaining to tendencies and audibles

Jack Sells

to Zook prior to the 1991 Florida-Tennessee game in Gainesville.

On at least two different occasions, Sells denied faxing anything to Zook, although the Knoxville News-Sentinel had acquired copies of some of the material he had faxed to Zook from Kinko's.

Sells, who by then had been punched out by at least one irate UT fan, continued to deny his involvement. Asked again, Sells said only that his father might've sent something to Zook.

Finally, after repeated denials, Zook admitted he received something from Sells, but denied it was plays.

Sells never admitted publicly that he faxed anything until he filed a lawsuit against Kinko's.

Zook, however, finally acknowledged it, and Florida Coach Steve Spurrier later found out and admonished Zook.

Sells' suit against Kinko's was settled out of court in 1995.

37. Name the only UT coach to win the American Football Coaches Association National Coach of the Year award.

Receiver Carl Pickens, who turned pro after his junior year, was defensive MVP of the 1989 Cotton Bowl win over Arkansas.

wondered to myself if he would cut and run when the going got tough. Chuck never had much to say but he was the consummate player on the field. I mean he'd look great in practice, then take it to another plateau on game day, and that day against Ole Miss, he was in a zone."

HIGH COTTON There was really no way to stop Arkansas' running game in the Cotton Bowl, except maybe to outrun them, which UT did. Arkansas finished with 320 rushing yards, but UT averaged a Cotton Bowl-best 8.4 yards per carry to finish with 361.

Chuck Webb picked up 78 yards in one run, the third-longest in Cotton Bowl history. But UT had learned to pass, too, and Andy Kelly and Anthony Morgan hooked up on an 84-yard score.

Former Vol Jim Bates gave up his job as linebackers coach after a run-in with Johnny Majors.

Webb, who scored twice, was the game's offensive MVP and Carl Pickens, though by now reluctant to play safety, was the game's defensive MVP after picking off a pass in the Vols' end zone to thwart a bid by the Razorbacks, the Southwest Conference champions who had by then announced plans of joining the SEC.

Though it didn't come to light until after he'd departed, linebackers coach and former Vol Jim Bates had a run-in with Majors over the latter's planned visit to a prospective recruit. It was a visit that never took place and Bates, deciding UT wasn't the place for him, became another of the numerous ex-Majors assistants. Also, Doug Mathews, who'd been Majors' defensive coordinator, decided to enter private business.

There was a house-cleaning and into the defensive coordinator's post stepped Larry Lacewell, who had coached a year for Majors at Iowa State before going on to an outstanding career first at Oklahoma, then at Arkansas State.

VOLUNTEER QUIZ

38. What were the original colors for Vol jerseys?

1990: SUGAR SWEET

For whatever reason, the even-numbered years weren't so kind to Majors. His teams posted a 44-38-5 record in even-numbered years as opposed to a 65-26-3 mark in odd-numbered seasons from 1977-91. The Vols went 5-5-1 in '78, 5-6 in '80, 6-5-1 in '82, 7-4-1 in '84, 7-5 in '86 and 5-6 in '88.

So Majors and UT faithful approached 1990 with cautious, guarded optimism.

In the early 1990s, before additions pushed the attendance over the 100,000 mark, an average home game crowd of 90,000 would partake of: 70,000 soft drinks, 60,000 pounds of ice, 17,000 hot dogs, 5,000 boxes of Cracker Jacks, 3,000 bags of nuts and 1,500 bags of potato chips.

The Vols were to open the year in a preseason gala on the West Coast, The Disneyland Pigskin Classic in Anaheim, Calif., against Colorado, which was coming off an 11-1 season. The game was billed as a duel of Heisman hopefuls: Darian Hagan, the Colorado quarterback who had ran and passed for 1,000 yards each the previous year, and Chuck Webb, around whom UT had built — imaginary or otherwise — national championship hopes.

Majors was anything but a fool, and he knew what UT had in Webb. He had also had another outstanding back at Pitt, a youngster named Tony Dorsett. He often called Dorsett a once-in-a-coach's-career player, but later amended that statement, referring to Webb in the same breath.

STEALING THUNDER It was neither Webb nor Hagan who ended up with top billing when the Pigksin Classic was in the books. It was quarterback Andy Kelly, the youngster from southeast Tennessee whose brain was as sharp as his feet were slow. Kelly, under fire from a pressing Colorado defensive line, suggested at halftime that maybe UT should go with its two-minute offense in the second half.

Andy Kelly, with a 368-yard passing performance, led a UT rally for a tie against Colorado in the Pigskin Classic.

PROFILE: KEITH DELONG (1985-88)

He came from a talented family — both his father and uncle had starred for the Volunteers — so expectations were high when Keith DeLong stepped onto the field at Tennessee.

A linebacker in the Vols' 5-2 defense, DeLong finished his senior season as a first-team All-America selection. He recorded 159 tackles, including 117 solo hits, for the 10th- and third-best performances in Tennessee history.

For two seasons he led the Vols in tackles and his best single-game performance came in 1988 when he registered 23 total tackles (19 solos).

"I've never had a player play any harder at any position that DeLong did," said Coach Johnny Majors. "A lot of people can play when everything is going well, but it takes someone special to play the way he did when things weren't going well."

DeLong, prior to being selected by the San Francisco 49ers in the first round of the NFL draft, played in the Japan and Senior bowl games.

He wound up completing 33 of 55 passes for 368 yards and three touchdowns as Tennessee rallied to tie the game at 31-31, then almost pulled out the win. Webb broke a 25-yard run that put the Vols in position for a winning field goal, but time elapsed before he could get out of bounds.

VOLUNTEER QUIZ

UN-WEBBED The Vols won handily the next week, drubbing former Vol offensive coordinator Walt Harris' Pacific team, 55-7. But when asked about Pacific even today, most UT fans will tell you rather quickly not the score but the fact that this was the game in which Chuck Webb's college career ended. The knee injury came on a short gainer in Pacific territory, and Webb didn't actually get hit with a solid blow. He planted to pivot and the next thing anyone knew was that he was down. Webb, a juggernaut of a running back, walked off the field.

"There's not been another one like him," UT assistant Randy Sanders would later say. "He had a style all his own and nobody, nobody has run like Chuck Webb."

AN OPENING He wasn't as big or as shifty as Chuck Webb, but little Mantoniel (Tony) Deion Thompson, a 5-foot-7, 180-pound senior from Lake Wales, Fla., saw an opportunity and made the most of it, becoming an unlikely hero as UT headed for its first back-to-back SEC championships since 1940.

The following week was UT's league-opener at Mississippi State and Thompson was up to the task. Sure, he had holes you could have driven a truck through on occasion. But Thompson responded with a

39. UT lost its first college football game to whom?

Johnny Majors was fond of saying, "Those who stay will play," and such was the case for Tony Thompson.

Bernard Dafney's (left) only touchdown as a Vol came on a "fumble-rooskie" against Mississippi State.

Phillip Fulmer recalls John Fisher (middle) as, "One of those tough players who'd do anything for you."

Greg Burke (right), a junior college transfer, made a name for himself as a consistent kicker.

248-yard effort before retiring to the UT bench in the third quarter, having scored on runs of 69 and 80 yards.

This also was big Bernard Dafney's moment to shine. Recruited to UT as a defensive tackle, Dafney (6-7, 300) had moved to offensive guard. He scored the Vols' third touchdown against State on a "fumble-rooskie" he picked up and toted 32 yards for a touchdown. It was this play that eventually caused NCAA rules-makers to amend the regulation regarding an offensive team advancing a fumble.

Andy Kelly wasn't needed, nor was Thompson, the next week as UT blistered Texas-El Paso, 56-0. The Vols were resting up for Auburn the next week.

"Listen, boys," Auburn Coach Pat Dye told a team that was down 19-3 at halftime, "I know this coach. He'll try to sit on the lead. Just keep plugging away."

Tennessee did indeed try to sit on its lead and Vol defenders, on a hot and humid night "on the Plains," began to cramp up from spending so much time on the field. Some, like linebacker Darryl Hardy (he also played special teams), played 80-plus snaps as Auburn rallied to tie the game at 26-26.

Still, UT had a chance to win. But record-setting Greg Burke's 34-yard field goal try faded left of the uprights as time expired.

Though he might tell you today he shouldn't have done it, UT center John Fisher was caught on camera by ESPN hurling a cup of ice. It hit Burke and the incident received much publicity. To be honest, Fisher proved why he was never a quarterback candidate — he was aiming at the camera man.

OPPORTUNITY KNOCKS AGAIN The critics were again out in force, busting Majors' chops for letting one get away against Auburn and for his teams' general inability to beat Auburn and Alabama.

But there already was another rivalry that had been rekindled and it was an opportunity for Majors to quell the unruly.

With nine bowl representatives on hand, UT scrambled to a 7-3 halftime lead over Florida. But with the second-half kickoff the game was all but over.

Dale Carter, an All-American, keyed UT's win over Florida with an amazing kickoff return.

Gathering in the kick at his own 9-yard line, Dale Carter, the junior college transfer, zigged and zagged his way through the first two waves of Gator defenders, then broke to the open spaces and polished off a 91-yard kickoff return with a flourish.

The Vols, who threw 21 points on the board in a 12-minute span of the third period, broke it wide open. Freshman Reggie Ingram scored on a 22-yard interception return and Carl Pickens completed a 47-yard touchdown pass play from tight end Von Reeves. The Gators finished with just 64 rushing yards and 194 total yards in one of the worst beatings (45-3) a Steve Spurrier team has ever absorbed.

As a freshman, Reggie Ingram intercepted a pass and returned it for a touchdown against Florida.

One of Majors' old thorns, Alabama, was next. The Vols, facing one of the stoutest defenses ever put together in Tuscaloosa, could muster only two field goals. It was the block of a 50-yard Greg Burke field goal try that led to Alabama's game-winning kick from Phillip Doyle. This was the first game since a scoreless tie in 1953 that neither the Volunteers nor the Crimson Tide scored a touchdown.

Tennessee by now was into November, Majors' favorite time of the season. He often said, "They remember what you do in November."

The Vols downed Temple, 41-20, with Pickens, by now solely a receiver, pulling in three passes for 141 yards. And Pickens and quarterback Andy Kelly put on a memorable show on Nov. 10 as Notre Dame, sparked by Raghib "Rocket" Ismail, foiled a UT comeback to win, 34-29. Kelly threw for 399 yards — the best single-game effort in UT history — and Pickens, setting a UT single-game catching record (13), accounted for 167 of those yards. It took an end-zone interception by Notre Dame's

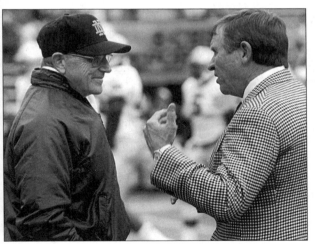

Johnny Majors was feeling the pressure from his critics, but the Vols came up with an amazing 35-34 victory over Lou Holtz's 1991 Notre Dame team.

VOLUNTEER QUIZ

40. The Vols' first win and their first home win came in different seasons against the same team. What team was it?

Rod Smith to ensure the win.

From there, though, it was win, win, win: Ole Miss, 22-13, with Kelly and Alvin Harper hooking up twice for touchdowns; Kentucky, 42-28, as Tony Thompson became the fifth Vol to crack the 1,000-yard rushing barrier and Kelly, who also dropped pooch punts dead at the UK 10- and 9-yard lines, passed for a school record five touchdowns; and Vanderbilt, 49-20, as Thompson ran for 236 yards and four touchdowns behind an offensive line that consisted of tight ends Von Reeves and Mark Adams, tackles Charles McRae and Antone Davis, guards Tom Myslinski and Doug Baird and center John Fisher.

SWEETNESS ONCE MORE As had been his trademark, Andy Kelly polished off the '90 season with a bang. So did Tony Thompson, who scored the winning touchdown late in the fourth quarter. They rallied the Vols, who finished with 20 fourth-quarter points (a Sugar Bowl record), to beat Virginia ,23-22, and finish the year ranked in the Top 10 in both writers' and coaches' polls.

THE PHONE IS RINGING Tennessee coaches had been busy recruiting, securing the commitments of players such as "Little Man" Stewart and Aaron Hayden. But no player has commanded as much interest as Heath Shuler, the quarterback from Bryson City, N.C., a small town just over the Smoky Mountains. On the day Shuler was to announce his decision between UT and Alabama, the sports department at the Chattanooga Free Press received more than 400 inquiries and the story was similar in Knoxville and Nashville.

And though he was the bell cow of an outstanding class, it was running backs Hayden and Stewart who stepped to the front the earliest.

Linebacker Darryl Hardy once put Murray Hill out of an Alabama game, but it opened the door for Siran Stacy, who had a field day against the Vols.

1991: FIESTA TIME

Vol coaches had been quite concerned about their running game in the spring of 1991 following the departure of Tony Thompson and Chuck Webb, who — bad knee and all — was drafted by Green Bay.

Into the gap stepped Stewart and Hayden, who became the first backfield duo to rush for 100 yards each in a game in 18 years. UT struck down Howard Schnellenberger's Louisville Cardinals in the '91 opener.

The watchword by now, though — even with the return of Andy Kelly and Carl Pickens and the arrival of Stewart and Hayden — was defense. There were linebackers Darryl Hardy, Earnest Fields and Shon Walker; Shazzon Bradley, by now having found a home at tackle;

PROFILE: HEATH SHULER (1991-93)

In the foothills of the Great Smoky Mountains on the North Carolina side is a road that once was to connect Bryson City, N.C., with Knoxville, Tenn. Because it cut through the Great Smoky Mountains National Forest, conservationists succeeded in having its construction halted. It became known as "The Road to Nowhere."

It was along this road, just a mile or two from his home, that Heath Shuler traveled as he debated his college choice, which had boiled down to Alabama and Tennessee.

"The Road to Nowhere" led Shuler to UT, where he became a runner-up in the Heisman Trophy balloting and a first-round pick in the NFL draft (Washington Redskins).

In between his decision to join UT and his decision to leave the Vols for the NFL after his junior season were a whole lot of exciting football games.

There were stories — they've become part of the Tennessee football lore — that accompany Shuler now wherever he goes. It's said that he once threw a football 80 yards … while on his knees; that he drank nothing stronger than juice, and that included going without soft drinks that contained caffeine; that he knocked out a karate instructor with one kick; that he threw a football so hard to a teammate that the ball burst when it hit a facemask screw. Then, too, there's the ESPN television footage of Shuler, urged on by an ESPN commentator to "throw harder" shattering a plexiglass shield that

was protecting the cameraman.

Had Shuler stayed for his final collegiate season, he would surely have displaced Andy Kelly as the Vols' all-time leading passer. Many fans still ponder how close UT would have chased a national title with Shuler, the senior, directing the Vols. And the debate still rages that had he remained for his senior season, he would have had much less to overcome when he went pro.

Regardless, the Shuler name is etched in UT football history.

Heath Shuler on "The Road to Nowhere," the abandoned road from Bryson City, N.C., to Knoxville where he made his decision to come to Tennessee.

UT's all-time leading rusher, James "Little Man" Stewart had a great day against Ole Miss, running for 215 yards.

Tracy Smith's interception return for a touchdown iced a win over UCLA.

and ends Chris Mims and Chuck Smith to name a few.

They knocked Louisville quarterback Jeff Brohm from the game and sharpened their claws for UCLA phenom Tommy "Machine" Gunn.

It was a mismatch. On a blazing hot Saturday afternoon, Tennessee's defense swarmed Gunn. Punter Tom Hutton averaged 51.6 yards on five boots, all of which went unreturned. Kelly and Pickens clicked on a 34-yard touchdown play, and former running back Tracy Smith, now in the secondary, picked off and returned a Gunn pass 34 yards for a touchdown.

Kelly, though a fifth-year senior, didn't score his first Vol touchdown until the Mississippi State game, which UT won, 26-24, to move to 3-0. But it took a late pass to tight end Mark Adams to bring the Vols back from the brink of disaster.

With a stadium record of 97,731 fans in the house, UT moved to 4-0 with a 30-21 victory over Auburn and again it was Kelly-to-Pickens — on touchdowns of 87 and 67 yards. But the game also was the coming-out party for true freshman kicker John Becksvoort, who nailed three field goals and began a string of consecutive PAT kicks that would became the NCAA standard.

Despite a 392-yard passing performance from Kelly the following week, UT saw its eight-game win streak

PROFILE: SHAZZON BRADLEY (1988-91)

His critics told him often he would never make it. Shazzon Bradley never listened.

Though handicapped by a learning disability, Bradley surprised those critics by passing the ACT and earning more than enough credits to surpass NCAA academic standards.

A running back and linebacker at McMinn County High in Athens, Tenn., Bradley became a starting linebacker at UT as a true freshman. He would play, before he graduated, fullback and defensive end before settling in at defensive tackle.

Bradley was an intelligent, motivated youngster. He served as the team philosopher in the late '80s, and he was one of the most often quoted of Vol players.

Though he didn't make it in the NFL, Bradley, who began dabbling with boxing in his junior and senior seasons, is now a heavyweight fighter.

And, despite being tagged with a "can't-make-it" label, Bradley earned his diploma in four years from UT.

Now a professional boxer, Shazzon Bradley always came up big on defense for UT. He also scored a Vol touchdown on a fake field goal.

broken as Florida cashed in on four of the Vols' six turnovers en route to a 35-18 victory.

It was after this game that Vicky Fulmer, wife of the assistant head coach, was accosted by a Gator fan as she made her way down to the locker room area. She literally

THE VOL NAVY

Tailgate parties have become a common occurrence at football games. But at Tennessee, there's a twist. One can find the world's largest *floating* tailgate party.

There are but two campuses in the nation with access to a water front — UT and Washington — and it is that unusual setting that spawned the Vol Navy.

Former Volunteer sports announcer George Mooney and a friend were the first to travel to games via the Tennessee River (in 1962). From that humble beginning, one can often see as many as 300 boats of all sizes and shapes docked along Neyland Drive.

Some arrive as early as Thursday, some have traveled the river from as far away as 600 miles and some from Alabama have made a three-day trip up the river through Florence and Muscle Shoals. And once within sight of Neyland Stadium on a football Saturday, one is likely to see skiers, canoes, house boats, pontoon boats and even larger crafts.

Once docked, some never hit the shore. They either can't get tickets or they prefer the cool breeze along the river and the colorful analysis of UT play-by-play man John Ward, another of the Tennessee legends.

"jacked his jaw," spraining her wrist in the process, before going on to the Vol area under the stands.

The record dropped to 4-2 the following week as UT was unable to make a 6-3 halftime lead — two Becksvoort field goals — over Alabama stand up. As a mater of fact, the two teams combined for 34 points in the fourth period as Alabama won, 24-19.

From there it was a lengthy stretch run but the Volunteers ran the table, clubbing Memphis State, escaping Notre Dame, blitzing Ole Miss, clamping Kentucky and destroying Vanderbilt.

The most entertaining game, and likely one of the top Vol performances all-time, came on Nov. 9 at South Bend, Ind. Behind 31-7, Tennessee began to right itself just before the half when Darryl Hardy crashed through to block an Irish field goal. Floyd Miley then picked up the loose ball and returned it 85 yards for a UT score.

John Becksvoort made his debut against Auburn and kicked three field goals.

Vol defensive coordinator Larry Lacewell, determined to stop a Notre Dame backfield that featured 255-pound Jerome Bettis, threw 10 men up on the line of scrimmage and dared the Irish to throw. But the pressure was overwhelming, and the Vols pulled back into the fray. In the game's final moments, Kelly found Hayden on a screen pass and Hayden finished off the 26-yard play in the end zone.

Notre Dame, which had lost its kicker earlier in the game, then had a last-second field goal bounce off the buttocks of a diving Jeremy Lincoln, who'd later thank his parents for what he called his "big butt."

Stewart followed up with one of his biggest days the next week, rushing for 215 yards against Ole Miss; and Becksvoort's three field goals pushed UT ahead for good against Kentucky as Vol defenders allowed the Wildcats a net 80 rushing yards after seven tackles for loss and five quarterback sacks.

In the regular-season finale, the Vols had for the first time in UT history three backs gain 100 yards each. Stewart had 145; Hayden, 115; and Nashville product Mose Phillips, 107. The game also marked the first offensive touchdown for senior Shazzon Bradley, who caught a scoring strike from Kelly on a fake field goal.

Defensive coordinator Larry Lacewell left UT after a disagreement with Johnny Majors at the Fiesta Bowl.

The Vols fell apart, however, in a Fiesta Bowl battle with Penn State after forging a 17-7 lead, suffering one interception but also losing three fumbles.

There was some unreported squabbling going on between Majors and his staff at the bowl site in Tempe, Ariz., and several assistants would go their own way — Lacewell to the Dallas Cowboys and defensive line coach Rex Norris to Texas — after UT finished the year 9-3.

It was a sure signal of the bubbling turmoil that was to erupt quite soon.

Changing of the Guard

Johnny Majors was coming off a three-year stretch of 29 wins, six losses and two ties with a major bowl appearance in each of the three seasons (Cotton, Sugar, Fiesta).

With the departures of Larry Lacewell and Rex Norris, Majors brought in Larry Marmie as defensive coordinator and hired Ray Hamilton for the defensive line. Marmie had served under Majors from 1983-84 and left for a head coaching job at Arizona State. Hamilton had been working in the pros.

Too, Majors and the university had lost trainer Tim Kerin, who'd served as advisor to and occasionally go-between for Majors.

Phillip Fulmer as a still-young offensive line coach at Tennessee. Fulmer progressed from the O-line to offensive coordinator to assistant head coach prior to taking over the football program.

Majors was also in the process of renegotiating his contract as UT's head coach and — despite six straight losses to Alabama — believed he was in a strong bargaining position regarding salaries and amenities. He made no bones about his value to the university and began alienating long-time friends and powerful supporters as he pleaded his case.

And then he had heart problems, undergoing a quintuple bypass before the beginning of the 1992 season. He contends that a contract had been on his desk but disappeared before his convalescent leave ended.

FULMER STEPS UP Assistant head coach Phillip Fulmer filled in for Majors, and UT defeated Southwestern Louisiana, 38-3; Georgia, 34-31; and Florida, 31-14.

Quarterback Heath Shuler didn't play long in his debut as a starter, but completed 8 of 9 passes for 130 yards with touchdown strikes to Craig Faulkner and Cory Fleming. He also scored a rushing touchdown against USL.

The Vols asked Fulmer if they could break out white pants for the road game at Georgia and Fulmer responded, "I don't care what you wear as long as we win."

That they did. Georgia rallied to take the lead but Shuler led the Vols back down the field, completing what was Ronald Davis' biggest catch as a Vol. It was a 22-yard completion on a fourth-and-14 at the Georgia 40-yard line before Shuler scored the game-winner from three yards out. The comeback overshadowed a 354-yard passing performance from Bulldogs quarterback Eric Zeier and a 150-yard receiving performance from the Bulldogs' Andre Hastings.

The defense stepped up against Florida although one of the game's most memorable plays — coming just before a monsoon swamped Neyland Stadium — was a 66-yard screen pass from Shuler to Mose Phillips. It boosted the Vols' lead to 24-7. The defense, led by tackle Paul Yatkowski, end Todd Kelly and linebacker Ben Talley, had eight lost-yardage tackles and three sacks.

He later moved to the defensive secondary and was a high draft choice by the Atlanta Falcons, but Ronald Davis made a name for himself with a clutch catch against Georgia in 1992.

DISMAL RETURN Some question why Majors returned as quickly as the fourth game, but the Vols already had won two games they weren't necessarily favored to win and Fulmer was gaining popularity while proving he was quite prepared for a head coaching job. He had, after all, already turned down more than a handful of job interviews.

When Majors did return, though, he found a rather disappointing homecoming. The contract was no longer on his desk and his problems with the administration carried over into staff and team meetings.

Still, with Heath Shuler solidly entrenched as Andy Kelly's successor, the Vols dispatched Cincinnati and Louisiana State with shutouts and appeared to have things going their way.

But then along came Arkansas, which left Knoxville as a 25-24 upset victor on a late field goal. Then Alabama, which won, 17-10.

Next the Vols headed for South Carolina. Majors got into it with defensive line coach Ray Hamilton on the sidelines — destroying a headset that connected to the coaches in the press box — and a couple of Vol assistants left the field so angry that day that there were tears of frustration and anger rolling down their cheeks.

South Carolina won, 24-23, despite an amazing run in

It wasn't the pressures of the job, according to Athletic Director Doug Dickey, that caused Johnny Majors' release, but rather Majors' relationships within the UT community.

which Mose Phillips broke eight tackles, and Tennessee's 5-0 start was spoiled by three straight losses.

CALLING IT QUITS It was at Memphis, as UT prepared to play Memphis State, that the pot finally boiled over. In its late editions of Friday, Nov. 13, the *Chattanooga Free Press* reported that Majors had scheduled a press conference to announce he was leaving, and that Fulmer was the odds-on favorite to replace him.

At his press conference that night, Majors indeed made the expected announcement, but said he was being forced out by UT's administration. UT officials basically remained silent, saying only that they felt a change was in order.

Somehow the players managed to maintain their composure long enough to dispatch Memphis, 26-21, and Kentucky, 34-13, to enter the Vanderbilt game with a 7-3 record.

FULMER STEPS IN Speculation was running wild, but Athletic Director Doug Dickey sent a memo to the media at halftime of the Vanderbilt game saying that UT would have a press conference the next day in Knoxville. Though UT defeated Vanderbilt, 29-25, the headlines state-wide Sunday carried the story: Fulmer would be announced as the Vols' new coach, ending a tough month for Majors and Fulmer and the entire UT family.

TOUGH TIMES "It wasn't a pleasant time for me, either," recalled Doug Dickey, who'd been shoved aside as Florida's head coach in '78.

But when asked what went into the decision to not extend Majors' contract, which was down to two years, Dickey defended the findings of himself, UT President Dr. Joe Johnson and several of the athletic board members, including Bill Johnson, a former Majors teammate, and Jim Haslam, who played for the Vols' national championship team of '51 and who captained the '52 team.

"I think you have to analyze first: You either have a coach whose winning has gotten so poor that you just can't tolerate it, or there are problems in the program, or the two combined have gotten really poor," Dickey said. "You know when you're not competitive that it's time to make a change. In this case there was a lot of discord in the program. A lot of people were coming to me with a lack of support on the street.

"It wasn't directed at John so much as people were uncomfortable with where we were. Now some of the individuals who I consider to be important to the program were uncomfortable with John. So we had to make a decision to unify our program. Would Phillip do that? It was our opinion, yes. He was unknown

VOLUNTEER QUIZ

41. In what year did organized cheerleading become a part of Vol football tradition?

VOLUNTEER QUIZ

42. What former U.S. Senator and vice-presidential candidate played for UT?

nationally but very popular locally. John was very popular nationally, but not strong at home and we had to make a decision on which one did we want."

The decision was reached over a period of three or four brutal weeks in which Majors supporters accused Fulmer of job-stealing, of selling out his former boss and in which Fulmer supporters cried out that Majors has lost his "people" skills where team, staff and supporters were concerned.

UT did get its eye blacked nationally, "but Phillip did unite the front and it has moved from there to where he is becoming a nationally-known coach, and it has proven to be a very sound decision," Dickey said in the spring of 1996.

Majors was offered an assistant athletic directorship at UT, but he eventually returned to Pittsburgh where he'd won a national championship.

Phillip Fulmer

NO COMMENT To this day Fulmer has refused to discuss any knowledge he has of what transpired, preferring to look forward rather than back. The only time he addressed accusations of wrong-doing on his part was the night his hiring was announced.

"I want to make it known to all concerned that at no time have I never demeaned or conspired against John Majors, or given anyone any sort of ultimatum. I was put in the middle of a situation not of my making. I have put my heart, my soul, my love into this program and that is the reason I'm standing here today. I appreciate all that Coach Majors has done for me. I wish him well."

Other assistants on Majors' final UT staff have said that Majors would speak to none of the coaches, that the situation was untenable and that most already were looking for other jobs prior to the change.

Those closest to Fulmer say one of two things: He didn't want to make a bad situation worse, or he was kept in the dark by the administration until after Majors' press conference in Memphis.

Regardless, UT football moved on, Fulmer officially assuming his duties on Nov. 29, 1992.

The only full-time assistant coach who went with Majors to Pittsburgh was running backs coach Charlie Coe. Larry Marmie had agreed to go, but then he backed out when Majors refused to let him select Pitt's defensive staff.

GOALS, ASPIRATIONS On the night he became the 20th head football coach at the University of Tennessee, Fulmer spoke almost as a visionary.

"I want our team to have fun, to be exciting along with being tough and poised. There is an edge out there and

VOLUNTEER QUIZ

43. At what game did Neyland Stadium first have more than 50,000 fans?

VOLUNTEER QUIZ

44. Only once have three UT players rushed for 100 yards each in the same game. Who were they and who was the opponent?

that edge is attitude," said Fulmer, whose head coaching record entering the 1996 season stood at 33-7-0 (.825).

"God blessed me with four children and I'm taking the approach that I have 100 more. When they need their necks hugged, I want to be there to hug their necks. And when they're not doing what they're supposed to be doing, I want to be there to encourage and guide them toward what they're supposed to be doing."

As for the emotional roller coaster on which he'd been forced to ride, Fulmer said, "I've felt every emotion possible over the last few months and now I'm looking forward to putting it behind me and moving forward.

"I look forward to the good times we have ahead."

Two players in particular gave a good read on the '92 season and the changes that took place.

"They've replaced Coach Majors with a very fine man. Coach Fulmer cares about his players and he wants 'em to do well. He's a good coach and I think we'll play an exciting style of football," said senior center Brian Spivey.

"Everybody has respect for Coach Fulmer," said defensive tackle Paul Yatkowski. "We already know his limits. But you don't want to walk the razor's edge with him. He'll work with you and respond to what you have to say, but there'll come a time when he'll cut straight to the chase and say, 'Hey, this is the way it is, bottom line.' I think guys respect that."

FIRST BOWL WIN The first game with Fulmer officially carrying the head-coaching title was little more than a postseason game to some. For Fulmer, though, it was so much more. He wanted to get his program off on a good start and lay the foundation for a solid recruiting season.

UT was invited to the Hall of Fame Bowl in Tampa, where its opponent would be Boston College. He had quarterback Heath Shuler throw a bomb, which went to the Eagles' 1-yard line on UT's first offensive play. Shuler, who passed for 245 yards on 18-of-23 passing with no interceptions and two touchdowns, was the game's MVP. The game, won by UT, 38-23, really served to launch an unofficial Heisman campaign for the North Carolina lad.

VOLUNTEER QUIZ

45. What's the single-game rushing record and who holds it?

MICRO-MANAGING As he looks back on his first couple of years, Fulmer sees mistakes he made.

"When I took over, I went almost into a micro-managing mode: do everything, make sure everything's perfect. I darn near killed myself from a time standpoint. We still work hard but people around me are not as jumpy.

"I'm more comfortable with what I'm doing, the day-to-day interactions with media, faculty, Dr. Johnson and Coach Dickey. I think we have a good direction and that's my main job — to facilitate success for the players

On the night he became head football coach, Phillip Fulmer said, "I want our teams to be exciting, tough and poised."

and to have a structured organization in which I know where to go to get answers rather than chasing my tail."

He feels organized enough now to the point where he can spend more time with players and coaches. "I trust a lot of it to David (Cutcliffe, the offensive coordinator) and John (Chavis, the defensive coordinator), the staff as a whole."

BE YOURSELF Where he had been working with a specific group of players as an assistant, Fulmer has since had to structure his schedule so that he can build relationships that came so easily as an assistant.

Fulmer also established a unity council, a group representing each position on the team, which meets periodically. It is something akin to an open forum where players are able to express concerns or ideas, "and I think that's very important to all of today's kids, not just athletes."

But, the bottom line with Fulmer?

"I think it's important to be yourself. You can't be like somebody you admire."

VOLUNTEER QUIZ

46. How many seasons did "Little Man" Stewart, UT's all-time rushing leader, reach the 1,000-yard rushing plateau?

Fulmer & the Next Level

Self-admittedly, Phillip Fulmer probably didn't belong at the University of Tennessee as a player.

"I was one of those guys, probably, who was signed because at the time you could sign 35-40 guys a year. I was recruited harder to go to a couple of other schools but I felt Tennessee was my school and that's where I needed to be," said Fulmer, who was born on Sept. 1, 1950, in Winchester, Tenn. "I had aspirations to be the next Steve Kiner.

"Then when I got here I realized two things: One, I was gonna have to fight like heck to play at all, and two, I was not gonna be the next Jack Reynolds."

Displaying the determination that is so much a part of his character, Fulmer, recruited as a tight end and linebacker, eventually found a home on the offensive line, starting at guard and serving as team co-captain his senior season.

Signed out of Franklin County High in Winchester, Tenn., as a linebacker-tight end, Phillip Fulmer found a home in the offensive line and served UT as a co-captain his senior season.

"I knew I was gonna make it. I knew I was going to stay and play at Tennessee. A lot of people were probably intimidated or overwhelmed by it, but it honestly never crossed my mind to do anything but make it," Fulmer said.

He had overcome obstacles earlier in his life, so he was fairly well prepared for serving UT as its football coach. And it's a good thing, for Fulmer was tested early. At the Hall of Fame Bowl in Tampa at the end of the 1992-93 season, his first game as the official head coach, Fulmer dismissed from the team and sent home a player because of alleged involvement with a prostitute and for having a gun.

And during his very first recruiting campaign, Fulmer was faced with a crisis when one of the UT players was arrested for possessing and firing a gun at a fraternity party. With a number of prospects and their families on campus for official visits, Fulmer was quickly put to the test. He called all of the prospects and their parents together before breakfast on Sunday morning, told them what he knew and laid out a couple of scenarios of what could happen.

His policy of hugging necks and pointing his players in the right direction was severely tested because other players were involved

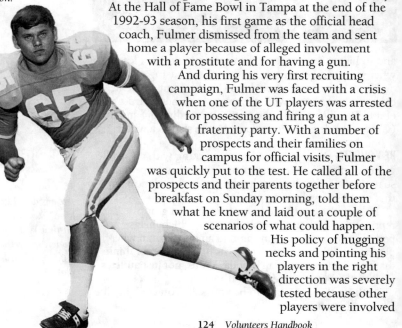

in what had started as a two-person scuffle. The matter was eventually resolved, the offending player being dismissed from the team and several others being placed on school probation and asked to perform community service by Fulmer.

Monstrous James "Little Man" Stewart, who played from 1991-94, became the Volunteers' all-time leading rusher.

1993: FULMER'S FIRST

The Volunteers opened with a blaze, snuffing Louisiana Tech, 50-0, as Heath Shuler threw two touchdown passes to Craig Faulkner and Cory Fleming before yielding to backup Jerry Colquitt, who then threw a touchdown pass to true freshman Benjie Shuler, Heath's younger brother.

Though Eric Zeier returned for Georgia at quarterback, he completed just 15 passes for 114 yards as the Volunteers broke from a 7-6 lead two minutes before the half to a 21-6 halftime bulge behind Shuler, Charlie Garner and Jason Parker, whose fumble recovery set up Garner's touchdown run. Seven different Vols caught passes and 10 different Vols accumulated part of Tennessee's 298 rushing yards as UT controlled the ball for more than 34 minutes.

But there stood Florida, waiting to host UT in "The Swamp," as Ben Hill Griffin Stadium is unofficially known. The Vols made a serious run, actually outgaining the Gators in total yardage, but they also lost two of three fumbles and had a pass intercepted during the 41-34 setback. As has been the case with the Gator-Vol

VOLUNTEER QUIZ

47. Who was the first back to gain 200 rushing yards?

games, though, UT quarterback Shuler had a field day in a losing cause. He threw for five scores and 355 yards, with three of the touchdowns pulled down by Billy Williams and one each by Fleming and Joey Kent.

REBOUNDING It has become a staple of Fulmer's philosophy: Never too high, never too low. UT rebounded the following week by slugging LSU, 42-20, a victory that started a three-game win streak and an unbeaten string that was to reach eight games. The Vols spotted the Tigers a 3-0 lead and then scored 42 straight points.

In a three-week stretch — Florida through Duke — Heath Shuler threw 12 touchdown passes, getting three in a 52-19 romp past Duke. There was even room for Charlie Garner to record another 100-yard rushing effort with 129 yards on 10 carries.

In UT's first trip to play Arkansas in Little Rock since 1907, the team came up with a 28-14 decision on a fourth-quarter scoring run from Shuler. This is the game in which ESPN TV cameras on the sidelines caught Arkansas Coach Danny Ford allegedly saying, "I hope he tears up a knee." Though many believed he was talking about Shuler still being in the game, Ford said he was getting on one of his assistants. However, he later apologized to Fulmer and to Tennessee.

It was one of those miracle finishes that kept UT from beating Alabama in Fulmer's debut season. The Crimson Tide tied the game late on a two-point conversion run by pesky David Palmer. Alabama, which had all but put Shuler out of the game with a bruise to his right (passing) shoulder, rallied for the tie despite a career-high 144-yard rushing effort from Garner.

The tie eventually became a UT victory when NCAA punishment called for Bama to forfeit its 1993 wins, including the tie. Regardless, another rebound was called for and the Volunteers, mindful of the previous season's setback to South Carolina, got busy.

Steve Taneyhill, the ponytail-wearing quarterback of the Gamecocks, never had a chance. Sacked seven times, twice by end Horace Morris, he finished the day with just 47 passing yards. Meanwhile, Garner broke a 60-yard scoring run on the game's second play and the Vols never looked back. "Little Man" Stewart, playing more of a backup role to Garner, finished with 114 yards to Garner's 105. Third-team quarterback Todd Helton, who later would play baseball in the Colorado Rockies' farm

VOLUNTEER QUIZ

48. How many sets of twins have lettered for UT?

Perhaps the most talented trio of backs to play at UT at the same time were Charlie Garner (30), James "Little Man" Stewart (33) and Aaron Hayden (24). They left only after cracking UT's all-time Top 10 rushing lists, Garner going to the Philadelphia Eagles, Stewart to the Jacksonville Jaguars, and Hayden to the San Diego Chargers.

A former Miami signee and a junior college standout, Charlie Garner moved to fifth on UT's all-time rushing list in just two seasons.

49. UT holds the record for largest attendance at a spring game. How many were there and when?

system, got the first touchdown passes of his college career — four yards to tight end John Sartelle and 51 yards to wideout Nilo Silvan.

Scoring on its first two possessions, UT cruised to a 41-10 rout of Louisville.

But by design no one could focus solely on Shuler and his receivers, as Kentucky found out the following week. UT passed for 291 yards and ran for 280 in running up a 48-0 score, the most lopsided victory against the Wildcats since the series began in 1893.

The Vols ended the season on a very high note, pinning a 62-14 thrashing on Vanderbilt as Stewart scored three touchdowns and Garner ran for 151 yards. It was the Vols' final game at home on plastic grass and they finished with a home artificial turf record of 125-38-7.

WILL HE GO? There had been much conversation throughout the season about Heath Shuler's departure for the NFL, although he had another year of eligibility. A runner-up finish in Heisman Trophy balloting just fueled the fires of discussion.

Though hounded by the media, Shuler was mum

throughout Citrus Bowl preparations for Penn State. His teammates — and probably his coaches — were distracted nevertheless, and the Vols wound up absorbing a 31-13 butt-kicking at the hands of Joe Paterno's Nittany Lions to finish the year 9-2-1.

Shuler finally had a press conference to announce his decision. Yes, he said, he was going pro. Though he never beat Alabama and though he finished third on the all-time passing charts behind Andy Kelly and Jeff Francis, Shuler had enhanced a foundation for quarterbacks at UT, and it was to pay off handsomely in the form of a lanky New Orleans youngster named Peyton Manning.

Heath Shuler tried to keep the great debate about his future from becoming a distraction as UT prepared to play Penn State in the Citrus Bowl.

1994: GOING FOR THE GUSTO

Though Heath Shuler had moved on to the Washington Redskins as a first-round draft pick and Charlie Garner was now a Philadelphia Eagle, the Vols were still highly-regarded entering the season.

The primary question was whether or not Jerry Colquitt, by now a fifth-year senior and a knowledgeable quarterback, could fill Shuler's shoes. It's a question that remains unanswered because in the first series of the Vols' first game of '94, Colquitt went down with a season-ending, career-threatening knee injury at UCLA.

UT lost to the Bruins, 25-23, severely damaging championship aspirations. But the Vols rallied for a win the next week.

The Vols won at Georgia, where "Little Man" Stewart rushed for 211 yards and Aaron Hayden 113. Stewart also scored four touchdowns as Todd Helton, originally the backup quarterback, made his starting debut. Stewart's performance overshadowed another great night for Georgia quarterback Eric Zeier, who passed for 401 yards and might have had more had UT not held the ball for 39:57. That night's crowd of 86,117 was the largest ever for a Georgia game and the largest crowd ever to see a football game in the state of Georgia.

Jerry Colquitt was a key to UT's hopes for the 1994 season, but he went down with a career-ending knee injury in the season-opener vs. UCLA.

OUCH With their passing game very much in question, the Vols knew they were going to face a rough road against Florida, which had traditionally clamped down on UT's ground game. But no one expected the Gators to walk away with a 31-0 shutout, the first home shutout for UT since a 1980 loss (27-0) to Alabama. It wasn't the way UT's players had envisioned the first game on grass at Neyland Stadium since 1967.

That was, though, the tip of the iceberg.

AN S.O.S. Mississippi State at Starkville was next, and for the second time in four weeks the Vols found themselves

Peyton Manning saw his first extensive action against Mississippi State in 1994, throwing for two touchdowns and more than 200 yards.

The Vols went to the black border around the orange numbers on their road uniform jerseys prior to the South Carolina came at Columbia, S.C., Oct. 29, 1994.

with their starting quarterback out of the game and on the sidelines.

UT lost four fumbles and gave up the game-winning score with a key defensive player on the sidelines

Branndon Stewart and Peyton Manning had been dueling for the backup role but they expected little more than that. Their plans changed when Todd Helton went down with a knee injury against State. Manning was called upon and responded with 256 passing yards and his first two touchdown passes (to Kendrick Jones and Joey Kent). In between, "Little Man" Stewart tossed a touchdown pass to tight end David Horn.

Despite losing Helton, it appeared that UT would win, 21-17. But as linebacker Tyrone Hines stood along the Tennessee sidelines screaming, "Watch the end, watch the end," a fellow linebacker stepped up, took the fake and got beat on a pass from State quarterback Derrick Taite to Kendall Watkins. State won, 24-21.

It was something for which the Vols had specifically prepared. Yet there was the 6-foot-2, 299-pound Watkins — with the ball — in the end zone shuffling his feet in a

John Becksvoort not only holds SEC and NCAA records for consecutive point-after kicks, but he's also UT's all-time leading scorer.

loose-jointed swan dance of celebration.

"Ain't nobody going belly up," growled an agitated, frustrated Fulmer after the game. "I don't want to hear the first excuse … from anybody."

With an inexperienced Manning at the controls to face a talented defense, UT held on to beat touted Washington State, 10-9. But Manning and Stewart got a little more freedom the next week. Mose Phillips got the first two scores against Arkansas as UT forged a 21-0 lead before Arkansas got on the board. The Volunteers then went up 38-7 before the Razorbacks scored two late touchdowns.

It was against Arkansas that John Becksvoort set a new SEC standard for consecutive PATS (137), breaking the previous mark of 135 held by Alabama's Van Tiffin.

BAMA, AGAIN! Though he'd said nothing publicly, Fulmer was disgusted with UT's defensive play-calling at Mississippi State, and a fourth-quarter, 80-yard drive by Alabama did nothing to improve his opinion. But that's the way it went, Bama was down 13-10 late, yet drove virtually untouched for the game-winning score midway through the final period.

CATCHING FIRE Though Aaron Hayden rushed for 129 yards and Mose Phillips scored twice, UT's 24-13 victory

VOLUNTEER QUIZ

50. Two Vols went on to become city mayors. Who were they?

One of the classiest of UT's football citizens during his time with the Vols, Aaron Hayden finished sixth on the all-time rushing list before moving on to the San Diego Chargers.

Jay Graham filled in well for the departed "Little Man" Stewart and Aaron Hayden.

against Memphis actually belonged to Nilo Silvan, who returned four Tiger punts for 136 yards and set up all four Vol scores. He broke a single-game record (owned by Bert Rechichar) that had stood since 1950.

With 143 yards in a 52-0 rout of Kentucky the next week, "Little Man" Stewart moved within 84 yards of Johnnie Jones' career rushing record. It was the first home shutout of Kentucky by the Vols since 1970 and the most lopsided win in the long-running series.

Stewart got the career rushing record against Vanderbilt, gaining 121 yards on the day to finish with 1,028 for the year and 2,890 for his career. Though Hayden suffered a broken leg, Jay Graham turned in his first 100-yard day with a 121-yard effort. In his last regular-season game as a Vol, Kendrick Jones had four catches for 108 yards.

NEVER-SAY-DIE Tennessee had refused to roll over despite losing two starting quarterbacks and having to turn to a true freshman at a critical position, and now the Vols were headed to the Gator Bowl.

"You lose two quarterbacks, you get banged up, yet you fight back and have a reasonably good season. Yep, I was really proud of our team," Fulmer said.

They refused to fold the tent though they'd been two games under .500 through the first four games. The reward was a trip to play Virginia Tech in the Gator Bowl. The Vols toyed with an experienced team, a team that would make the Sugar Bowl the next season.

The vaunted Virginia Tech blitz did not hinder Peyton Manning, and he had a fine performance in an event in which his father, Archie, had shone years earlier. He threw for 189 yards and a touchdown as the Vols coasted to a 45-23 victory to finish the year 8-4.

ANOTHER QB LOST Tennessee coaches contended that Peyton Manning did not have the starting job sewn up and that spring practice would go a long way toward deciding the Vols' starting quarterback for 1995. Just weeks after the Gator Bowl, though, Branndon Stewart packed his bags and headed back to Texas, transferring to Texas A&M.

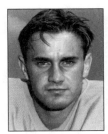

When asked about the short-lived duel, most who were around the Vol program at the time will tell you: Manning wanted to be a starting quarterback, Stewart wanted to be a freshman. Did Stewart get a fair shake? Yes. Stewart probably was the more athletic of the two quarterbacks, but Manning stayed on the field after practice to hone his skills, studied his playbook rigorously and probably saw as much video in a year's time as movie critics Siskel and Ebert.

After just one season at Tennessee, Branndon Stewart decided to return to his native Texas, transferring to Texas A&M.

"I think Branndon just felt career-wise it was the best move for him if he's going to have a chance to go to the next level. They don't draft guys that watch," said Art Briles, Stewart's high school coach in Stephenville, Texas. "We'd been in contact throughout the season, especially the last half, and I think the UT coaches were fair and honest with Branndon in their dealings with him. But Branndon feels the writing is on the wall, and he knows how to read."

Stewart completed 34 of 55 passes (61.8 percent) with one touchdown and two interceptions. He completed 7 of 7 passes in the regular season finale against Vanderbilt, getting his first collegiate touchdown. He completed all three of his passes for 42 yards in the Gator Bowl victory against Virginia Tech.

"I appreciate the opportunity the folks at UT gave me because it has been a tremendous experience. The coaches and players at UT, and all the folks I have been associated with, have been extremely nice to me. I feel it is in my best interest to transfer to Texas A&M, but I wish the Vol coaches, players and fans continued

51. The longest non-scoring pass play in UT history was 81 yards. Who were the passer and receiver?

Leonard Little came across the mountain from Asheville, N.C., to be a dominating defensive end.

VOLUNTEER QUIZ

52. Who was UT's first All-American?

success," Stewart said.

Still, it left the Vols with but one quarterback on scholarship. They wound up signing Jeremy Bates, the diminutive quarterback from nearby Sevier County, and the son of former Vol player and assistant coach Jim Bates, along with Harriman standout Jeremaine Copeland. Too, they talked Shawn Snyder, another former Knoxville-area quarterback, into walking on.

By the time spring practice rolled around, Fulmer had said adios to defensive coordinator Larry Marmie, who moved to UCLA, elevated John Chavis into the coordinator's post and hired Andy McCollum from Baylor to coach defensive ends. McCollum, though, returned to Baylor after spring practice and Fulmer brought in Steve Caldwell from Ole Miss.

STILL MORE ADVERSITY Before the Vols could get back on the competitive field, word leaked out during the latter part of spring practice that Tennessee was conducting an in-house investigation. Players from football, basketball and baseball had been using a university access code to make long-distance telephone calls illegally. Some players were suspended, a couple for a year, and all had to make restitution.

But there was more to come.

The Volunteers opened the season by shutting down East Carolina and slipping past Georgia, but on the eve of the Florida game in Gainesville, senior offensive tackle Leslie Ratliffe was suspended from the team amidst allegations that he had taken money from a booster. Ratliffe would not return to the field.

Then the day after the Vols were humbled in Gainesville by Florida, senior wide receiver Nilo Silvan was arrested and charged with rape and sodomy. Though he was acquitted, Silvan also never returned to the team.

So there it was. A 2-1 team had just been blistered by Florida and within three days had lost two of its key ingredients.

"I'm most proud of the way the team reacted to the adversity we faced at the beginning of the season and how we responded in practice the Monday after the Florida game. That, to me, was a mark that the leadership was in place," Fulmer recalled.

The Volunteers reeled off eight straight wins, including a 41-14 triumph over Alabama, to gain a Citrus Bowl berth opposite Ohio State, which had been in the national championship picture until a last-game loss to rival Michigan knocked the Buckeyes out of the Rose Bowl.

Stepping in for the now graduated "Little Man" Stewart and Aaron Hayden, Jay Graham came out of the chutes quickly, gaining 144 yards against ECU and 137 versus Georgia. But it took a 34-yard field goal from Jeff Hall with 10 seconds remaining to lift the Vols over the Bulldogs.

"When Georgia missed a field goal, I started getting nervous. When Jay made that good run to get it down close I got more nervous. And when Peyton stopped the clock with 10 seconds left, I went black," said Hall, who had three field goals and three extra points against the Bulldogs.

Tennessee's defense, which had looked so good against ECU in John Chavis' debut as defensive coordinator, got run ragged by Georgia's Robert Edwards, who had 156 yards before leaving the game late in the third period with a bruised foot.

HERE'S THE ALAMO A Florida fan stood outside Ben Hill Griffin Stadium in Gainesville, repeatedly stomping on a coonskin cap. "Are you from Tennessee?" he asked. "Well, you're getting ready to go back to the Alamo."

It didn't appear early on that such would be the case. UT, sporting new white pants without the twin orange

53. Who was Tennessee's first NFL first-round draft pick?

54. Only once has UT had three players selected in the first round of an NFL draft. Who were they?

VOLUNTEER QUIZ

55. Of the 116 schools UT has played over the years, name those the Vols have never defeated.

stripes up the sides but with an orange "T" on the left hip, broke on top 30-14 and held a 30-21 lead at the half.

And then the wheels fell off as Florida, thanks to four Vol fumbles and back-to-back shanked punts, danced through Tennessee for a 62-37 victory. It was the worst whipping UT had suffered since the 56-28 beating from Bama in 1986 and the most points UT had given up in more than 100 years, since Duke scored 70 in a shutout.

"The Florida game really gets you — the fact that they didn't beat us but that we beat ourselves. We had two turnovers back-to-back, two bad punts back-to-back," Fulmer said.

PROFILE: PEYTON MANNING (1994-PRESENT)

There have been some awfully good folks pass through the University of Tennessee's football program, as players and simply as just good people.

Of late, names like Jeff Smith, Kevin Mays and Bubba Miller —

Peyton Manning threw for four touchdowns and 384 yards, the fifth- best passing performance in UT history, against Top 25-ranked Arkansas.

the big linemen — come to mind, along with Thomas Woods, the little wide receiver; Joey Kent, the wideout from Huntsville, Ala.; defensive linemen such as Chuck Smith, Paul Yatkowski and Shane Bonham; running backs Aaron Hayden, Little Man Stewart, Eric Lane and Jay Graham and quarterbacks like "The Pearl," Sterling Henton, Jeff Francis, Andy Kelly and Heath Shuler.

Another such gem is Peyton Manning. Sure, he's captured the imagination of most every Tennessee fan, and he's headed for the top of the charts in every conceivable passing and total offense category.

Plucked away from Ole Miss — where his father, Archie, etched his name — and out of New Orleans, Manning had almost instant success at UT, becoming a starting quarterback in his first year and successfully entrenching himself there.

As he entered the 1996 season, Manning already stood third on the career passing yardage list behind only Kelly and Francis with 4,095 yards; his 33 career passing touchdowns were good for third behind the 36 thrown by Kelly and Shuler; he was third on the all-time

REGROUPING The Vols dropped from eighth to 15th in the national polls after the Florida debacle, but Monday's practice was hell on wheels. Seniors like Bubba Miller, Jason Layman, Jeff Smith, Shane Burton and DeRon Jenkins saw to it. They weren't just running from one drill to another, they moved at a flat-out dead sprint. The contact drills were cut short for fear someone was going to get hurt.

Mississippi State never had a chance. A Top 30 team, State's first four series were three downs and out. UT, led by a fired-up defense aiming to shut up John Chavis' critics, led 31-0 at the half, keyed by Burton's block and

56. Only two players have served UT as multi-year captains. Who are they?

completions list (333) and fourth on the all-time attempts chart (524).

And in that career is a completion percentage mark of 64 percent. In only one of his starts did Manning fail to complete at least 50 percent of his passes, that behind a 5-of-12 afternoon against Memphis in '94. But then in '95, looking back at some of his headline-commanding performances, Manning completed 80 percent of his passes (16-of-20) with four touchdowns against South Carolina and then threw for 384 yards and four touchdowns (35-46-1) against Arkansas. For '95, Manning threw but four interceptions in 380 attempts, which ties the NCAA record held by former Florida State standout Charlie Ward, and the single-year effort is by far the best the Southeastern Conference has ever seen.

David Cutcliffe, UT's offensive coordinator and assistant head coach, can't seem to say enough about his quarterback, but said after the 1995 win over Arkansas, "I'm not afraid to say Peyton Manning is the best player in college football."

Said former Georgia coach Ray Goff, "If you give Peyton Manning time, he'll eat you alive. He's a very cool guy and that big offensive line doesn't hurt him either."

What impressed Alabama's Gene Stallings was Manning's unerring judgment. "He recognizes defenses, audibles properly and throws the ball to the right people," Stallings said.

And said Arkansas' Danny Ford after Manning's '95 performance against his Razorbacks, "I played against his daddy in 1969 (when Ford was a player at Alabama) when his daddy was pretty good on national TV. He (Peyton) was as sharp (against Arkansas) as his daddy was that night."

After the 1995 season, Joel Buchsbaum wrote in Pro Football Weekly, "Manning is just a sophomore, but he probably deserves the Heisman, and if he were in the NFL draft, he would be the first player picked."

Is there is a weakness?

"Peyton needs help with his wardrobe — he has trouble matching clothes," Olivia Manning, Peyton's mom, told a sportswriter. "I think he needs flash cards. We even thought about sending him Polaroids of matched outfits. I don't think he worries about it too much, though. He's got more important things to think about."

Jay Graham became only the seventh Vol in UT history to reach the 1,000-yard rushing mark in a season. But Graham also rushed for at least 100 yards in 10 of the Vols' 11 regular-season games in 1995.

VOLUNTEER QUIZ

57. Only two Vol head coaches served as captains during their UT playing careeers. Who are they?

scoring return of a MSU punt. The final score was 52-14.

"The defense is doing it," Fulmer said after UT took a 31-0 homecoming win over Oklahoma State the next week. And indeed they were. OSU came in with a Top 20 rushing attack and left having gained just 92 yards on 39 attempts. Too, the Cowboys managed just 58 yards and their leading receiver, tight end Alonzo Mayes, was held without a catch.

Making the adjustment from linebacker to end, Leonard Little recorded a tackle for loss, two quarterback sacks and caused a fumble. Offensively, Jay Graham picked up his fourth 100-yard effort in five games.

MURDERER'S ROW It was back to SEC play the next three weeks — Arkansas, Alabama and South Carolina — and UT's veterans remembered well that Arkansas and South Carolina had both plagued the Vols only a couple of years earlier. Alabama was, well, Alabama.

The Vols' No. 10 national ranking appeared to be in

jeopardy early on at Fayetteville, Ark., as 18th-ranked Arkansas built a 24-14 lead. But by halftime, Peyton Manning had thrown his fourth touchdown pass and UT led, 28-24. The Vols went on to a 49-31 victory as Manning completed 35 of 46 passes for 384 yards, the fifth-best passing effort in Vol history. Jay Graham added three more scores on 130 yards rushing. The performance by Manning pushed him past Randy Wallace and into the Vols' Top 10 all-time passing list. Too, Joey Kent's 13 receptions tied the single-game standard set in 1990 by Carl Pickens.

UT borrowed a tradition from Alabama the next week, handing out victory cigars to all parties involved. Why? Because the Vols literally thundered past the Crimson Tide, winning, 41-14, and ending a winless streak that dated back to 1986.

Fourteen seconds into the game Tennessee led 7-0 after an 80-yard hook-up between Manning and Kent, an Alabama native. The Vols made it 21-0 on a Manning pass to Marcus Nash and a 1-yard Manning run before the first quarter had ended.

And then every time the Tide scored, Tennessee answered. Bama's Montoya Madden finished off a 15-play drive with a 15-yard scoring run. "But that touchdown didn't mean a thing," said Madden. "When we would make a play, they would match it. They kept coming at us, and it took the air out."

Madden's score made it 28-14, and then Graham bounced outside and ran 75 yards to boost UT's advantage to 35-14. A couple of Jeff Hall field goals closed out the scoring.

"That game will never be forgotten," Fulmer said. "Some people have told me I didn't smile during the whole game. Well, I wasn't going to let it get away. It wasn't fun until it was over."

Defense, Chavis' defense, rocked South Carolina quarterback Steve Taneyhill the next week. Taneyhill was coming off a three-game stretch in which he'd thrown for more than 1,000 yards with 12 touchdowns. Tennessee intercepted him three times, knocked him down repeatedly.

Leonard Little blocked a field goal try that Tyrone Hines plucked out of the air at the UT 10-yard line and raced 90 yards for a score. Tackle Shane Burton batted, then intercepted, a Taneyhill pass to set up another UT score.

Offensively, Manning completed 80 percent of his passes (16 of 20) with four touchdown strikes — two to Kent and one each to tight end Scott Pfeiffer and Graham, who also contributed 126 rushing yards.

Defensively, senior co-captain Scott Galyon had 10

VOLUNTEER QUIZ

58. Since the SEC was formed (1933), there has been only one season in which every UT game was decided by a shutout. What season was it and what was the Vols' record that year?

VOLUNTEER QUIZ

59. Two coaches have taken Tennessee teams to the Rose Bowl. Obviously, one was Gen. Neyland but who was the other?

Jay Graham

tackles as the Vol defense broke up five passes and intercepted three throws and recorded three quarterback sacks.

SHUTOUT CITY Ten weeks into the season there had been but three shutouts in all the games played by SEC teams. Tennessee, thanks to a 42-0 whitewashing of Southern Mississippi, had two of 'em.

UT moved to 8-1 with the win over the Golden Eagles, who had scored at least 20 points in each of their first eight games. Defense again set the pace as Vol defenders sacked Southern Mississippi quarterback Heath Graham five times and intercepted him four.

Though he had something of an off day, completing *only* 50 percent of his passes, Peyton Manning moved into the Top Five on the Vols' all-time passing list in just his 19th game as a Vol, passing Tony Robinson, Dewey

NICKNAMES

To look at the gangly youngster with peach fuzz on his cheeks — in a few places, anyway — one wonders how or when anyone will refer to Vol quarterback Peyton Manning as "sir."

Around Tennessee, they either call him Peyton or "Coach."

Nicknames are part of the colorful tradition we know as Tennessee football and Manning is just one of few who have been pegged over the years.

Years ago, long before he became dean of the school of engineering, N.W. Dougherty, one of the first Vol standouts, was called "Big 'Un," as befitted his size.

And over the years there have been Alonzo "Goat" Carroll, W.O. "Chink" Lowe, Roy "Pap" Striegel and Robert "Tarzan" Holt. Gene McEver was known as "The Wild Bull," but there also were George "Bad News" Cafego, John "Skeeter" Bailey, Harold "Herky" Payne, Frank "Boomer" Boring, Bill "Moose" Barbish, Jim "Young

'Un" Haslam, Bill "Pug" Pearman.

In the more recent era, Johnny Majors was called "Drum"; Jack Reynolds was called "Hacksaw"; quarterback Joe Wyche was better known as "Bubba." Punter Herman Weaver was known as "Thunderfoot" and his teammates called Bobby Scott "Lassie"; Dewey Warren will forever be remembered as the "Swamp Rat"; Condredge Holloway "The Artful Dodger"; Jimmy Streater as "The Sylva (N.C.) Streak" or "Bird"; and James Stewart as "Little Man," a moniker placed on him by his father.

Jeff Smith was called "Big Country"; Kevin Mays, "Big Chevy"; and nobody except his momma ever heard of Stephen DeJuan Miller. We all knew him as "Bubba".

And two of the best from the modern era are Jeff "Tool Shed" Tullis and Andy "Mammaw" Kelly.

Warren, Bobby Scott and Jimmy Streater.

Also, Jay Graham became only the seventh player in UT history to rush for 1,000 yards in a season, and Joey Kent moved into UT's Top 10 receivers list with 99 career receptions.

The Vols seemed to lose a little bit of their zip in the final two regular-season contests. Recording mediocre performances, they had to rally and then hold on against both Kentucky and Vanderbilt to finish the year 10-1.

CITRUS SWEETNESS The Volunteers were underdogs to a team that boasted the Heisman Trophy winner, Eddie George, on its roster. Ohio State had been up as high as No. 2 in the national rankings most of the season before losing to Michigan in its final regular-season game.

Fulmer's pregame management of team activities and the bowl site practice schedule paid dividends. The Vols, especially the defense, were ready to play, and UT wound up No. 2 in the coaches' poll and No. 3 in the writer's poll after clipping the Buckeyes, 20-14. The Vols' win streak reached nine en route to the 11-1 record, the fifth time a Tennessee team had reached the 11-win plateau.

Jay Graham was named the game's MVP after rushing for 154 yards, including a 69-yard scoring jaunt near the close of the first half. Peyton Manning and Joey Kent combined for a 47-yard touchdown, and Jeff Hall had field goals of 29 and 25 yards.

It wasn't long after the Citrus Bowl that UT lost offensive line coach Steve Marshall to UCLA. Fulmer promoted Mark Bradley into that position and hired ex-Auburn standout Rodney Garner to coach tight ends and assist with the offensive line.

Entrenched by now, Fulmer had united and solidified the program.

Tennessee headed into the 1996 season considered a contender for the national title and was ranked in some preseason publications as the No. 1 team in the country.

There were plenty of top players returning for the Vols, including tailback Graham, who set a single-season rushing record in '95, and wide receiver Kent, who was coming off a season in which he set a school single-season receiving record.

But the optimism for Tennessee's success centered on Manning, who finished sixth in Heisman Trophy voting as a sophomore after the 1995 season. Volunteer fans were banking on Manning wowing the country with his Heisman campaign while leading Tennessee to that next level in 1996.

Joey Kent

VOLUNTEER QUIZ

60. *Where and against whom did UT play its first actual night game?*

Peyton Manning

By the Numbers

SEASON-BY-SEASON SUMMARY

PRE-CONFERENCE SEASONS

Year	W-L-T	Coach	Captain(s)
1891	0-1-0	none	H.K. Denlinger
1892	2-5-0	none	Charles Moore
1893	2-4-0	none	H.A. Ijams
1894	No team		
1895	No team		

SOUTHERN INTERCOLLEGIATE ATHLETIC ASSOCIATION

Year	W-L-T	Coach	Captain(s)
1896	4-0-0	none	Strang Nicklin
1897	4-1-0	none	James A. Baird
1898	No team (Spanish-American War)		
1899	5-2-0	J.A. Pierce	William L. Terry
1900	3-2-1	J.A. Pierce	Bill Newman
1901	3-3-2	George Kelley	C.E. Holopeter
1902	6-2-0	H.F. Fisher	Nash Buckingham
1903	4-5-0	H.F. Fisher	T.B. Green
1904	3-5-1	S.D. Crawford	Roscoe Word
1905	3-5-1	J.D. DePree	Roscoe Word
1906	1-6-2	J.D. DePree	Roscoe Word, E.P. Proctor
1907	7-2-1	George Levene	Roscoe Word
1908	7-2-0	George Levene	Walker Leach
1909	1-6-2	George Levene	N.W. Dougherty
1910	3-5-1	Alex Stone	W.C. Johnson
1911	3-4-2	Z.G. Clevenger	H.C. Branch
1912	4-4-0	Z.G. Clevenger	C.H. Fonde
1913	6-3-0	Z.G. Clevenger	Sam Hayley
1914	9-0-0	Z.G. Clevenger	Farmer Kelly
1915	4-4-0	Z.G. Clevenger	E.A. McLean
1916	8-0-1	John R. Bender	J.G. Vowell
1917	No Team (World War I)		
1918	No Team (World War I)		
1919	3-3-3	John R. Bender	W.O. Love
1920	7-2-0	John R. Bender	Buck Hatcher

SOUTHERN CONFERENCE

Year	W-L-T	Coach	Captain(s)
1921	6-2-1	M.B. Banks	Hal Blair
1922	8-2-0	M.B. Banks	Roy Striegel
1923	5-4-1	M.B. Banks	Tarzan Holt
1924	3-5-0	M.B. Banks	J.G. Lowe
1925	5-2-1	M.B. Banks	J.G. Lowe
1926	8-1-0	R.R. Neyland	Billy Harkness
1927	8-0-1	R.R. Neyland	John Barnhill
1928	9-0-1	R.R. Neyland	Roy Witt
1929	9-0-1	R.R. Neyland	Howard Johnson
1930	9-1-0	R.R. Neyland	Harry Thayer
1931	9-0-1	R.R. Neyland	Eugene Mayer
1932	9-0-1	R.R. Neyland	Malcolm Aitken

SOUTHEASTERN CONFERENCE YEARS

Year	Overall	Conf.	Coach	Captain(s)
1933	7-3-0	5-2-0	R.R. Neyland	Talmadge Maples
1934	8-2-0	5-1-0	R.R. Neyland	Ralph Hatley
1935	4-5-0	2-3-0	W.H. Britton	Toby Palmer
1936	6-2-2	3-1-2	R.R. Neyland	DeWitt Weaver
1937	6-3-1	4-3-0	R.R. Neyland	Joe Black Hayes
1938	11-0-0	7-0-0	R.R. Neyland	Bowden Wyatt
1939	10-1-0	6-0-0	R.R. Neyland	Sam Bartholomew
1940	10-1-0	5-0-0	R.R. Neyland	Norbert Ackermann
1941	8-2-0	3-1-0	John Barnhill	Ray Graves
1942	9-1-1	4-1-0	John Barnhill	Al Hust
1943	No team (World War II)			
1944	7-1-1	5-0-1	John Barnhill	Bob Dobelstein

1945	8-1-0	3-1-0	John Barnhill	Billy Bevis
1946	9-2-0	5-0-0	R.R. Neyland	Walter Slater
1947	5-5-0	2-3-0	R.R. Neyland	Denver Crawford
1948	4-4-2	2-3-1	R.R. Neyland	Jim Powell
1949	7-2-1	4-1-1	R.R. Neyland	Ralph Chancey, Hal Littleford
1950	11-1-0	4-1-0	R.R. Neyland	Jack Stroud
1951	10-1-0	5-0-0	R.R. Neyland	Bert Rechichar
1952	8-2-1	5-0-1	R.R. Neyland	Jim Haslam
1953	6-4-1	3-2-1	Harvey Robinson	Mack Franklin
1954	4-6-0	1-5-0	Harvey Robinson	Darris McCord
1955	6-3-1	3-2-1	Bowden Wyatt	Jim Beutel
1956	10-1-0	6-0-0	Bowden Wyatt	John Gordy
1957	8-3-0	4-3-0	Bowden Wyatt	Bill Johnson, Bill Anderson
1958	4-6-0	4-3-0	Bowden Wyatt	Bobby Urbano
1959	5-4-1	3-4-1	Bowden Wyatt	Joe Schaffer
1960	6-2-2	3-2-2	Bowden Wyatt	Mike LaSorsa
1961	6-4-0	4-3-0	Bowden Wyatt	Mike Lucci
1962	4-6-0	2-8-0	Bowden Wyatt	Pat Augustine
1963	5-5-0	3-5-0	Jim McDonald	Buddy Fisher
1964	4-5-1	1-5-1	Doug Dickey	Steve DeLong
1965	8-1-2	3-1-2	Doug Dickey	Hal Wantland
1966	8-3-0	4-2-0	Doug Dickey	Austin Denney, Paul Naumoff
1967	9-2-0	6-0-0	Doug Dickey	Bob Johnson
1968	8-2-1	4-1-1	Doug Dickey	Dick Williams
1969	9-2-0	5-1-0	Doug Dickey	Bill Young
1970	11-1-0	4-1-0	Bill Battle	Tim Priest
1971	10-2-0	4-2-0	Bill Battle	Jackie Walker
1972	10-2-0	4-2-0	Bill Battle	Jamie Rotella
1973	8-4-0	3-3-0	Bill Battle	Eddie Brown
1974	7-3-2	2-3-1	Bill Battle	Jim Watts, Condredge Holloway
1975	7-5-0	3-3-0	Bill Battle	Ron McCartney
1976	6-5-0	2-4-0	Bill Battle	Larry Seivers, Andy Spiva
1977	4-7-0	1-5-0	Johnny Majors	Greg Jones, Pert Jenkins, Brent Watson
1978	5-5-1	3-3-0	Johnny Majors	Dennis Wolfe, Robert Shaw
1979	7-5-0	3-3	Johnny Majors	Craig Puki, Jimmy Streater, Roland James
1980	5-6-0	3-3-0	Johnny Majors	Jimmy Noonan
1981	8-4-0	3-3-0	Johnny Majors	Lemont Holt Jeffers, Lee North, James Berry
1982	6-5-1	3-2-1	Johnny Majors	Mike L. Cofer
1983	9-3-0	4-2-0	Johnny Majors	Reggie White
1984	7-4-1	3-3-0	Johnny Majors	Johnnie Jones, Carl Zander
1985	9-1-2	5-1-0	Johnny Majors	Tim McGee, Tommy Sims, Chris White
1986	7-5-0	3-3-0	Johnny Majors	Joey Clinkscales, Dale Jones, Bruce Wilkerson
1987	10-2-1	4-1-1	Johnny Majors	Harry Galbreath, Kelly Ziegler
1988	5-6-0	3-4-0	Johnny Majors	Keith DeLong, Nate Middlebrooks
1989	11-1-0	6-1-0	Johnny Majors	Eric Still
1990	9-2-2	5-1-1	Johnny Majors	Tony Thompson
1991	9-3-0	5-2-0	Johnny Majors	Earnest Fields, John Fisher
1992	9-3-0	5-3-0	Majors/Fulmer	Todd Kelly, J.J. McCleskey
1993	10-2-0	7-1-0	Phillip Fulmer	Craig Faulkner, Cory Fleming, Horace Morris, James Wilson
1994	8-4-0	5-3-0	Phillip Fulmer	Kevin Mays, Ben Talley
1995	11-1-0	7-1-0	Phillip Fulmer	Jason Layman, Bubba Miller, Scott Galyon

COACHING RECORDS

Coach	Years	W-L-T	Pct.	Coach	Years	W-L-T	Pct.
J.A. Pierce	1899-1900	8-4-1	.654	W.H. Britton	1935	4-5-0	.444
George Kelley	1901	3-3-2	.500	John Barnhill	1941-45	32-5-2	.846
H.F. Fisher	1902-03	10-7-0	.588	Harvey Robinson	1953-54	10-10-1	.500
S.D. Crawford	1904	3-5-1	.389	Bowden Wyatt	1955-62	49-29-4	.622
J.D. DePree	1905-06	4-11-3	.305	Jim McDonald	1963	5-5-0	.500
S. George Levene	1907-09	15-10-3	.589	Doug Dickey	1964-69	46-15-4	.738
Andrew (Alex) Stone	1910	3-5-1	.389	Bill Battle	1970-76	59-22-2	.723
Z.G. Clevenger	1911-15	26-15-2	.628	Johnny Majors	1977-92	116-62-8	.645
John Bender	1916-20	18-5-4	.741	Phillip Fulmer	1992-present	33-7-0	.825
M.B. Banks	1921-25	27-15-3	.633				
Robert Neyland	1926-34	76-7-5					
	1936-40	43-7-3					
	1946-52	54-17-4					
	Total	173-31-12	.829				

BOWL APPEARANCES

Year	Bowl, Opponent (Result)
1931	New York Charity Game, NYU (W, 13-0)
1939	Orange Bowl, Oklahoma (W, 17-0)
1940	Rose Bowl, Southern Cal (L, 14-0)
1941	Sugar Bowl, Boston College (L, 19-13)
1943	Sugar Bowl, Tulsa (W, 14-7)
1945	Rose Bowl, Southern Cal (L, 25-0)
1947	Orange Bowl, Rice (L, 8-0)
1951	Cotton Bowl, Texas (W, 20-14)
1952	Sugar Bowl, Maryland (L, 28-13)
1953	Cotton Bowl, Texas (L, 16-0)
1957	Sugar Bowl, Baylor (L, 13-7)
1957	Gator Bowl, Texas A&M (W, 3-0)
1965	Blue Bonnet Bowl, Tulsa (W, 27-6)
1966	Gator Bowl, Syracuse (W, 18-12)
1968	Orange Bowl, Oklahoma (L, 26-24)
1969	Cotton Bowl, Texas (L, 36-13)
1969	Gator Bowl, Florida (L, 14-13)
1971	Sugar Bowl, Air Force (W, 34-13)
1971	Liberty Bowl, Arkansas (W, 14-13)

Year	Bowl, Opponent (Result)
1972	Astro-Bluebonnet Bowl, LSU (W, 24-17)
1973	Gator Bowl, Texas Tech (L, 28-19)
1974	Liberty Bowl, Maryland (W, 7-3)
1979	Bluebonnet Bowl, Purdue (L, 27-22)
1981	Garden State Bowl, Wisconsin (W, 28-21)
1982	Peach Bowl, Iowa (L, 28-22)
1983	Florida Citrus Bowl, Maryland (W, 30-23)
1984	Sun Bowl, Maryland (L, 28-27)
1986	Sugar Bowl, Miami (W, 35-7)
1986	Liberty Bowl, Minnesota (W, 21-14)
1988	Peach Bowl, Indiana (W, 27-22)
1990	Cotton Bowl, Arkansas (W, 31-27)
1991	Sugar Bowl, Virginia (W, 23-22)
1992	Fiesta Bowl, Penn State (L, 42-17)
1993	Hall of Fame Bowl, Boston College (W, 38-23)
1994	Citrus Bowl, Penn State (L, 31-13)
1994	Gator Bowl, Virginia Tech (W, 45-23)
1996	Citrus Bowl, Ohio State (W, 20-14)

MILESTONE VICTORIES

No.	Date	Score	Opponent	Site
1	Oct. 15, 1892	25-0	Maryville	Maryville
50	Oct. 17, 1908	7-0	Kentucky St.	Knoxville
100	Nov. 6, 1920	49-0	Transylvania	Knoxville
150	Oct. 27, 1928	26-7	Washington & Lee	Knoxville
200	Oct. 13, 1934	27-0	Ole Miss	Knoxville
250	Nov. 16, 1940	41-14	Virginia	Knoxville
300	Oct. 16, 1948	21-6	Alabama	Knoxville
350	Oct. 15, 1955	20-0	Alabama	Birmingham
400	Nov. 9, 1962	26-0	Tulane	New Orleans
450	Oct. 3, 1970	48-3	Army	Knoxville
500	Nov. 22, 1975	17-13	Kentucky	Lexington
550	Nov. 19, 1983	10-0	Kentucky	Lexington
600	Nov. 25, 1989	31-10	Kentucky	Lexington
650	Sep. 30, 1995	31-0	Oklahoma State	Knoxville
657	Jan. 1, 1996	20-14	Ohio St.	Orlando

MILESTONE DEFEATS

No.	Date	Score	Opponent	Site
1	Nov. 21, 1891	24-0	Sewanee	Chattanooga
50	Nov. 13, 1909	10-0	Alabama	Knoxville
100	Nov. 2, 1935	19-6	Duke	Durham
150	Oct. 15, 1958	21-7	Georgia Tech	Atlanta
200	Sep. 28, 1974	21-0	Auburn	Auburn
250	Sep. , 1988	28-17	Georgia	Athens

YEARLY LEADERS

Year	Rushing	Yards	Passing	Yards	Receiving	Catches/Yards
1950	Andy Kozar	648	Hank Lauricella	364	Bert Rechichar	9-205
1951	Hank Lauricella	881	Hank Lauricella	352	John Davis	8-160
1952	Andy Kozar	660	Pat Shires	252	John Davis	14-297
1953	Jimmy Wade	675	Jimmy Wade	451	Jerry Hyde	8-173
1954	Tom Tracy	794	Johnny Majors	107	Hugh Garner	5-57
1955	Johnny Majors	657	Johnny Majors	476	Buddy Cruze	12-232
1956	Tommy Bronson	562	Johnny Majors	552	Buddy Cruze	20-357
1957	Bobby Gordon	526	Bobby Gordon	260	Tommy Potts	10-123
1958	Bill Majors	294	Bill Majors	215	Murray Armstrong	14-195
1959	Glenn Glass	261	Gene Etter	298	Cotton Letner	8-92
1960	Bunny Orr	267	Glenn Glass	167	Ken Waddell	8-60
1961	Mallon Faircloth	475	Mallon Faircloth	460	Hubert McClain	11-149
1962	George Canale	455	Bobby Morton	305	John Bill Hudson	15-259
1963	Mallon Faircloth	652	Mallon Faircloth	509	Buddy Fisher	12-242
1964	Stan Mitchell	325	Art Galiffa	338	Hal Wantland	21-284
1965	Stan Mitchell	464	Dewey Warren	588	Johnny Mills	23-328
1966	Charlie Fulton	463	Dewey Warren	1,716	Johnny Mills	48-725
1967	Walter Chadwick	645	Dewey Warren	1,053	Richmond Flowers	41-585

Year	Rushing	Yards	Passing	Yards	Receiving	Catches/Yards
1968	Richard Pickens	736	Bubba Wyche	1,539	Ken DeLong	34-393
1969	Curt Watson	807	Bobby Scott	1,352	Gary Kreis	38-609
1970	Curt Watson	791	Bobby Scott	1,697	Joe Thompson	37-502
1971	Curt Watson	766	Jim Maxwell	544	Joe Thompson	15-247
1972	Haskel Stanback	890	Condredge Holloway	807	Emmon Love	20-280
1973	Haskel Stanback	682	Condredge Holloway	1,149	Stanley Morgan	22-511
1974	Stanley Morgan	723	Condredge Holloway	1,146	Larry Seivers	25-347
1975	Stanley Morgan	809	Randy Wallace	1,318	Larry Seivers	41-840
1976	Bobby Emmons	462	Randy Wallace	1,046	Larry Seivers	51-737
1977	Kelsey Finch	770	Jimmy Streater	742	Reggie Harper	30-331
1978	Jimmy Streater	593	Jimmy Streater	1,418	Reggie Harper	31-356
1979	Hubert Simpson	792	Jimmy Streater	1,256	Anthony Hancock	34-687
1980	James Berry	543	Steve Alatorre	747	Anthony Hancock	33-580
1981	James Berry	500	Steve Alatorre	1,171	Anthony Hancock	32-437
1982	Chuck Coleman	600	Alan Cockrell	2,021	Willie Gault	50-668
1983	Johnnie Jones	1,116	Alan Cockrell	1,683	Clyde Duncan	33-640
1984	Johnnie Jones	1,290	Tony Robinson	1,963	Tim McGee	54-809
1985	Keith Davis	684	Tony Robinson	1,246	Tim McGee	50-947
1986	William Howard	787	Jeff Francis	1,946	Joey Clinkscales	37-511
1987	Reggie Cobb	1,197	Jeff Francis	1,512	Thomas Woods	26-335
1988	Reggie Cobb	547	Jeff Francis	2,237	Thomas Woods	58-689
1989	Chuck Webb	1,236	Andy Kelly	1,299	Thomas Woods	34-511
1990	Tony Thompson	1,261	Andy Kelly	2,241	Carl Pickens	53-917
1991	James Stewart	939	Andy Kelly	2,759	Carl Pickens	49-877
1992	Charlie Garner	928	Heath Shuler	1,712	Cory Fleming	40-490
1993	Charlie Garner	1,161	Heath Shuler	2,353	Craig Faulkner	40-680
1994	James Stewart	1,028	Peyton Manning	1,141	Joey Kent	36-470
1995	Jay Graham	1,438	Peyton Manning	2,954	Joey Kent	65-1,055

TEAM RECORDS (* indicates modern NCAA record)

OFFENSE, RUSHING — GAME

Most rushes — 75, vs. Kentucky, 1980
Most net yards — 513, vs. Washington & Lee, 1951
Highest avg. per rush — 10.7, vs. Tenn. Tech, 1951

OFFENSE, PASSING — GAME

Most attempts — 60, vs. Notre Dame, 1990
Most completions — 35, vs. Notre Dame, 1990
Most had intercepted — 5, Duke, 1949
Most yards gained — 399, vs. Notre Dame, 1990

OFFENSE, TOTAL OFFENSE — GAME

Most rushing, passing plays — 95, vs. Miss. State, 1991
Most rushing, passing yards — 665, vs. Vanderbilt, 1994
Highest avg. per play — 10.6, vs. Louisville, 1953

OFFENSE, PUNTING — GAME

Most punts — 14, vs. Alabama, 1944; Kentucky, 1976
Highest avg. per punt (min. 5 punts) — 52.0, vs. Vanderbilt, 1956; LSU, 1982; Auburn, 1983

OFFENSE, PUNT RETURNS — GAME

Most punts returned — 10, vs. Tenn. Tech, 1947
Most yards returned — 192, vs. Chattanooga, 1951

OFFENSE, KICKOFF RETURNS — GAME

Most kickoffs returned — 8, vs. Southern Cal, 1981; Alabama, 1989
Most yards returned — 192, vs. Florida, 1993, 7 returns

OFFENSE, SCORING — GAME (FROM 1937)

Most points scored — 68, vs. Tenn. Tech, 1951
Most touchdowns scored — 10, vs. Tenn. Tech, 1951
Most field goals scored — 5, vs. Kentucky, 1979; Memphis St., 1982; Kentucky, 1982
Most PATs kicked — 9, vs. Vanderbilt, 1994
Most 2-point conversions — 2, Clemson, 1974; Alabama, 1982; Alabama, 1987; UCLA, 1994
Most points scored by kicking — 17, Kentucky, 1978; Memphis St., 1982; 5-6 FGs, 2 PATs
Most points scored one quarter — 31, vs. Oregon St., 1977; Pacific, 1990

OFFENSE, MISCELLANEOUS — GAME

Most first downs by rush — 24, vs. Wofford, 1952
Most first downs by pass — 18, vs. Florida, 1984; Alabama, 1987; Colorado, 1990; Florida, 1991; Memphis St. 1991
Most total first downs — 32, vs. UCLA, 1968; Memphis St., 1991; Vanderbilt, 1991
Most penalties against — 13, vs. Chattanooga, 1948; North Carolina, 1955
Most yards penalized — 155, vs. Miss. State 1954 (12 penalties)
Fewest penalties against — 0, vs. Miss. State, 1990
Fewest yards penalized — 0, vs. Miss. State, 1990
Most fumbles — 8, vs. Alabama, 1949; Chattanooga, 1949; Santa Barbara, 1972; Ole Miss, 1975; Ole Miss, 1977; Kentucky, 1981
Most fumbles lost — 6, vs. Alabama, 1963; Santa Barbara, 1971

OFFENSE, RUSHING — SEASON (SINCE 1936)

Most attempts — 593, in 1976
Most net yards gained — 3,068, in 1951
Highest avg. per rush — 5.9, in 1993
Most TDs by rush — 40, in 1951
Highest avg. per game — 306.8, in 1951

OFFENSE, PASSING — SEASON (SINCE 1936)

Most attempts — 391, in 1995
Most completions — 250, in 1995
Highest percent completions — 65, 208-320 in 1993
Most yards gained — 3,031, in 1995
Most TDs by passing — 31, in 1993

Highest avg. per game — 275.5, in 1995

TOTAL OFFENSE — SEASON (SINCE 1936)

Most rushing, passing plays — 881, in 1970
Most rushing, passing yards — 5,285, in 1993
Highest avg. per play — 6.9, in 1993
Highest avg. per game — 480.5, in 1993

OFFENSE, PUNTING — SEASON (SINCE 1936)

Most punts — 139, in 1937
* Most punts per game — 13.9, in 1937
   (139 in 10 games)
Highest avg. per punt — 45.1, in 1982

OFFENSE, INTERCEPTIONS — SEASON (SINCE 1936)

Most passes opp. intercepted — 18, in 1948, 1970
Most yards interceptions returned by opponent —
   367, in 1991
Fewest passes opp. intercepted — 4, in 1961, 1992,
   1995
Fewest yards interceptions returned by opponent —
   8, in 1986

OFFENSE, KICKOFF RETURNS — SEASON (SINCE 1936)

Most kickoff returns — 47, in 1987
Most yards returned — 1,023, in 1990

OFFENSE, PUNT RETURNS — SEASON (SINCE 1936)

Most punts returned — 68, in 1939, 1940
Most yards returned — 974, in 1940

OFFENSE, SCORING — SEASON (SINCE 1936)

Most points scored — 471, in 1993
Highest avg. points per game — 42.8, in 1993 (471 in
   11 games)
Most touchdowns scored — 62, in 1993
Most field goals scored — 27, in 1982
Most PATs (kick) — 59, in 1993

OFFENSE, MISCELLANEOUS — SEASON (SINCE 1936)

Most first downs by rush — 150, in 1987
Most first downs by pass — 145, in 1995
Most total first downs — 280, in 1995
Most penalties against — 75, in 1991
Most yards penalized — 748, in 1955
Most fumbles — 50, in 1977
Most fumbles lost — 31, in 1971
Fewest fumbles — 13, in 1990
Fewest fumbles lost — 3, in 1990

DEFENSE, RUSHING (SINCE 1946)

Fewest rushes allowed — 14, Georgia, 1994
Fewest net yards allowed — minus-9, Wofford, 1952
Lowest avg. allowed — minus-0.4, Wofford, 1952; 24
   rushes, minus-9 yards

DEFENSE, PASSING (SINCE 1946)

* Fewest attempts allowed — 0, Georgia Tech, 1977
* Fewest completions allowed — 0, Miss. State, 1950
Fewest yards allowed — minus-3, vs. Kentucky, 1946
   (1 completion)

TOTAL DEFENSE (SINCE 1946)

Fewest rushing, passing plays allowed — 33, vs.
   Vanderbilt, 1946
Fewest rushing, passing yards allowed — 13, vs.
   Vanderbilt, 1952
Lowest avg. per play alowed — 0.3 yards, vs.
   Vanderbilt, 1952 (43 plays for 13 yards)

DEFENSE, INTERCEPTIONS (SINCE 1946)

Most passes intercepted — 8, vs. Alabama, 1970
Most yards returned — 214, vs. South Carolina, 1971
   (on 5 interceptions)

Most touchdowns by interception returns — 2, vs.
   Hawaii, 1972; Florida, 1970; Penn State, 1971;
   South Carolina, 1971

DEFENSE, PUNTING (SINCE 1946)

Most times opponent forced to punt — 15, vs. Duke,
   1946
Lowest avg. per punt (min. 5 punts) — 24.8, vs.
   Chattanooga, 1946; 8 punts-198 yards
Most punts blocked — 2, vs. Kentucky, 1986

DEFENSE, MISCELLANEOUS (SINCE 1946)

Fewest total first downs allowed — 2, vs. Vanderbilt,
   1946; Kentucky, 1946; Wofford, 1952
Most fumbles by opponent — 9, Kentucky, 1950;
   Miss. State, 1955
Most fumbles lost by opponent — 8, vs. Kentucky,
   1950
Most field goals blocked — 2, Notre Dame, 1991
Most sacks — 8, vs. Kentucky, 1986; Georgia Tech,
   1979

DEFENSE, RUSHING — SEASON (SINCE 1936)

Fewest rushes allowed — 231, in 9 games, 1945
Fewest net yards allowed — 385, in 1945
Fewest TDs allowed by rush — 0, in 1939
Lowest avg. per rush allowed — 1.7, in 1945
Lowest avg. per game allowed — 55.0, in 1945

DEFENSE, PASSING — SEASON (SINCE 1936)

Fewest attempts against — 109, in 1937
Fewest completions allowed — 44, in 1937
Lowest comp. percentage against — 37.9, in 1952
Fewest yards allowed — 392, in 1939
Lowest average per game allowed — 39.2, in 1939
Most QB sacks — 42, in 1995
Most passes broken up — 60, in 1987

DEFENSE, TOTAL DEFENSE — SEASON (SINCE 1936)

Fewest rushing, passing plays allowed — 368, in
   1945
Fewest rushing, passing yards allowed — 1,023, in
   1939
Lowest avg. per play allowed — 2.2, in 1939
Lowest avg. per game allowed — 102.3, in 1939
Most tackles for lost yardage — 69, in 1976

DEFENSE, PUNTING — SEASON (SINCE 1936)

Most times opponent forced to punt — 123, in 1940
Lowest avg. per opponent punt — 32.9, in 1940, 1961
Most punts opponent had blocked — 6, in 1940, 1949

DEFENSE, INTERCEPTIONS — SEASON (SINCE 1936)

Most passes intercepted — 36, in 1970
* Most yards returned — 782, 1971
* Highest avg. per interception return — 31.2, 1972
   (25-782)
* Most TDs by interception return — 7, 1971

DEFENSE, SCORING — SEASON (BY OPP. SINCE 1936)

* Fewest points allowed — 0, 1939
* Fewest rushing, passing TDs allowed — 0, 1939
* Most consecutive shutouts 17, 1938-40
* Most consecutive shutout quarters — 71, 2nd qtr
   LSU '38 through 2nd qtr Alabama '40

DEFENSE, MISCELLANEOUS — SEASON

Fewest total first downs allowed — 55, 1945
Fewest total first downs allowed per game — 6.0, 60
   in 1939
* Most opponent turnovers — 57, 1970 (36
   interceptions, 21 fumbles)
Turnover margin — Plus 1.916 per game, 1990
   (plus 23 in 12 games)

INDIVIDUAL RECORDS

SCORING—TOTAL POINTS CAREER

John Becksvoort*	1991-94	317	Beattie Feathers	1931-33	198
Fuad Reveiz*	1981-84	314	Greg Burke*	1989-9	182
Gene McEver	1928-31	276	Alan Duncan*	1978-80	180
James Stewart	1991-94	240	Reggie Cobb	1988-89	176
Stanley Morgan	1973-76	236	* placekicker		
George Hunt*	1969-71	203			

CAREER TOTAL OFFENSE LEADERS

1.	6,427	Andy Kelly, QB	1988-91	6,397 pass, 30 run
2.	5,900	Jeff Francis, QB	1985-88	5,867 pass, 33 run
3.	4,807	Jimmy Streater, QB	1976-79	3,433 pass, 1,374 run
4.	4,483	Heath Shuler, QB	1991-93	4,088 pass, 283 run, 12 rec.
5.	4,075	Peyton Manning, QB	1994-present	4,095 pass, 20 run
6.	4,068	Condredge Holloway, QB	1972-74	3,102 pass, 966 run
7.	3,807	Alan Cockrell, QB	1981-83	3,823 pass
8.	3,580	Bobby Scott, QB	1968-70	3,371 pass, 209 run
9.	3,527	Tony Robinson, QB	1982-85	3,332 pass, 195 run
10.	3,519	Dewey Warren, QB	1965-67	3,357 pass, 162 run
11.	3,367	James Stewart, RB	1991-94	14 pass, 2,890 run, 463 rec.
12.	3,108	Randy Wallace, QB	1974-76	2,356 pass572 run
13.	3,072	Johnnie Jones, RB	1981-84	2,852 run, 220 rec.
14.	3,038	Stanley Morgan, WB	1973-76	11 pass, 1,952 run, 1,075 rec.
15.	2,757	Johnny Majors, SW-TB	1954-56	1,135 pass, 1,622 run
16.	2,733	Mallon Faircloth, SW-TB	1961-63	1,230 pass, 1,503 run
17.	2,568	Hank Lauricella, SW-TB	1949-51	1,105 pass, 1,463 run
18.	2,476	Curt Watson, RB	1969-71	2,364 run, 112 rec.
19.	2,293	Steve Alatorre, QB	1980-81	1,918 pass, 375 run
20.	2,210	Beattie Feathers, RB	1931-33	126 pass, 1,888 run, 196 rec.
21.	2,195	Charlie Garner, RB	1992-93	2,089 run, 106 rec.
22.	2,139	George Cafego, RB	1931-33	550 pass, 1,598 run
23.	2,114	Bubba Wyche, QB	1966-68	2,018 pass, 96 run
24.	2,088	Anthony Hancock, WB	1978-81	262 run, 1,846 rec.
25.	2,029	Tim McGee, WR	1982-85	13 run, 2,042 rec.

YARDAGE LEADERS—GAME

Tony Robinson, 1985, 417 vs. UCLA
Andy Kelly, 1990, 407 vs. Notre Dame
Tony Robinson, 1984, 389 vs. Florida
Andy Kelly, 1991, 386 vs. Florida
Andy Kelly, 1991, 383 vs. Auburn
Bobby Scott, 1970, 375 vs. Florida
Peyton Manning, 1995, 373 vs. Arkansas
Heath Shuler, 1992, 359 vs. South Carolina
Jeff Francis, 1987, 356 vs. Alabama
Steve Alatorre, 1981, 353 vs. Vanderbilt
Heath Shuler, 1993, 349 vs. Florida
Andy Kelly, 1990, 348 vs. Colorado
Peyton Manning, 1995, 342 vs. Georgia
Jeff Francis, 1986, 335 vs. Army
Bob Lund, 1945, 329 vs. Vanderbilt
Jeff Francis, 1988, 325 vs. Georgia
Peyton Manning, 1995, 312 vs. Florida
Jeff Francis, 1986, 306 vs. Alabama
Tony Robinson, 1984, 284 vs. Vanderbilt
Darryl Dickey, 1985, 281 vs. Vanderbilt
Tony Robinson, 1985, 281 vs. Florida

OFFENSIVE PLAYS—GAME

Andy Kelly, 1990, 66 vs. Notre Dame
Andy Kelly, 1991, 65 vs. Florida
Bubba Wyche, 1968, 62 vs. Auburn
Andy Kelly, 1990, 59 vs. Colorado
Andy Kelly, 1991, 54 vs. Mississippi St.
Alan Cockrell, 1982, 53 vs. Iowa (Peach Bowl)
Steve Alatorre, 1981, 53 vs. Wisconsin (Garden St. Bowl)
Bubba Wyche, 1968, 50 vs. Georgia
Tony Robinson, 1984, 50 vs. Florida
Peyton Manning, 1995, 48 vs. Arkansas
Jeff Francis, 1987, 48 vs. Alabama
Heath Shuler, 1993, 47 vs. Florida
Bobby Scott, 1970, 47 vs. South Carolina
Heath Shuler, 1992, 46 vs. Vanderbilt
Tony Robinson, 1985, 46 vs. Florida
Tony Robinson, 1985, 45 vs. UCLA
Bobby Scott, 1970, 45 vs. Florida
Jimmy Streater, 1977, 45 vs. Florida
Dewey Warren, 1966, 45 vs. Mississippi
Bobby Scott, 1969, 44 vs. Florida

2,000-YARD TOTAL OFFENSE—SEASON

2,928 — Peyton Manning, 1995 (-26 run, 2,954 pass)
2,819 — Andy Kelly, 1991 (60 run, 2,759 pass)
2,426 — Heath Shuler, 1993 (73 run, 2,353 pass)
2,289 — Jeff Francis, 1988 (52 run, 2,237 pass)
2,259 — Andy Kelly, 1990 (18 run, 2,241 pass)
2,089 — Tony Robinson, 1984 (126 run, 1,963 pass)
2,011 — Jimmy Streater, 1978 (593 run, 1,418 pass)

CAREER RUSHING LEADERS

Pos. Name, Years	Atts.	Yds.	Avg.
1. James Stewart, 1991-94	531	2,890	5.40
2. Johnnie Jones, 1981-84	517	2,852	5.50
3. Curt Watson, 1969-71	529	2,364	4.50
4. Reggie Cobb, 1987-89	445	2,360	5.30
5. Charlie Garner, 1992-93	313	2,089	6.67
6. Aaron Hayden, 1991-94	393	2,061	5.20
7. Stanley Morgan, 1973-76	353	1,952	5.50
8. Beattie Feathers, 1931-33	309	1,888	7.20
9. Andy Kozar, 1950-52	355	1,850	5.20
10. Jay Graham, 1993-	363	1,802	4.96
11. Haskel Stanback, 1971-73	391	1,730	4.40
12. James Berry, 1978-81	419	1,721	4.10
13. William Howard, 1984-87	398	1,711	4.30
14. Keith Davis, 1985-88	322	1,704	5.30
15. Richard Pickens, 1966-68	306	1,644	5.30
16. Johnny Majors, 1954-56	386	1,622	4.20
17. George Cafego, 1937-39	259	1,589	6.10
18. Kelsey Finch, 1975-78	348	1,587	4.60
19. Hubert Simpson, 1976-79	309	1,516	4.90
20. Mallon Faircloth, 1961-63	400	1,503	3.80

RUSHING YARDAGE — SEASON

Jay Graham, 1995	1,438
Johnnie Jones, 1984	1,290
Tony Thompson, 1990	1,261
Chuck Webb, 1989	1,236
Reggie Cobb, 1987	1,197
Charlie Garner, 1993	1,161
Johnnie Jones, 1983	1,116
James Stewart, 1994	1,028
James Stewart, 1991	939
Charlie Garner, 1992	928
Haskel Stanback, 1972	890
Hank Lauricella, 1951	881
Aaron Hayden, 1994	819
Stanley Morgan, 1975	809
Curt Watson, 1969	807
Tom Tracy, 1954	794
Hubert Simpson, 1979	792
Curt Watson, 1970	791
William Howard, 1986	787
Kelsey Finch, 1977	770
Curt Watson, 1971	766
Richard Pickens, 1968	736
Stanley Morgan, 1974	723
Aaron Hayden, 1991	704
Keith Davis, 1985	684

LONGEST RUSHING SCORING PLAYS

99 — Kelsey Finch, 1977 vs. Florida
91 — Dick Dodson, 1927 vs. Transylvania
87 — Dick Dorsey, 1933 vs. Virginia Tech
82 — Steve Wold, 1969 vs. Vanderbilt
81 — Hank Lauricella, 1950 vs. Tenn. Tech
80 — Tony Thompson, 1990 vs. Miss. State
80 — Jimmy Streater, 1977 vs. California
80 — Stanley Morgan, 1975 vs. Kentucky
80 — John Majors, 1954 vs. Miss. State
80 — Jay Graham, 1995 vs. Alabama

200-YARD RUSHING GAMES

294 — Chuck Webb, 1989 vs. Ole Miss
250 — Chuck Webb, 1990 vs. Arkansas
248 — Tony Thompson, 1990 vs. Miss. St.
236 — Tony Thompson, 1990 vs. Vanderbilt
234 — Johnnie Jones, 1983 vs. Rutgers
225 — Reggie Cobb, 1989 vs. Auburn
215 — James Stewart, 1991 vs. Ole Miss
211 — James Stewart, 1994 vs. Georgia
211 — Jay Graham, 1995 vs. Vanderbilt
203 — Johnnie Jones, 1984 vs. Washington St.
201 — Stanley Morgan, 1975 vs. Hawaii

CAREER PASSING LEADERS

Name, Years	Att./Comp.	Pct.	Yards	TD
1. Andy Kelly, 1988-91	846-514	60.8	6,397	36
2. Jeff Francis, 1985-88	768-476	62.0	5,867	31
3. Peyton Manning, 1994-	524-333	64.0	4,095	33
4. Heath Shuler, 1991-93	513-316	61.6	4,088	36
5. Alan Cockrell, 1981-83	568-317	55.8	3,823	26
6. Jimmy Streater, 1976-79	467-241	51.6	3,433	17
7. Bobby Scott, 1968-70	498-236	47.4	3,371	32
8. Dewey Warren, 1965-67	440-258	58.6	3,357	27
9. Tony Robinson, 1982-85	411-253	61.6	3,332	23
10. C. Holloway, 1972-74	407-238	58.5	3,102	18
11. Randy Wallace, 1974-76	301-153	50.8	2,536	13
12. Bubba Wyche, 1966-68	312-173	55.4	2,018	18
13. J.B. Proctor, 1946-48	193-93	48.2	1,308	14
14. Mallon Faircloth, 1961-63	176-77	43.8	1,230	13
15. Johnny Majors, 1954-56	148-80	54.1	1,135	11

PASSING ATTEMPTS — CAREER

Andy Kelly, 1988-91	846
Jeff Francis, 1985-88	768
Alan Cockrell, 1981-83	568
Peyton Manning, 1994-present	524
Heath Shuler, 1991-93	513
Bobby Scott, 1968-70	498
Jimmy Streater, 1976-79	467
Dewey Warren, 1965-67	440
Condredge Holloway, 1972-74	407
Bubba Wyche, 1966-68	312
Randy Wallace, 1974-76	301
J.B. Proctor, 1946-48	193
Hank Lauricella, 1949-51	179
Mallon Faircloth, 1961-63	176
Johnny Majors, 1954-56	148

PASSING COMPLETIONS — CAREER

Andy Kelly, 1988-91	514
Jeff Francis, 1985-88	476
Peyton Manning, 1994-present	333
Alan Cockrell, 1981-83	317
Heath Shuler, 1991-93	316
Dewey Warren, 1965-67	258
Tony Robinson, 1982-85	253
Jimmy Streater, 1976-79	241
Condredge Holloway, 1972-74	238
Bobby Scott, 1968-70	236
Bubba Wyche, 1966-68	173
Randy Wallace, 1974-76	153
J.B. Proctor, 1946-48	93
Johnny Majors, 1954-56	80
Mallon Faircloth, 1961-63	77

SINGLE-SEASON PASSING LEADERS

Name, Year	Att/Comp./Pct.	Yards	TD
Peyton Manning, 1995	380-244-64.0%	2,954	22
Andy Kelly, 1991	366-231-63.2%	2,759	15
Heath Shuler, 1993	285-184-64.6%	2,353	25
Andy Kelly, 1990	304-179-58.9%	2,241	14
Jeff Francis, 1988	314-191-60.8%	2,237	13
Alan Cockrell, 1982	294-174-59.2%	2,021	12
Tony Robinson, 1984	253-156-61.7%	1,963	14
Jeff Francis, 1986	233-150-64.4%	1,946	9
Dewey Warren, 1966	229-136-59.0%	1,716	18
Bobby Scott, 1970	252-118-46.9%	1,697	14
Alan Cockrell, 1983	243-128-52.7%	1,683	13
Bubba Wyche, 1968	237-134-56.1%	1,539	14
Jeff Francis, 1987	201-121-60.2%	1,512	8
Jimmy Streater, 1978	198-101-51.0%	1,418	4

PASSING ATTEMPTS—GAME

60 — Andy Kelly, 1990 vs. Notre Dame
56 — Andy Kelly, 1991 vs. Florida
55 — Andy Kelly, 1990 vs. Colorado
46 — Peyton Manning, 1995 vs. Arkansas
45 — Bubba Wyche, 1968 vs. Auburn
44 — Jeff Francis, 1987 vs. Alabama
43 — Tony Robinson, 1984 vs. Florida
42 — Bobby Scott, 1970 vs. South Carolina
39 — Jeff Francis, 1988 vs. Georgia
38 — Bobby Scott, 1970 vs. Florida
38 — Jeff Francis, 1988 vs. Washington St.
37 — Alan Cockrell, 1982 vs. LSU
37 — Jeff Francis, 1988 vs. Alabama
36 — Dewey Warren, 1966 vs. Ole Miss
36 — Tony Robinson, 1985 vs. Florida
35 — Tony Robinson, 1985 vs. UCLA
35 — Bobby Scott, 1970 vs. UCLA
34 — Alan Cockrell, 1983 vs. Pittsburgh
34 — Bubba Wyche, 1968 vs. Georgia
34 — Bobby Scott, 1969 vs. Florida (Gator Bowl)

PASSING COMPLETIONS—GAME

35 — Andy Kelly, 1990 vs. Notre Dame
35 — Peyton Manning, 1994 vs. Arkansas
33 — Andy Kelly, 1990 vs. Colorado
33 — Andy Kelly, 1991 vs. Florida
29 — Tony Robinson, 1984 vs. Florida
27 — Jeff Francis, 1988 vs. Kentucky
26 — Jeff Francis, 1987 vs. Alabama
26 — Tony Robinson, 1985 vs. Florida
25 — Bubba Wyche, 1968 vs. Auburn
25 — Tony Robinson, 1985 vs. UCLA
25 — Jeff Francis, 1988 vs. Georgia
24 — Jeff Francis, 1986 vs. Army
23 — Jeff Francis, 1986 vs. Alabama
23 — Jeff Francis, 1988 vs. Washington St.
22 — Daryl Dickey, 1985 vs. Vanderbilt

300-YARD PASSING GAMES

399 — Andy Kelly, 1990 vs. Notre Dame
392 — Andy Kelly, 1991 vs. Florida
387 — Tony Robinson, 1985 vs. UCLA
385 — Bobby Scott, 1970 vs. Florida
384 — Peyton Manning, 1995 vs. Arkansas
371 — Tony Robinson, 1984 vs. Florida
368 — Andy Kelly, 1990 vs. Colorado
358 — Jeff Francis, 1987 vs. Alabama
355 — Heath Shuler, 1993 vs. Florida
355 — Andy Kelly, 1991 vs. Auburn
354 — Jeff Francis, 1988 vs. Georgia
349 — Peyton Manning, 1995 vs. Georgia
338 — Bubba Wyche, 1968 vs. Auburn
334 — Jeff Francis, 1986 vs. Army
330 — Andy Kelly, 1991 vs. Miss. St.

326 — Peyton Manning, 1995 vs. Florida
319 — Steve Alatorre, 1981 vs. Vanderbilt
319 — Andy Kelly, 1991 vs. Memphis
315 — Steve Alatorre, 1981 vs. Wisconsin
309 — Jeff Francis, 1986 vs. Alabama
307 — Heath Shuler, 1993 vs. Arkansas
301 — Peyton Manning, 1995 vs. Alabama
300 — Tony Robinson, 1985 vs. Florida
300 — Andy Kelly, 1990 vs. Kentucky

CAREER RECEPTIONS LEADERS

Name, Years	No.	Yards	TD
Thomas Woods, 1986-89	124	1,617	7
Tim McGee, 1982-85	123	2,042	15
Larry Seivers, 1974-76	117	1,924	8
Joey Kent, 1992-present	115	1,734	18
Craig Faulkner, 1990-93	110	1,705	9
Carl Pickens, 198-91	109	1,875	13
Anthony Hancock, 1978-81	106	1,826	12
Alvin Harper, 1987-90	102	1,547	16
Richmond Flowers, 1966-68	101	1,172	11
Reggie Harper, 1977-80	98	1,141	7
Cory Fleming, 1990-93	94	1,266	18
Willie Gault, 1979-82	89	1,482	10
Jim Powell, 1946-48	80	1,186	12
Johnny Mills, 1964-66	76	1,120	4
Ken DeLong, 1967-69	76	844	9
Lester McClain, 1968-70	70	1,003	10
Gary Kreis, 1967-69	69	1,043	9
Joe Thompson, 1969-71	56	791	5
John Yarbrough, 1973-75	56	776	6
Stanley Morgan, 1973-76	48	1,075	8

SINGLE-SEASON RECEPTIONS LEADERS

Name, Year	No.	Yards	Avg.	TD
Joey Kent, 1995	65	1,055	16.23	9
Thomas Woods, 1988	58	689	11.88	5
Tim McGee, 1984	54	809	14.98	6
Carl Pickens, 1990	53	917	17.30	6
Larry Seivers, 1976	51	737	14.45	2
Tim McGee, 1985	50	947	18.94	7
Willie Gault, 1982	50	668	13.36	4
Carl Pickens, 1991	49	877	17.89	5
Johnny Mills, 1966	48	725	15.10	4
Larry Seivers, 1975	41	840	20.48	4
Richmond Flowers, 1967	41	585	14.27	4
Gary Kreis, 1969	38	609	16.03	5
Joe Thompson, 1970	37	502	13.57	4
Joey Clinkscales, 1986	37	511	13.81	3
Alvin Harper, 1988	37	487	13.16	5
Jim Powell, 1948	36	502	13.57	4
Richmond Flowers, 1966	35	407	11.63	5
Ken DeLong, 1968	34	393	11.56	3
Lester McClain, 1968	29	329	11.34	6
Larry Seivers, 1974	25	347	13.88	2
Gary Kreis, 1968	25	334	13.36	4
Richmond Flowers, 1968	25	180	7.20	0

RECEPTIONS—GAME

13 — Carl Pickens, 1990 vs. Notre Dame
13 — Joey Kent, 1995 vs. Arkansas
12 — Alvin Harper, 1988 vs. Washington St.
11 — Thomas Woods, 1988 vs. Kentucky
11 — Johnny Mills, 1966 vs. Auburn
11 — Gary Kreis, 1969 vs. Kentucky
11 — Anthony Hancock, 1981 vs. Wisconsin
11 — Larry Seivers, 1976 vs. Clemson
10 — Jim Powell, 1948 vs. Ole Miss
10 — Johnny Mills, 1965 vs. UCLA
10 — Lenny Taylor, 1983 vs. Auburn
10 — Tim McGee, 1984 vs. Florida
10 — Tim McGee, 1984 vs. Vanderbilt
10 — Carl Pickens, 1990 vs. Kentucky

RECEIVING YARDS — GAME

225 — Johnny Mills, 1966 vs. Kentucky
217 — Willie Gault, 1981 vs. Vanderbilt
201 — Carl Pickens, 1990 vs. Kentucky
201 — Stanley Morgan, 1973 vs. Texas Christian
196 — Anthony Hancock, 1981 vs. Wisconsin
190 — Tim McGee, 1984 vs. Vanderbilt
174 — Willie Gault, 1982 vs. Auburn
172 — Carl Pickens, 1991 vs. Auburn
163 — Carl Pickens, 1990 vs. Notre Dame
163 — Anthony Hancock, 1979 vs. Vanderbilt
163 — Tim McGee, 1985 vs. Auburn
161 — Larry Seivers. 1975 vs. North Texas St.
161 — Joey Kent, 1995 vs. Arkansas
159 — Anthony Miller, 1986 vs. Alabama
157 — Tim McGee, 1984 vs. Florida
151 — Gary Kreis, 1969 vs. South Carolina
146 — Stan Trott, 1970 vs. Florida
145 — Gary Kreis, 1969 vs. Kentucky
142 — Jim Powell, 1948 vs. Ole Miss
142 — Tim McGee, 1985 vs. UCLA

ALL-PURPOSE YARDS—CAREER

(Rushing, Receiving, Kickoff Returns, Punt Returns)
1. Stanley Morgan, 1973-76 — 4,642
2. Willie Gault, 1979-82 — 4,035
3. James Stewart, 1991-94 — 3,353
4. Johnnie Jones, 1981-84 — 3,072
5. Reggie Cobb, 1987-89 — 3,046
6. George Cafego, 1937-39 — 2,863
7. Carl Pickens, 1989-91 — 2,798
8. Thomas Woods, 1986-89 — 2,617
9. Mallon Faircloth, 1961-63 — 2,500
10. Curt Watson, 1969-71 — 2,493
11. Johnny Majors, 1954-56 — 2,404
12. Aaron Hayden, 1991-95 — 2,383
13. Beattie Feathers, 1931-33 — 2,347
14. Charlie Garner, 1992-93 — 2,334
15. Anthony Hancock, 1978-81 — 2,291

CAREER KICK/PUNT RETURN LEADERS

Willie Gault, 1979-82	2,513
Dale Carter, 1990-91	1,652
Stanley Morgan, 1973-76	1,615
Bobby Majors, 1969-71	1,530
George Cafego, 1937-39	1,274

SINGLE-SEASON PUNT RETURNS

Name, Year	No.	Yards	Avg.
Bobby Majors, 1969	37	457	12.1
Bobby Majors, 1971	42	437	10.1
Eddie Brown, 1972	42	429	10.2
Dale Carter, 1990	29	381	13.1
Willie Gault, 1981	31	381	12.3

SINGLE-SEASON KICKOFF RETURNS

Name, Year	No.	Yards	Avg.
Willie Gault, 1980	24	662	27.6
Dale Carter, 1991	27	623	23.1
Willie Gault, 1981	28	606	21.6
Carl Pickens, 1989	26	594	22.8
Anthony Morgan, 1988	24	580	24.2

CAREER PUNTING LEADERS

Name, Years	Avg.
Jimmy Colquitt, 1981-84	43.8
Craig Colquitt, 1975-77	42.5
Ron Widby, 1964-66	42.3
Kent Elmore, 1986-88	42.2
Neil Calbo, 1972-74	41.7
Tom Hutton, 1991-94	40.7
Bob Garmon, 1984-87	40.6
George Canale, 1960-62	40.5
Herman Weaver, 1967-69	40.1
John Warren, 1979-82	39.8

DEFENSE

INTERCEPTIONS — CAREER

Tim Priest, 1968-70 — 18
Mike Jones, 1967-69 — 16
Conrad Graham, 1970-72 — 15
Bill Young, 1966-69 — 15
Bobby Majors, 1969-71 — 13
J.W. Sherrill, 1948-50 — 13
Charles Davis, 1983-86 — 13

INTERCEPTIONS — SEASON

J.W. Sherrill, 1949 — 12
Bobby Majors, 1970 — 10
Tim Priest, 1970 — 9
Bill Young, 1968 — 9
Chris White, 1985 — 9

TOTAL TACKLES — CAREEER

Andy Spiva, 1973-76 — 547
Jamie Rotella, 1970-72 — 413
Earnest Fields, 1987-91 — 407
Greg Jones, 1974-77 — 377
Craig Puki, 1975-79 — 358
Jim Noonan, 1976-80 — 355
Kelly Ziegler, 1983-87 — 353
Dale Jones, 1983-86 — 350
Steve Poole, 1973-75 — 349
Russ Williams, 1974-77 — 332

Carl Zander, 1981-84 — 332
Keith DeLong, 1985-88 — 330

TOTAL TACKLES — SEASON

Andy Spiva, 1976 — 194
Jamie Rotella, 1972 — 190
Steve Poole, 1974 — 182
Ray Nettles, 1971 — 174
Carl Zander, 1984 — 167

TOTAL TACKLES — GAME

Tom Fisher — 28, 1964 vs. Auburn
Greg Jones — 25, 1977 vs. Vanderbilt
Greg Jones — 25, 1976 vs. Alabama
Andy Spiva — 25, 1975 vs. Vanderbilt
Kelly Ziegler — 24, 1987 vs. Boston Coll.
Lemont Holt Jeffers — 24, 1981 vs. Auburn
Andy Spiva — 24, 1976 vs. Kentucky

QB SACKS — CAREER

Reggie White, 1980-83 — 32
Todd Kelly, 1989-92 — 22.5
James Wilson, 1989-93 — 20.5
Steve White, 1992-95 — 20
Brad White, 1978-80 — 19
Mark Hovanic, 1983-87 — 19
Ronnie McCartney, 1973-75 — 17.5

QB SACKS — SEASON

Reggie White, 1983 — 15
Leonard Little, 1995 — 11
Todd Kelly, 1992 — 11
Ronnie McCartney, 1975 — 10
Manley Mixon, 1970 — 9.5
Chuck Smith, 1991 — 9

QB SACKS — GAME

Reggie White — 4, 1983 vs. The Citadel
Shane Bonham — 3, 1992 vs. Arkansas
Chuck Smith — 3, 1991 vs. Louisville
Mark Hovanic — 3, 1985 vs. Florida
Dennis Wolfe — 3, 1976 vs. TCU
David Page — 3, 1974 vs. Clemson

AWARDS

ALL-AMERICANS

1929 Gene McEver, halfback
1930 Bobby Dodd, quarterback
1931 Herman Hickman, guard
1933 Beattie Feathers, halfback
1938 Bowden Wyatt, end; George Cafego, halfback; Bob Suffridge, guard
1939 George Cafego, halfback; Ed Molinski, guard; Bob Suffridge, guard; Abe Shires, tackle
1940 Bob Suffridge, guard; Bob Foxx, halfback; Ed Molinski, guard
1944 Bob Dobelstein, guard
1946 Dick Huffman, tackle
1950 Ted Daffer, guard; Bud Sherrod, end
1951 Hank Lauricella, halfback; Ted Daffer, guard; Bill Pearman, tackle
1952 John Michels, guard; Doug Atkins, tackle
1954 Darris McCord, tackle
1956 John Majors, halfback; Buddy Cruze, end
1957 Bill Johnson, guard
1963 Steve DeLong
1964 Steve DeLong
1965 Frank Emanuel, linebacker
1966 Paul Naumoff, linebacker; Austin Denney, end; Ron Widby, punter; Bob Johnson, center
1967 Bob Johnson, center; Albert Dorsey, back; Richmond Flowers, wingback
1968 Charles Rosenfelder, guard; Steve Kiner, linebacker; Jim Weatherford, back
1969 Steve Kiner, linebacker; Chip Kell, guard; Jack Reynolds, linebacker
1970 Chip Kell, guard; Jackie Walker, linebacker
1971 Bobby Majors, back; Jackie Walker, linebacker
1972 Conrad Graham, back; Ricky Townsend, placekicker; Jamie Rotella, linebacker
1973 Eddie Brown, back; Ricky Townsend, placekicker
1975 Larry Seivers, end
1976 Larry Seivers, end
1979 Roland James, back
1982 Willie Gault, wide receiver; Jimmy Colquitt, punter
1983 Reggie White, tackle; Jimmy Colquitt, punter
1984 Bill Mayo, guard
1985 Tim McGee, wide receiver; Chris White, back
1987 Harry Galbreath, guard
1988 Keith DeLong, linebacker
1989 Eric Still, guard
1990 Antone Davis, tackle; Dale Carter, back
1991 Dale Carter, back; Carl Pickens, wide receiver
1993 John Becksvoort, Placekicker

ACADEMIC ALL-AMERICANS

(GTE First Team Selections Only)
1956 Charles Rader, Tackle, Chemistry
1957 Bill Johnson, Guard, Business Administration
1965 Mack Gentry, Tackle, Business Administration
1967 Bob Johnson, Center, Industrial Engineering
1970 Tim Priest, defensive back, Pre-Law
1980 Tim Irwin, Tackle, Pre-Law
1982 Mike Terry, DE, Business Administration

LETTERMEN

A Abernathy, George "Owl" T. 1926-27; Ackermann, Norbert J. Sr. 1939-40 (Capt.); Ackermann, Norbert J. Jr. 1963-64; Adams, Mark 1988-89-90-91; Adams, Ralph 1952; Adkins, Stockton 1955-56-57; Aguillard, Kyle 1977-78-79; Aiello, Sam 1982; Aiken, Malcolm 1930-31-32 (Capt.); Aitchison, Bret 1979; Akin, Brent 1978 (Service); Alatorre, Steve 1980-81; Alexander, Frank 1950-51-52; Alexander, W. C. 1900; Allen, David C. 1970-71-72; Allen, Jimmy 1970; Allen, John H. 1929-30-31; Alley, E. H. "Herc" 1927-28; Alston, Chris 1992; Amonette, Jason 1993 (Service); Amsler, Greg 1986-88-89-90; Anderson, Bill 1955-56-57 (Co-Capt.); Anderson, Charles 1974-75-76; Anderson, Malcolm S. 1932-33-34; Anderson, Wendell 1980 (Service); Andes, Julian (Mgr.) 1942-44; Andridge, Bob "Breezer" 1938-39-40; Applewhite, J. M. 1911; Arbo, Billy 1975-76-77-78; Archibald, Doug 1964-65-66; Armstrong, Carlton 1979-80-81; Armstrong, Jack 1946-47-48; Armstrong, Murray 1956-57-58; Asbury, E. J. 1944-45; Aszman, Jim 1986; Atchley, Randy 1984 (Service); Atkins, Doug 1950-51-52; Attkisson, Eugene R. (Mgr.) 1896-97; Augustine, Pat 1959-61-62 (Capt.); Austelle, Alfred 1934; Austin, Raymond 1993-94-95; Autry, Keith 1974; Aymett, Julian 1902-03.

B Bacon, J. B. 1899; Bacon, Pryor E. 1938-39; Bailey, Carey 1988-89-90-91; Bailey, Howard H. 1932-33-34; Bailey, John "Skeeter" W. 1938; Baird, Doug 1987-88-89-90; Baird, James A. 1896-97 (Capt.); Baird, Robert R. 1896-97; Baker, Bill 1966-67-68; Baker, Carey 1990; Baker, Charles F. 1947-48-49; Baker, Charles B. 1960; Baker, Tommy (Mgr.) 1967-68-69-70; Baker, W. G. 1906-07-08; Baldini, Ralph 1961; Balitsaris, George 1946-47-48; Balitsaris, Mike 1939-40-41; Balthis, R. F. 1901; Balthrop, Joe 1969-70-71; Bandemier, Bill 1973; Banks, Randy 1990; Baracca, Marty 1960-61; Barbish, Bill "Moose" 1951-52-53; Barker, Grey 1995; Barksdale, Val 1977-78-79-80; Barnes, William "Billy" 1937-38-39; Barnes, W. O. 1896; Barnhill, John H. 1925-26-27 (Capt.); Barron, David 1974-75-76-77; Bartholomew, Sam 1937-38-39 (Capt.); Bass, Ben 1969; Bass, Vernon 1984-85-86; Bates, Bill 1979-80-81-82; Bates, Jim 1966-67; Bates, William M. 1893; Batey, Jack S. 1924; Baucom, Tom

1967-68-69; Baugh, William M. 1893; Bayer, J. T. 1909; Bayer, S. D. 1913-14-15; Bayless, John D. 1931-32-33; Beard, Ed 1961; Becker, Hubert 1947; Beckler, David 1970; Becksvoort, John 1991-92-93-94; Beene, F. R. 1906; Beene, Jones C. Jr. 1901-02-03-04-05; Beene, L. Phillip 1928-29-30; Beene, Patton 1901-02; Begnaud, Shane 1993-1995; Behrens, John 1975-76 (Service); Bell, C. A. 1897; Bell, J. D. 1897; Bell, L. L. 1896; Bellis, Leonard 1945; Bellmont, L. T. 1904; Belote, Lew (Mgr.) 1978-79; Bender, Joe (Mgr.) 1949; Bennett, Andy 1969-71; Bennett, David 1989-90-91-92; Bennett, Fred 1984-85-86; Bennett, William R. "Bill" 1956-57; Bennett, Tom L. 1969-70-71; Benson, Chris 1989; Benton, Charles 1983-84-85-86; Benton, Steve (Mgr.) 1975; Bergmeier, Ron 1947-48-49; Berkhan, Rick 1977 (Service); Bernard, George R. 1893; Beron, Billy 1994-95; Berry, James 1978-79-80-81 (Tri.-Capt.); Beutel, Jim 1954-55 (Capt.); Bevans, Mike 1968-69-70; Bevis, William "Billy" 1942-44-45 (Capt.); Bibee, M. Bert 1932-33; Bible, Alvah 1970 (Service); Binion, Larry 1995; Bird, Terry 1964-65-66; Blackburn, David (Mgr.) 1989; Blackstock, William "Bill" 1951; Blair, Hal Edward 1919-20-21 (Capt.); Blair, Reuben Moore 1919; Blake, Tom 1945; Blankenship, Warren, 1959-60-61; Blessing, Hugh 1944; Bolton, Chris 1977-78-79-80; Bond Robert U. 1924; Bone, William "Bill" 1923-24; Bonham, Shane 1992-93; Booker, Ronnie 1982; Bordinger, Don 1951; Borgognone, Dirk 1987; Boring, Frank "Boomer" 1949-50-51; Bourches, Joe E. 1893; Bourkard, Harrison O. 1934-35; Bourne, T. P. 1900; Bowman, Larry 1974; Boyd, Samuel B. 1893; Boynton, John 1965-66-67; Brackett, H. B. "Deke" 1931-32-33; Brackney, Rick 1989 (Service); Bradford, Jim B. 1919-20; Brady, David 1973-74-75-76; Bradley, Shazzon 1988-89-90-91; Branch, Rufus C. 1910-11 (Capt.) 12; Brandau, Arthur A. 1942; Brandt, Frederic "Fritz" P. 1928-29-30; Brann, Ray O. 1958; Breeding, Ken 1960-61; Brengle, Bobby 1952-53-54; Bridges, Greg 1980; Bridges, Hal 1956; Briggs, Jesse 1977; Brixey, Tom 1948-49; Bronson, Tommy E. 1955-56-57; Brooks, Albert O. (Mgr.) 1932; Broome, W. Lloyd 1938-40; Broug, J. L. 1900-01; Brown, Bob G. 1960; Brown, C. D. 1892; Brown, Earle W. 1939-45; Brown, Eddie 1971-72-73 (Capt.); Brown, Fred "Bo" 1923-24-25; Brown, Herbert T. 1928-29-30; Brown, James P. 1892-93; Brown Jonathan 1994-95; Brown, Kenny 1960-61-62; Brown, Laron 1983; Brown, Richard 1984-85; Brown, Terry 1983-84-85-86; Brown, Victor 1992-93; Brown, W. C. 1906; Brown, W. P. 1908; Browne, David 1968-69-70; Brozowski, John 1969 (Service); Bruhin, John 1985-86-87; Brunson, Mario 1990-91-92-93; Bryan, C. L. 1899; Bryson, G. G. 1899; Bryson, Shawn 1995; Bryson, William J. 1940'; Buckingham, H. L. 1910; Buckingham, T. N. "Nash" 1901-02 (Capt.); Bullard, Ralph 1974-75-76-77; Burdette, A. M. 1906-07; Burdette, George M. 1923-24-25; Burgess, Robert E. 1927; Burke, Greg 1989-90; Burklow, Sammy 1956-57-58; Burnett, Jon 1973; Burnham, Bruce 1954-55-56; Burnley, Danny (Mgr.) 1980; Burns, Mark 1979-80 81; Burton, Lee Otis 1978; Burton, Shane 1992-93-94-95; Bush, Wayne 1962-63; Butcher, Elvin, 1925-26-27; Butler, Dan 1951-53; Butler, Johnny W. 1939-40-41; Bybee, Joe T. 1927; Byrd, Ray 1951-52.

Cafego, George 1937-38-39; Caldwell, Chan 1945-46-47; Caldwell, J. A. 1902-03-04-05; Caldwell, J. H. Jr. 1903-04-05; Caldwell, Lamar 1970-71-72; Caldwell, Mike 1972-73-74; Callahan, P. H. 1914; Callaway, Richard 1967-68-69; Callaway, Tom 1967-68-69; Cameron, Bill 1963-64-65; Cameron, A. D. "Scotty" 1912-14-15; Campbell, Bo 1995; Campbell, David 1971-72-73; Campbell, Earl 1950-51-52; Campbell, Kenneth 1990-91; Campbell, M. R. 1896-99; Campbell, L. Roe 1920-21-22-24; Canale, Frank 1962; Canale, George 1960-61-62; Canale, Whit 1962-64; Canini, Pat 1963; Cannon, Gary 1960-61; Cannon, R. L. 1892; Cantrell, Craig 1979; Cantrell, Edd M. 1953-54-55-56; Careathers, Paul 1972-73-74; Carmichael, Nick 1971-72-73; Carpenter, Don 1969-70; Carr, Hilrey 1969; Carroll, Alonzo M. Jr. "Goat" 1911-12-13-14; Carroll, Steve 1967-68-69; Carter, Al 1955-56-57; Carter, Dale 1990-91; Carter, George 1950; Carter, Howard 1976 (Service); Carter, J. W. 1959-60-61; Carter, Tony 1984 (Service); Carter, Vince 1984-85-86; Cartwright, Jim 1958-59-60; Casteel, Mike 1980-81-82; Cates, Clifton B, 1914-15; Chadnock, John 1944-45; Chadwell, James J. 1942; Chadwick, Dennis 1970-71-72; Chadwick, Walter 1965-66-67; Chambers, Harold 1960; Chancey, Ralph E. 1946-47-48-49 (Co-Capt.); Chancey, Steve 1971-72-73; Chandler, Allen E. 1942; Chandler, H. C. 1913; Chapman, D. C. 1896; Chapman, Joey 1990-91-92-93; Chapman, Ray M. 1953; Chavis, Johnny 1977-78; Childers, Ray (Mgr.) 1960; Christian, Bill 1977-79; Christmas, E. K. 1924; Cifers, Robert G. 1941-42; Cifers, Ed 1938-39-40; Cissell, Don 1959-60; Clabo, Neil 1972-73-74; Clabo, Phil 1973-74-75; Clark, Vince 1982-83-84; Claxton, J. O. "Jim" 1932-33-34; Clay, Boyd 1937-38-39; Clayton, Rufus 1922; Clements, H. H. (Mgr.) 1930; Clemmens, Bob B. 1921; Clemmer, James H. 1930-31; Cleveland, Terence 1986-87-88-89; Clinkscales, Joey 1984-85-86 (Tri.-Capt.); Cloninger, Bob O. 1952-53; Cobb, Reggie 1987-88; Cochran, E. R. 1906; Cockrell, Alan 1981-82-83; Cody, J. R. 1907; Cofer, Joe 1982-83-84; Cofer, Mike E. 1979-80-81; Cofer, Mike L. 1979-80-81-82 (Capt.); Coffey, Bryan 1985; Coffey, Charles 1953-54-55; Coffman, Leonard 1937-38-39; Coggins, Roger 1948-49; Cole, Bill 1973-74-75; Cole, Jeff 1983 (Service); Cole, Harry A. 1910; Coleman, Chuck 1981-82-83; Coleman, Jimmy L. 1938-39-40; Coleman, Jeff 1995; Coleman, Lee 1969; Coleman, Wayne A. 1960-61-62; Colhoun, Adams 1897; Collier, Harris T. 1893; Colquitt, Craig 1975-76-77; Colquitt, Jerry 1991-92-93-94; Colquitt, Jimmy 1981-82-83-84; Combs, Lewis 1982 (Service); Cone, Steve 1973-74; Connelly, Robert C. 1941; Cook, John 1982-83-84; Cook, Xavier 1982; Cooper, J. S. 1901-03 (Mgr.); Cooper, Kenneth 1981-82-83-84; Cooper, Richard 1984-85-87; Cooper, W. C. 1948-49-50; Copeland, Jeremaine 1995; Cornick, T. R. 1899; Costello, Mike 1959; Cotton, Jackie 1963-64-65; Cottrell, C. B. 1907; Covington, C. L. 1903; Cox, J. T. 1901-02; Cox, John B. 1891-92; Cox, William G. 1929-31; Cozart, Joe 1981-82; Craddock, Charles E. (Mgr.) 1911; Craig, George P. 1933-34-35; Craig, T. E. 1899; Crawford, Denver 1942-46-47 (Capt.); Crawford, Edwin S. 1934-35; Crawford, Frank J. 1935-36-37; Crawford, S. D. 1901-02; Creamer, Andre 1984-85-86-87; Creasey, George (Mgr.) 1945; Cross, Roy L. 1942-45; Crowson, Larry 1951; Crutchfield, Todd 1987 (Service); Cruze, Kyle "Buddy" 1955-56; Cummins, Charles L. Sr. 1919-21; Cummins, Charles H. 1949; Cunningham, Mike 1976; Cunningham, Rory 1980; Cvetnick, John 1954.

Daffer, Ted 1949-50-51; Dafney, Bernard 1990-91; Dalton, Benny 1968-69; Dalton, Bob 1961-62-63; Dalton, Ray 1962; Dalton, Terry 1966-67-68; Daniels, Terry 1979-80-81; Daniels, Tim 1979; Danychuk, Bill 1964; Darty, Landon 1955-56-57; Davis, Antone 1987-88-89-90; Davis, Bob 1949-50-51; Davis,

Charles 1983-84-85-86; Davis, Harlan 1990; Davis, John "Tex" 1951-52; Davis, Keith 1985-86-87-88; Davis, Kevin 1974-75-76; Davis, Ronald 1991-92-93-94; Davis, Steve L. 1977-78-79; Davis, Vando 1986-87-88; Davis, Willie (Mgr.) 1941; Dawson, D. A. 1912-13; Days, Kelly 1987-88-89-90; Deaver, Everett E. H. 1924; Decker, James Quinn 1928-29-30; DeFillippo, Joe 1975 (Service); DeHart, Dick 1966 (Service); DeLong, Keith 1985-86-87-88 (Capt.); DeLong, Ken 1967-68-69; DeLong, Steve 1962-63-64 (Capt.); DeLucca, Jerry 1954-55; Demastus, Mike 1974-75 (Service); DeMelfi, Joe 1962; Denbo, Don 1968-69-70; Denlinger, H. K. 1891 (Capt.); Denney, Austin, 1965-66 (Co-Capt.); Denson, Keith 1988-89; Derryberry, F. Woodrow 1935-36; Derryberry, O. Merton 1930-31; Derryberry, W. Everett 1925-27; Derwin, Jim 1963; Dickens, Phil W. 1934-35-36; Dickerson, Calvin 1981; Dickey, Daryl 1984-85; Dietzen, Walter N. 1919-20-21; Dilemme, Bill 1991; Dinges, D. C. 1907; Dingus, Vic. 1967-68-69; Disney, Theodore E. "Ty" 1929-30-31; Disspayne, Elmer 1939; Ditmore, Frank M. 1934-35; Ditmore, J. M. 1958; Doak, Alf 1920; Dobelstein, Robert 1942-44 (Capt.) 45; Dobelstein, Russ 1944-45-46; Dockery, Rex 1963; Dodd, Robert Lee "Bobby" 1928-29-30; Dodson, Richard B. 1925-26-27; Donahue, Ken 1949-50; Donaldson, R. C. 1896; Donaldson, W. J. 1906; Donelson, A. J. Jr. 1911-12; Doolin, Phil 1973; Dorsey, Albert 1965-67; Dorsey, Richard T. 1932-33-34; Dotson, Dewayne 1989-90; Dougherty, Joe Q. 1933-35-36; Dougherty, Nathan W. 1906-07-08-09 (Capt.); Douglas, A. H. 1901-02; Douglas, David 1984-85; Douglas, Steve 1983-84; Dowling, Clark (Mgr.) 1932-33; Downey, Pat 1962-63; Drost, Ray 1942-46-47; Drummond, Keith 1954-55; Drummonds, Ronnie 1968-69-70; Dudley, Bubba 1969; Duff, Bill 1994-95; Duncan, Alan 1978-79-80; Duncan, Clark 1977-78-80; Duncan, Clyde 1981-82-83; Duncan, Edwin Cheek 1936-37-38; Dunkin, Jim 1983-84; Dutton, Cliff 1992; Duvall, Jim 1975-76-77.

Earl, Richard 1970-71-72; Eblen, R. Hooper 1935; Edmiston, Don "Speedy" 1939-40-41; Edmonds, H. M. 1896-97-1900; Edmonds, Oscar 1944; Edwards, Anthony 1969-70-71; Edwards, Skip 1964-66; Eichholtz, Bill 1984; Eldred, Ralph E. 1936-37-38; Eldridge, Robert "Dink" (Mgr.) 1939-40; Elkas, Ray 1948-49; Elkins, L. E. 1910; Elliott, Frank S. 1925-27; Ellis, Carl 1963-64; Ellis, Dick 1967; Ellis, J. B. 1931-32-33; Ellspermann, Steve 1966 (Service); Elmore, James W. 1925-26-27; Elmore, Kent 1988-89; Emanuel, Frank 1963-64-65; Embry, Jim 1974; Emendorfer, Bill 1970-71-72; Emmons, Bobby 1976-77-78; Emery, John 1993-94; Emory, Bill 1915-16; Emory, David 1957; England, Lee 1987-88-89; Ensley, Jerry 1960-61-62; Epperson, Harry G. 1935-36; Epps, Cortney 1994; Epstein, Adam 1988; Epstein, Jason 1992; Ernsberger, Dick 1949-50-51; Etter, Gene 1958-59-60; Evans, Joe 1919-20; Evey, Dick 1961-62-63.

Fair, Dale 1974; Fair, Terry 1994-95; Faircloth, Mallon 1961-62-63; Fairfield, C. D. 1897; Falco, Joe 1963-64; Farmer, Joel 1983-84-85; Farrar, Scot 1976-77; Faulkner, Craig 1990-91-92-93 (Co-Capt.); Faust, Hugh D. 1930; Feathers, Beattie 1931-32-33; Felty, Gene 1949-50; Fender, M. W. 1912; Ferris, Charles E. 1892; Fielden, Alan 47-48-49; Fields, Brad 1979 (Service); Fields, Earnest 1988-89-90-91 (Co-Capt.); Filson, Dave 1990; Finch, H. B. (Mgr.) 1902; Finch, Kelsey 1976-77-78; Finney, James I. 1928-29; Fisher, Armandos 1993; Fisher, Bob 1951-52-53; Fisher, Buddy 1961-62-63 (Capt.); Fisher, James C. 1892-93; Fisher, Jody 1941-42;

Fisher, John 1988-89-90-91 (Co-Capt.); Fisher, Lavoisier 1982-83-84-85; Fisher, Tom 1964-65; Fitchpatrick, Tim 1973-74-75; Fleming, Cory 1990-91-92-93 (Co-Capt.); Fleming, Jeff (Mgr.) 1986-87; Flenniken, Hector (Mgr.) 1933; Fletcher, Mark 1988-89-90-91; Flora, Charles 1949-50; Flowers, George 1924; Flowers, Richmond 1966-67-68; Folsom, Derrick 1989; Fonde, C. H. 1910-11-12 (Capt.); Ford, Chester 1994-95; Ford, Glenn 1979-80; Ford, Howard (Mgr.) 1931; Foster, Clifton 1983 (Service); Fourman, Nate (Mgr.) 1950; Fowler, Harley (Mgr.) 1908; Fowler, W. S. "Monk" 1947; Fox, D. N. 1904; Fox, R. E. 1904; Foxall, Joe 1960-61-62; Foxx, Bob 1938-39-40; Foxx, Frank 1976-77-78; Francis, Hugh 1919; Francis, J. H. 1910; Francis, Jeff 1985-86-87-88; Francis, John 1941-46-47; Frank, Milton 1931-32-33; Frank, Richard (Mgr.) 1936; Franklin, Coy 1958; Franklin, John 1930-31-32; Franklin, L. D. 1908-09; Franklin, Mack 1951-52-53 (Capt.); Franklin, Robbie 1964-65-66; Frazier, Bobby 1963-64-65; Freeman, Dewayne 1992; French, F. D. 1900; Frere, Rob 1970-71-72; Frere, Ron 1972 (Service); Frost, Ken 1959-60; Frost, Tim 1992; Fugate, Stanley (Mgr.) 1964-65-66; Fuhler, Tom 1990-91; Fuller, Ben F. 1927-28-29; Fuller, C. J. 1902-03; Fulmer, Phillip 1969-70-71; Fulton, Charles 1965-66-67; Fulton, Robert W. 1935-36; Furnas, Doug 1981-82; Furnas, Mike 1982-83; Fuson, Clyde 1942.

Gaffney, James T. 1941-42; Gaines, Cory 1995; Gaines, Greg 1978-80; Galbreath, Harry 1984-85-86-87 (Co-Capt.); Galbreath, John (Mgr.) 1926; Galiffa, Art 1964-66; Gallagher, Joe 1973-74-75-76; Galyon, Scott 1992-93-94-95 (Capt.); Gamble, A. M. 1899; Gamble, R. M. 1901-02; Gammage, Elliott 1965-66-67; Gann, Gene 1960-61; Garmon, Bob 1985-86-87; Garner, Charlie 1992-93; Garner, Hugh 1952-53-54; Gault, Willie 1979-80-81-82; Gaut, David (Mgr.) 1907; Gauze, J. W. 1911; Gayles, Mike 1974-75-76; Gaylor, Jim 1975-76-77; Gearing, Paul 1946-47-48-49; Gebhardt, W. T. 1892; Geisler, J. V. 1911-12; Gentry, Mack 1964-65-66; Gerardi, Greg 1990; Getaz, David (Mgr.) 1916; Getteys, P. W. 1902; Gettys, R. E. 1899; Gibson, Brent 1993-94-95; Giddens, Clarence E. 1934-35; Gillespie, Charles 1979-82; Gilliam, Jim 1991; Glascott, Bob 1956; Glass, Glenn 1959-60-61; Gleaves, Bob 1956; Glover, Jimmy 1965-66-67; Godzak, Ed 1952; Gold, Bill 1941-42-43; Gonce, J. W. 1903; Gooch, Mike 1965-67-68; Goodin, Chad 1989; Goodrich, Guinn B. 1932-33; Gordon, Bobby 1955-56-57; Gordon, Milton 1986; Gordon, Rodney 1990-91-92; Gordy, John 1954-55-56 (Capt.); Gowdy, Jerry 1962-63; Graddy, Sam 1985-86; Graham, Conrad 1970-71-72; Graham, J. H. 1910; Graham, Jay 1993-94-95; Graham, Joe 1964-67; Grant, H. P. (Mgr.) 1905; Grant, Stan 1976; Gratz, Bobby 1963-64-65; Graves, Samuel Ray 1940-41 (Capt.); Gravitt, Mitchell 1973; Gray, Glenn 1963-64-65; Green, Louis A. 1926; Green, T. B. 1900-01-02-03 (Capt.); Green, Ron 1995; Greenwood, B. J. 1912; Greer, R. A. 1899; Grider, Heath (Mgr.) 1993; Griesbach, Bob 1952; Griffith, Dave 1952-53; Grim, Joe 1901-02-03; Grim, W. H. 1904; Grizzard, Kenneth 1921-22; Grubb, Jim 1956-57; Grubb, Wayne 1958-59-60; Gruble, John 1947-48-49-50; Gudalis, Bill 1958; Gudger, V. L. 1902-03; Gunn, Carlton 1979; Gunther, J. A. 1906; Gust, Ron 1952-53-54.

Hackman, J. S. "Buddy" 1928-29-30; Hagy, Everett 1896; Hahn, Jimmy C. 1966-67-68 (Service); Hahn, Jimmy R. 1949-50-51; Hair, Sammy 1972-73-74; Hale, Troy 1985; Hall, Jeff

1995; Hambaugh, P. C. 1915-16; Hamilton, H. T. 1900; Hamilton, Mercedes 1995; Hammond, Bill 1962-63; Hampton, Anthony 1994-95; Hancock, Anthony 1978-79-80-81; Hannah, Carl 1956; Hardy, Darryl 1988-89-90-91; Haren, Kyle 1991; Hargiss, Joseph E. 1893; Harkleroad, Rod 1966 (Service); Harkness, W. S. "Bill" 1923-24-25-26 (Capt.); Harp, Thomas "Red" 1935-36-37; Harper, Alvin 1987-88-89-90; Harper, Daryl 1980-81; Harper, Reggie 1977-78-79-80; Harris, Chris 1993 (Service); Harris, Jack (Mgr.) 1935; Harrison, Jim 1979 (Service); Harrison, W. R. (Mgr.) 1899; Haslam, Jim 1950-51-52 (Capt.); Hatcher, Adolphus H. "Buck" 1915-16-19-20 (Capt.); Hatcher, Bill 1923; Hatcher, O. C. 1916; Hatley, Ralph L. 1932-33-34 (Capt.); Havely, Casco (Mgr.) 1961-62-63; Hawkins, David 1983 (Service); Hayden, Aaron 1991-92-93-94; Hayes, Joe Black 1935-36-37 (Capt.); Hayley, Samuel B. 1911-12-13 (Capt.); Haynes, Samuel H. 1893; Hays, Johnny (Mgr.) 1990-91; Hays, Robert L. 1891; Hayworth, Tracy 1986-87-88-89; Hazen, T. Flem (Mgr.) 1914; Heard, Scott 1984 (Service); Heath, Ricky 1973; Hedgecock, Leland (Mgr.) 1922; Helton, L. T. 1960-62; Helton, Todd 1993-94; Henderson, Joseph Ray "Possum" 1916-19; Henderson, Sam 1982-83-85; Hendricks, Gerald S. 1936-37-38; Hendrix, Tim 1983-84-85-86; Henry, Duan 1982; Hensley, Tom 1952-53; Henson, Tavio 1989-90-91-92; Henton, Sterling 1987-89-90; Herndon, L. Houston 1927-28-29; Herring, Melvin G. 1936-37; Herrmann, Gary 1951; Herzbrun, Lon 1955-56-57; Heydrick, Paul D. 1929; Hibbard, Bob 1954-55-56; Hibbett, Johnny 1983-84-85-86; Hickman, Herman 1929-30-31; Hicks, Bob 1947; Hidinger, Lee 1973-74-75; Higginbotham, Roger 1974; Hill, Claude 1946-47-48; Hill, Gaylon 1970-71-72; Hill, Jimmy 1948-49-50; Hillman, Bill 1942-46; Hines, Tyrone 1994-95; Hite-Smith, Van O. 1896; Hobby, Marion 1986-87-88-89 (Alt.-Capt.); Hodge, Bonnie 1937; Holland, Mark 1992-93-94; Hollopeter, C. E. 1899-1900-01 (Capt.); Holloway, Condredge 1972-73-74 (Co-Capt.); Holloway, Jerry 1967-68; Holohan, Francis 1950-51-52; Holsclaw, Claude 1944; Holt, Laird 1929-30-31; Holt, Ricky 1981-82-83; Holt, Robert "Tarzan" 1920-21-22-23 (Capt.); Honea, Ken 1961-62-63; Hood, Merlyn 1970-71; Hooser, P. Hobart "Hobe" 1927; Horn, David 1992-93-94-95; Horner, Amos J. 1927-28; Hough, Joe 1976-77; Hovanic, Mark 1985-86-87; Howard, Anthony 1985-86; Howard, Chip 1971-72-73; Howard, Ermal 1946-47-48; Howard, Joey 1986-87; Howard, William 1984-85-86-87; Howe, Bubba 1954-55-56; Howell, Frank 1970-71; Hubbard, Bill 1953-54; Hubbard, Hal 1951-52-53; Hubbell, Franklin S. "Bud" 1941-42-46; Hubbell, Webster E. 1941; Hubbuck, Carl 1937; Huddleston, Ben 1946-47; Hudson, John Bill 1960-61-62; Hueser, Vernon 1946-47-48; Huff, Avery 1980; Huffman, Dick 1942-46; Hug, Paul N. 1928-29-30; Humphreys, Cecil C. "Sonny" 1933-34-35; Hundley, Elmo E. 1927; Huneycutt, Ralph 1947-48-49; Hunt, Brian 1985-86-87; Hunt, George 1969-70-71; Hunt, Walter (Mgr.) 1935; Hunter, George L. 1936-37-38; Hurley, Leonard F. 1920-21-22; Husband, Tom 1958-60; Hust, Al 1940-41-42 (Capt.); Hust, Emil R. 1939-41; Hutchinson, Byron 1942; Hutton, Tom 1991-92-93-94; Hyde, Jerry 1951-52-53.

Ijams, Howard A. 1891-92-93 (Capt.); Inglett, Paul 1959-60; Ingram, Brian 1977-78-79; Ingram, Mark 1995; Ingram, Phil 1978-79; Ingram, Reggie 1990-91-92-93; Irwin, Tim 1978-79-80.

Jackson, Howard 1956-57-58; Jackson, Leonard 1980-81; Jakobik, Jack 1991-92; James, David 1980-81-82; James, Roland 1976-77-78-79 (Tri.-Capt.); Janes, Palmer 1919-20-21; Jared, W. Bennett 1915; Jarnagin, F. W. 1899-1900-01; Jarvis, Ron 1965-66-67; Jasper, Bill 1949-50-51; Jeffers, Lemont Holt 1978-79-80-81 (Tri.-Capt.); Jeffries, Danny 1970-71-72; Jellicorse, Reggie 1964-65; Jenkins, Danny "Pert" 1975-76-77 (Tri.-Capt.); Jenkins, DeRon 1992-93-94-95; Jenkins, Lee 1980-81-82; Jernigan, Tom 1967-68; Jester, Mike 1978-79; Jester Nick 1992-93-94; Johnson, Bill 1955-56-57 (Co-Capt.); Johnson, Bob 1965-66-67 (Capt.); Johnson, Carl 1970-71-72; Johnson, David 1987-88; Johnson, Frank 1905; Johnson, Greg 1993-94-95; Johnson, Harold 1948-49-50; Johnson, Howard 1926-27-28 (Capt.); Johnson, L. B. "Farmer" 1926-27-28; Johnson, Paul 1973-74-75; Johnson, Steve 1994-95; Johnson, Steven 1993 (Service); Johnson, Stewart (Mgr.) 1946; Johnson, Tom 1963; Johnson, Tom D. 1970-71-72; Johnson, W. C. 1906-07-08-09-10 (Capt.); Johnston, James G. 1928-29; Jolley, Jack 1979-80; Jones, Dale 1983-84-85-86 (Tri.-Capt.); Jones, Frank D. 1926; Jones, Greg 1974-75-76-77 (Tri.-Capt.); Jones, Johnnie 1982-83-84 (Co-Capt.); Jones, Kendrick 1991-92-93-94; Jones, Kenny 1978-79-81-82; Jones, Marc 1989-90; Jones, Mike E. 1967-68-69; Jones, Mike S. 1971; Jones, Philip E. 1924; Jones, Richard H. 1923; Jones, Sam W. 1923-24-26; Jones, Wilbert 1978-79-80; Jordan, Dick 1942-46; Julian, Jason 1988-89-90-91; Jumper, Tommy 1950.

Kaseta, Vince 1949-50-51; Keener, Samuel 1906; Keever, Wade 1934; Kefauver, Estes 1922-23; Kell, Chip 1968-69-70; Keller, John 1968-69-70; Kelley, Mike 1986-87-88; Kelly, Andy 1988-89-90-91; Kelly, Farmer 1911-12-13-14 (Capt.); Kelly, Todd 1989-90-91-92 (Co-Capt.); Kelly, Van W. 1936-37; Kemp. C. M. 1915; Kennedy, Edwin M. 1919; Kennerly, Robert (Mgr.) 1927; Kent, Joey 1993-94-95; Kern, R. A. 1905; Kerney, Neal 1994 (Service); Kerr, R. V. 1911-12-13-14; Kesterton, T. O. 1909; Kidd, George 1992-93-94-95; Kile, Jack 1959; Killian, Gene 1971-72-73; Kilpatrick, Brent 1994 (Service); Kimbro, Bryan 1985-86-87-88; Kimbrough, Charles 1985-86-87; Kincaid, Bill 1956; Kiner, Steve 1967-68-69; King, Craig 1994-95; King, Harry F. 1922-23-24; King, William B. 1941; Kingman, Dan (Mgr.) 1901; Kipp, S. S. 1909; Kirk, Todd 1985-86-87; Klarer, Rudolph "Rudy" 1941-42; Kline, Cedric 1986-87-88-89; Kluge, Steve 1979-80-81-82; Knapp, Alan (Mgr.) 1995; Knappe, E. C. 1900; Knight, Steve 1981-82-83; Kohlhase, Charles E. 1929-30-31; Koleas, George L. 1935-36; Kolenik, Vic 1951-52; Kolinsky, Frank 1955-56-57; Kozar, Andy 1950-51-52; Krause, Dick 1958; Kreis, Gary 1967-68-69; Kremser, Karl 1967-68; Krouse, Henry W. 1932-34-35; Kyler, Greg 1995.

Labach, Joe E. 1893; Lacore, John O. 1893; LaCoste, Kelley 1967; Lambert, Ken 1971-72; Lane, Eric 1993-94-95; Lane, Hunter 1919-20-21-22; Lanter, Bill 1956-57; LaSorsa, Mike 1958-59-60 (Capt.); Lassiter, Robert 1970-72-73; Latham, F. S. Jr. 1909-10; Lathrop, Herbert A. 1891; Lauricella, Hank 1949-50-51; Lavin, Robert 1924; Law, Allen 1944; Lawder, Rynd, Jr. 1893; Layman, Jason 1992-93-94-95 (Capt.); Leach, J. Walker 1905-06-07-08 (Capt.); Leach, Sonny 1970-71-72; Leachman, Lamar 1952-53-55; Leake, David 1963-64-65; Leake, Don 1958-59-60; Ledford, Dennis Marshall 1941; Lee, Alan 1974; Leffler, Willie T. 1936-37; Lenoir, Patrick 1988-89-90-91; Letner, Cotton 1958-59-60; Levine, Mark 1995; Levine, Sam 1936-37;

Lewis, Roderick 1990-91; Lincoln, Jeremy 1987-88-90-91; Lindsay, Charles 1919-21; Lindsay, Robert M. "Russ" 1911-12-13-14; Linebarier, Chip 1976-77-78; Lippe, William T. 1934-35; Lipscomb, Paul 1942; Lis, Stan 1952; Little, Joseph P. "Joe" 1936-37-38; Little, Leonard 1995; Littleford, Hal 1947-48-49 (Co-Capt.); Lloyd, Owen C. 1941-42; Lockett, W. E. 1911; Logan, J. G. 1899-1900; Logan, Kim 1975-76-77; Logan, Nicholas E. 1893; Long, R. A. 1942-45-46; Longmire, Charlie 1990; Longmire, Wayne 1900-01; Lothrop, D. B. 1915; Loucks, J. C. 1906-07-08; Love, Emmon 1971-72-73; Lovingood, Frank 1934; Lowe, Andy 1916-21; Lowe, J. G. 1922-23-24 (Capt.) 25 (Capt.); Lowe, Jim 1963-65; Lowe, Theodore 1927; Lowe, W. O. "Chink" 1914-15-16-19 (Capt.); Lowe, Wes 1989; Lucci, Mike 1960-61 (Capt.); Luck, James K. 1915-16; Lukowski, Joe 1957-58-59; Lund, Bob 1945-46-47-48; Luttrell, Bill 1938-39-40; Lyman, Elbert J. 1896-1900; Lynn, Alan 1979; Lyons, Vernon 1950-51.

Madden, L. J. 1911; Mainous, Beau 1987-88; Maiure, Joe 1950-51-52; Major, Mark 1944-45-46-47; Majors, Bill 1958-59-60; Majors, Bobby 1969-70-71; Majors, John 1954-55-56; Malone, Robert 1976-78; Maloney, Frank 1896-97; Mankin, Carr 1892; Manning, John 1944-45; Manning, Peyton 1994-95; Maples, Talmadge R. "Sheriff" 1931-32-33 (Capt.); Marfield, George R. 1892; Marino, Rick 1966-67-68; Mark, Alton S. 1931-32-33; Markloff, Dave 1949; Marks, Arthur (Mgr.) 1952; Marquart, Cliff 1959-60-61; Marren, Bill 1977-78-79-80; Marsh, Pat (Mgr.) 1971; Martin, Craig 1990-91; Martin, Danny 1979-80; Martin, Fred 1963-64; Martin, Ray 1951-52; Marvin, Mickey 1973-74-75-76; Massey, R. H. 1910; Matthews, John 1981-82-83; Mattox, Bruce 1961-62; Mauck, Mike 1974-75-76; Mauriello, Bob 1966; Maxwell, Jim 1970-71; May, W. E. "Bill" 1913-14-15; Mayer, Eugene S. 1930-31 (Capt.); Mayes, J. C. 1908; Mayes, Vin 1966 (Service); Mayo, Bill 1981-82-83-84; Mayock, Dick 1952; Mays, Kevin 1991-92-93-94 (Co-Capt.); McAdams, Johnny 1981-84; McAllester, Sam J. 1903-04; McAllister, W. L. 1909; McArthur, Dave E. 1925-26-27; McBrayer, Brett 1987-88; McBride, Junior 1981; McCabe, Willis 1919; McCallum, Chip 1988; McCarren, William 1936-37-38; McCartney, Ronnie 1973-74-75 (Capt.); McClain, Hubert 1961; McClain, Lester 1968-69-70; McClellan, Bob "Skeet" (Mgr.) 1928; McCleneghan, Frank (Mgr.) 1921; McClennon, John 1982; McCleskey, J. J. 1989-90-91-92- (Co-Capt.); McCloud, Ted (Mgr.) 1959-62; McClung, C. J. (Mgr.) 1904; McClure, Robert L. (Mgr.) 1929; McClure, W. K. "Bill" 1912-13-15; McCollum, Clarence H. 1907-08; McConnell, E. M. 1900; McCord, Darris 1952-53-54 (Capt.); McCroskey, Clemmons 1989-90; McCroskey, Frank 1952-53; McCullough, Andy 1994-95; McDaniel, Terry 1984-85-86-87; McDaniel, Victor 1983; McDonald, Jim 1966-67-68; McDougal, Ed 1974 (Service); McEver, Gene 1928-29-31; McFadden, Bud 1955; McGee, Tim 1983-84-85 (Tri.-Capt.); McGeehan, Chick. 1968; McGlothin, Bill 1970-71-72; McGuire, Kennard 1986-87; McGuire, R. L. 1910-11-12; McKeen, E. Allyn 1925-26-27; McKelvy, Jerry 1965; McKenzie, Raleigh 1982-83-84; McKenzie, Reggie 1981-82-83-84; McLean, Evan A. 1912-13-14-15 (Capt.); McLeary, Don 1968-69-70; McMeans, Neal 1966-67-68; McMichael, Jeff 1981-82; McNamara, Jim 1966; McPherson, C. L. 1932; McQuady, Claude 1945; McRae, Charles 1987-88-89-90; McRee, Kenny 1945; McSpadden Malcolm 1914; McWilliams, John 1954; Meek, Bill 1940-41-42; Melas, Alex 1966 (Service); Melton, Gary 1966-67; Meneses, Oscar 1944; Merritt, J. B. 1968 (Service);

Meseroll, Norman 1946-47-48-49; Messimer, Jesse 1984; Meyer, Charles 1951; Michels, John 1950-51-52; Middlebrooks, Nate 1986-87-88 (Co-Capt.); Middleton, Albert 1932; Milam, Kevin 1970; Milchin, Jerry 1961-62-63; Miley, Floyd 1988-89-90-91; Miller, Anthony 1986-87; Miller, Ben 1944-45; Miller, Bubba 1992-93-94-95 (Capt.); Miller, Darrin 1984-85-86-87; Miller, Jim 1983-84-85-86; Miller, Michael 1980-81-82; Miller, Randy 1985 (Mgr.); Mills, Joe 1973-74; Mills, Johnny 1964-65-66; Milner, Orvis 1946-47; Mims, Chris 1990-91; Miner, Jim 1947-48-49; Minnick, Hagen (Mgr.) 1948; Mitchell, Charles T. 1941-42-43; Mitchell, Cleon 1993; Mitchell, D. K. 1931; Mitchell, Stan 1963-64-65; Mitchell, Steve 1971-72-73; Mixon, Manley 1968-69-70; Moeller, Gene 1951-52; Mohrman, Mike 1972-73-74; Molaskey, Ron 1965; Molck, Ricky 1971-72; Molinski, Ed 1938-39-40; Mondelli, Jim 1967-68; Mooers, Charles A. 1891; Moon, David 1984; Moore, Charles C. Jr. 1891-92 (Capt.); Moore, Dustin 1995; Moore, Gary 1977-78-79; Moore, Jeff 1975-76-77-78; Moore, Mark 1988-89; Moore, Owen Bud 1926; Moore, Terry 1972-73-74-75; Moore, Vincent 1987-89-90; Moran, Charley B. 1897; Morel, Bobby 1964-65-66; Morgan, Anthony 1988-89-90; Morgan, Ed. 1950-51-52; Morgan, Stanley 1973-74-75-76; Morris, Horace 1991-92-93 (Co-Capt.); Morris, B. Y. 1922-23; Morris, Randall 1980-81-82-83; Morris, W. W. 1915-16; Morrow, Russ 1944-45; Morton, Bobby 1962-63; Morton, Robert 1975; Moses, Fred J. 1933-34-35; Moss, Ray 1956-57-58; Mulliniks, Jack (Mgr.) 1955; Mulloy, Richard 1939-40-41; Munro, Colin 1951-53; Murdic, Jon 1972-73-74; Murphy, David 1966-67; Murphy, John 1975-76-77; Murrell, W. J. 1911; Murrell, William 1936; Murriel, Martin 1977-78; Mutter, Mitch 1967; Myers, Andy 1950-51-52; Myers, James A. "Jim" 1941-42-46; Myslinski, Tom 1988-89-90-91.

Nails, Brett 1985 (Service); Nash, Marcus 1994-95; Naumoff, Paul 1964-65-66 (Co-Capt.); Neal, G. F. 1896; Neal, Ray (Mgr.) 1947; Needham, Kenneth L. "Shorty" 1933-34-35; Neff, Herbert Artie 1922-23-24-25; Nelson, Lance 1990; Nelson, Ralph 1993; Nelson, Tony 1986-87-88; Nettles, Ray 1969-70-71; Newman, Clay (Mgr.) 1994; Newman, Fred 1939-40; Newman, W. M. 1896-99-1900 (Capt.); Newton, H. R. (Mgr.) 1909; Neyland, Bob Jr. 1952-53; Nichols, Jack 1960-61; Nicholson, Jacob H. "Jake" 1920-21; Nickla, Ed 1951-52; Nicklin, Strang 1896 (Capt.) 97; Noe, Richie 1992; Noel, Henry W. 1940-41; Noel, Tori 1993-95; Noonan, Jim 1976-77-78-80 (Capt.); North, Lee 1978-79-80-81 (Tri.-Capt.); Nowling, William E. 1940-41-42.

OOldham, Donnie 1977; Oleksiak, Pat 1952-54; Olmstead, H. S. 1899; Olszewski, Jeff 1979-80-81; O'Neal, Art 1963; Orr, Bunny 1959-60-61; Overbey, Beasley 1920; Overholt, Bobby 1957; Overton, Mike 1973-74-75-76.

Pafford, R. W. 1904-05; Page, David 1973-74-75; Paidousis, Mike 1944-45-46; Palmer, Edwin C. 1933-34-35 (Capt.); Panuska, Pete 1984-85-86; Parker, Jason 1992-93-94; Parker, S.Y. 1903-04-05; Parman, D. C. 1910; Parrish, Doug 1979-80-81-82; Parsons, David 1974-75-76; Parsons, Newt (Mgr.) 1957-58; Partin, Maxwell R. 1941-45-46; Patterson, Bobby 1967-69; Patterson, Don 1958-59-60; Patterson, Jack 1964-65; Patterson, Ryan 1990-92-93; Paty, John M. 1962-63-64; Paty, John W. 1934-35; Payne, Harold "Herky" 1949-50-51; Pearce, Lanny 1968; Pearman, Bill 1947-49-50-51; Peay, Johnny (Mgr.) 1956; Pedersen, Arnold 1962-63; Peel, Ike

1939-40-41; Peery, Arnall 1906-07-08-09; Penland, J. D. 1910; Peoples, Carlton 1979-80-81-82; Peppers, Victor 1984-85-86-87; Perkins, Marion 1936-37; Perry, Robbin 1987; Persinger, Tim 1969; Peterson, Trey 1993-94-95; Petrella, Bob 1963-64-65; Petruzzi, Leo 1932-33; Pettway, William D. (Mgr.) 1925; Pfeiffer, Scott 1993-94-95; Phillips, Ed 1963; Phillips, Frederick H. 1893; Phillips, Greg 1975-76; Phillips, Jimmie R. 1920-22; Phillips, Marvin 1958-59-60; Phillips, Mose 1991-92-93-94; Phillips, Vernon 1980; Phipps, F. L. (Mgr.) 1910; Pick, Jack M. 1934-35; Pickens, Carl 1989-90-91; Pickens, Richard 1966-67-68; Pickle, Joe 1983 (Service); Pierce, Phil 1969-70-71; Pierce, W. W. 1899; Pike, Patrick "Buddy" 1944-45-46; Pillow, Ronnie 1994-95; Poe, Matt 1994 (Service); Poles, Roland 1987-88-89-90; Poley, David 1973-74; Polofsky, Gordon 1949-50-51; Poole, Robert 1994-95; Poole, Steve 1973-74-75; Pope, Jackie 1960; Porter, James W. 1934-36; Porter, Steve 1976-77-78; Potts, Tommy 1956-57-58; Pounders, Louis E. 1932-33-34; Powe, Roc 1991; Powell, Don 1923; Powell, Jeff 1985; Powell, Jim 1942-46-47-48 (Capt.); Powell, John 1951-52-53; Powers, Eddy 1975-76-77; Powers, Rick 1976-77; Powers, William K. 1919; Prater, Tracy (Mgr.) 1938; Price, Jason 1995; Price, Mike 1966-67-68 (Service); Price, Peerless 1995; Price, Royal 1942-46-47; Priest, Tim 1968-69-70 (Capt.); Priest, Tom 1953-55; Prigmore, Quincy 1992-93-94-95; Pritchard, Ken 1962-63; Proctor, E. B. 1904-05-06 (Capt.); Proctor, J. B. 1946-47-48; Pruett, Kenneth 1949-50; Pryor, Wesley 1983-85-86; Puki, Craig 1975-76-78-79 (Tri.-Capt.); Pulliam, Robert 1972-73-74.

Q Quillen, Ford 1958.

R Rabenstein, Russ 1973-74-75; Rader, Charles 1954-55-56; Ragsdale, T. M. 1905-06; Rainey, Horace "Red" 1913-14; Rakestraw, Wes 1985; Ransey, Allen C. 1936-37; Ramsey, R. W. 1909; Rapien, Mike 1988-89-90; Ratliffe, Leslie 1992-93-94; Raulston, C. S. 1909; Rayburn, Virgil H. 1930-31-32; Reado, Jarvis 1995; Rechichar, Bert 1949-50-51 (Capt.); Redding, Jack 1944; Reed, C. H. 1892; Reeder, Claude S. 1906; Reeves, Von 1988-89-90-91; Regen, Dick 1944; Register, Arch 1921; Reich, Phil 1987; Reid, Junior 1977-78-80; Reineke, Charles W. 1928-29-30; Reveiz, Carlos 1985-86; Reveiz, Fuad 1981-82-83-84; Reviere, Dee 1976-77-78; Reyes, Orlando 1986; Reynolds, Art 1971-72-73; Reynolds, Jack 1967-68-69; Reynolds, Mike 1964; Rhea, Charles McClung 1891; Rice, Alvin 1937; Rice, Charles P. 1925-26; Rice, E. B. 1909; Rice, J. C. 1897; Richards, Larry 1960-61-62; Richards, Willie 1992; Richardson, Jim 1973-74; Richardson, W. A. 1903-04; Riffer, Eric 1990-91; Rike, Jim 1938-39; Ring, J. J. 1906-09; Ring, N. S. "Ned" 1915-16; Ritchey, Jim 1954; Roach, Gary 1975; Roberts, Louis T. 1928-29-30; Roberts, Rusty (Mgr.) 1981-82-83; Robertson, Sam 1963-64-65; Robinson, Antonio 1993; Robinson, Charles 1956; Robinson, Dick (Mgr.) 1953-54; Robinson, Diron 1995; Robinson, Edwin G. 1893; Robinson, Fred 1923-24; Robinson, Harvey L. 1931-32; Robinson, Ray 1985-86-87-88; Robinson, Steve 1968-69-70; Robinson, Tom 1923-24-25; Robinson, Tony 1983-84-85; Robinson, Tyrone 1985-86; Robison, Charles W. 1916-19-20; Rodgers, Kacy 1988-89-90-91; Roe, Joe 1957; Rogan, C. B. 1896-97; Rogers, E. N. 1908-09; Rollins, John 1987-88; Romine, Dave 1940; Rose, Roy Eugene 1933-34-35; Rosenfelder, Charles 1966-67-68; Ross, G. W. 1897; Rotella, Al 1942-46-47; Rotella, Jamie 1970-71-72 (Capt.); Rotroff, Roger 1951-52-53; Rowan, Bill Joe 1946-47; Rowe, Gary

1974-75-76; Rowsey, Thomas 1975-76-77; Rubin, W. P. 1911; Rudder, Bill 1971-72-73; Rudder, David 1978-79; Rumsey, Tim 1979-80-81-82; Rushin, Don 1954; Russas, Al 1946-47-48; Russell, Don 1919; Ruth, Rodney 1992; Ryan, Pat 1977.

S Sabato, Al 1942; Sadler, Ken 1958-59; Sanders, Jesse 1992-93-94-95; Sanders, Randy 1985-86-87-88; Sanders, William 1937; Sanderson, Dale 1983; Sanderson, Glenn (Mgr.) 1934; Sanderson, Ken 1976-77-78; Sandlin, Bobby 1956-57-58; Sartelle, John 1993-94-95; Satterfield, Larry 1972-73-74; Saunders, W. Raymond 1929-30-31; Saxton, N. L. 1907-08; Scandrett, David 1982-83; Schaffer, Joe 1957-58-59 (Capt.); Schenk, C. G. 1900; Schleiden, Roy 1944; Schneitman, Dale 1978-79 (Service); Schoenle, Bill 1991; Scholes, Charles 1954; Schubert, H. A. (Mgr.) 1920; Schultz, Don 1958; Schwanger Ted 1952-53; Schwartzinger, Jimmy 1940-41; Scott, Bob 1953-54-55; Scott, Bobby 1968-69-70; Scott, Robby 1983-84-85-86; Seivers, Larry 1974-75-76 (Co-Capt.); Sekanovich, Dan 1951-52-53; Sellers, Larry (Mgr.) 1972; Sells, Jack 1983-84; Session, Steve 1991-92; Severance, Charles 1959-60; Sewell, Tim 1995; Sexton, Scott 1994 (Service); Shafer, Bo 1956-57-58; Shaffer, David 1971-72-73; Shannon, H. I. 1908-09; Sharp, Sam J. 1935; Sharpe, W. P. 1900; Shaw, Robert 1975-76-77-78 (Co-Capt.); Shaw, William H. 1904-05; Shelby, A. G. 1916; Sherrill, J. W. 1948-49-50; Sherrod, Horace "Bud" 1947-48-49-50; Shields, David 1961; Shields, Lebron 1958-59; Shires, Marshall "Abe" 1938-39 40; Shires, Pat 1950-52-53; Shofner, Austin C. 1936; Shoulders, William 1915-16; Showalter, Nick 1966-67-68; Shuford, George 1962; Shuler, Benjie 1993-95; Shuler, Heath 1991-92-93; Shull, F. E. 1930-31-32; Siberman, Dow 1934-35; Silcox, J. H. 1902; Silvan, Nilo 1992-93-94; Silvey, George 1968-70-71; Simerly A. E. 1902; Simionetti, Leonard 1940-41; Simmonds, R. M. 1915; Simmons, Tony 1982-83-84; Simons, Kevin 1985-86-87-88; Simonton, Claud 1970-71-72; Simpson, Hubert 1976-78-79; Simpson, T. N. (Mgr.) 1919; Sims, Burt L. 1892; Sims, Tommy 1982-83-84-85 (Tri.-Capt.); Singer, Curt 1980-81-82-83; Sivert, Jim 1949; Sizemore, Bernie 1949-50; Slack, Tom 1948; Slater, Walter 1941-42-46 (Capt.); Sloan, Ira 1920-21; Smargiasso, Heath 1994-95; Smartt, Leon 1958-59-60; Smelcher, Jim 1955-56-57; Smith, Alfred E. 1892; Smith, Billy 1961; Smith, Boyd M. 1932; Smith. C. H. 1899; Smith, Carl E. 1956-57-58; Smith, Chuck 1990-91; Smith, Daryle 1984-85-86; Smith, Geric 1995 (Service); Smith, Gordon E. 1931-32-33; Smith, H. W. 1896-97; Smith, Jeff 1981-82-84-85; Smith, Jeff 1992-93-94-95; Smith, Jerry 1964-65-66; Smith, Jimmie F. 1920-21-22-23; Smith, Larry 1989; Smith, Mike 1973-75 (Service); Smith, Roy "Looney" 1947-48-49-50; Smith, Thomas 1938-39; Smith, Tracy 1990-91-92; Smith, Wayne 1968-69; Smith, Wiley Corry (Mgr.) 1924; Smithers, Bob 1956; Sneed, Robert 1936-37-38; Sneed, W. Bush 1923; Snipes, Herman 1931; Snowden, Robert B. 1919; Sollee, Neyle 1958-59; Sorrells, Frank G. 1913-14-15; Spain, Wayne 1969-70; Sparks, Scott 1987-88; Spence, J. W. 1906; Spence, Shirley E. 1891; Spiva, Andy 1973-74-75-76 (Co-Capt.); Spivey, Brian 1989-90-91-92; Spivey, Jeremy 1992; Spoone, Bill 1953; Spradlin, Danny 1977-78-79-80; Stafford, Tim 1986-87; Staley, Maurice 1994-95; Stanback, Haskel 1971-72-73; Stancell, Harold 1964-65-66; Stansell, Ken 1972; Stapleton, Clayton 1941-46-47; Starling, Marcus 1977-78; Starr, Lee (Mgr.) 1951; Steffy, Joe 1944; Steiner, Max 1938-39-40; Stephens, Buster 1944-45; Stephens, Don 1958; Stephenson, Casey

1944-45; Stephenson, Dave 1946; Stephenson, Guy 1922; Stewart, Bo 1944; Stewart, Branndon 1994; Stewart, Clifton 1967-68; Stewart, Howard L. 1931-32-33; Stewart, James 1991-92-93-94; Stewart, Lyonel 1977-78; Still, Eric 1986-87-88-89 (Capt.); Still, J. Ralph 1930-31; Stokes, Charles 1950-51; Stone, Cory 1993-94; Stottlemyer, Dave 1955-56-57; Stowell, Mike 1989-90-91-92; Stowers, Donnie 1977 (Service); Stratton, Mike 1959-60-61; Streater, Jimmy 1977-78-79 (Tri.-Capt.); Streno, Glenn 1981-82-83; Striegel, Roy B. "Pap" 1919-20-21-22 (Capt.); Stroud, Jack 1947-48-49-50 (Capt.); Stuart, Mark 1910; Stuart, Phil 1985-86-87-88; Studaway, Mark 1979-80-81-83; Stupar, Francis 1949; Suffridge, Robert "Bob" 1938-39-40; Sullivan, Jimmy 1962-64; Sullivan, Ned 1961-62-63; Summers, Shawn 1992-93-94-95; Summers, T. P. (Mgr.) 1906; Sumpter, Nate 1977-79; Surlas, J. J. 1989-90-91-92; Suttle, Chevette 1980; Sutton, Phil 1978-79; Swafford, J. H. 1908; Swanson, Eric 1984-85; Sweeney, Terry 1953; Symonds, Brad 1994 (Service); Szawara, Al 1976.

T Tade, Herbert 1935; Talbot, Joe 1923; Talley, Ben 1991-92-93-94 (Co-Capt.); Tanara, Al 1962-63-64; Tanner, Don 1949; Tanner, Larry 1939; Tansil, Vernon G. 1934-35; Tarwater, A. B. 1897; Taylor, Leland 1993-94; Taylor, Lenny 1981-82-83; Taylor, R. L. "Bob" 1912-13-14-15; Taylor, W. H. 1901; Teague, Trey 1994-95; Tedford, Gene 1963; Teel, Jerry 1991; Templeton, Conrad C. 1929-30; Templeton, Rick 1995 (Service); Terry, Mike 1979-81-82; Terry, William L. 1899 (Capt.); Thayer, Harry J. "Hobo" 1928-29-30 (Capt.); Theiler, Gary 1969-70-71; Thomas, Alfred 1937-38-39; Thomas, Bobby 1971; Thomas, Dave 1990; Thomas, Houston 1987-88-89; Thomas, Jimmy 1967-68-69; Thomason, R. F. "Tommy" 1912-13-14-15; Thompson, Joe 1969-70-71; Thompson, Johnny 1970-72; Thompson, Tony 1988-89-90; Thompson, Van 1939-40; Thornton, D. B. 1903-04-05; Thornton, Matthew 1989 (Service); Tidwell, Blane 1976; Tilson, Paul 1959-61-62; Toles, Alvin 1981-82-83-84; Todd, Robert 1991-92; Tomlinson, Billy 1963-64-65; Tompkins, F. M. 1910-11; Townes, Tim 1970-71-72; Townsend, Ricky 1972-73-74; Tracy, Tom 1953-54; Treece, Chris 1987; Tripp, Arthur M. 1926-27-28; Trott, Stan 1970-71-72; Trupovnieks, Jani 1980-81; Truss, Shawn 1989; Tucker, Glen 1976-77; Tucker, Homer 1988; Tucker, Willis 1940; Tudor, D. Vincent 1927-28; Tullis, Jeff 1989-90-91-92; Tunnell, S. M. (Mgr.) 1915; Turnage, Gordon 1969-71-72; Turnbow, Jesse 1975-77; Twifold, H. H. 1916.

U Upton, Mark 1993; Upton, Todd 1983-84; Urbano, Bobby 1956-57-58 (Capt.); Urbano, Roger 1954-55-56; Urubek, Steve 1971-72-73; Ussery, Bob 1952-53.

V Valbuena, Gary 1972-73; Vaughan, Charles W "Pug" 1932-33-34; Venable, Sam A. 1932; Verner, Randy 1974-1975; Vest, Roger 1951-52; Via, Mike 1986 (Service); Vick, Warren 1941; Vituccio, Gary 1965; Vowell, J. Graham 1914-15-16 (Capt.) 21; Vowell, Morris A. 1913-14-15-16; Vowell, Richie 1924; Vugrin, James 1946-47-48-49.

W Waddell, Ken 1959-60; Wade, Jimmy 1951-52-53-54; Wade, John 1979; Waff, Wayne 1962; Wagster, John 1970-71-72; Walker, David 1987; Walker, Jackie 1969-70-71 (Capt.); Walker, Jeff 1975; Walker, Shon 1988-89-90-91; Wallace, Randy 1974-75-76; Wallen, Joe 1936-38-39; Walter, Hank

1972-73-74; Walters, John M. 1906-07-08-09; Wampler, Chris 1980-81-82; Wantland, Hal 1963-64-65 (Capt.); Ward, Ernie 1973-74-75; Warmath, Murray 1932-33-34; Warner, E. T. 1896; Warren, Buist 1938-39-40; Warren, Dewey 1965-66-67; Warren, James 1992-93; Warren, John 1979-80-81-82; Warren, Phil 1905; Warren, Preston 1987-88-89-90; Washington, Anthony 1976; Watkins, Arthur B. 1897; Watkins, T. R. 1903-04; Watson, Bob (Mgr.) 1923; Watson, Brent 1974-75-76-77 (Tri.-Capt.); Watson, Curt 1969-70-71; Watts, Brad 1976; Watts, Jim 1972-73-74 (Co-Capt.); Watts, Johnny 1977-78-79; Weatherford, Derrick 1965-66-67; Weatherford, Jim 1966-67-68; Weaver, DeWitt T. 1934-35-36 (Capt.); Weaver, Herman 1967-68-69; Webb, Charlton 1975-77-78; Webb, Chuck 1989-90; Webb, Danny 1958; Weber, Nick 1939-40; Webster, Chris 1977; Wegener, Albert B. 1892-93; Weisenberg, Andrew 1908-09; Welch, F. W. 1915; Welch, Tim 1983-84-85; Wemlinger, Gary 1969; Wendelboe, Kevin 1991; Wert, Lee K. 1907; Wert, R. Y. 1900-01; Werts, Edwin S. 1891-92; West, Hodges "Burr" 1938-39-40; West, Tom 1973-74-75; Wheaton, Lance 1992-93-94; Wheeler, Ronnie 1973-74-75; Whitaker, James A. 1929; Whitaker, Walter C. (Mgr.) 1913; White, Brad 1978-79-80 (Co-Capt.); White, Chris 1983-84-85 (Tri.-Capt.); White H. Benton 1907-08; White, Lynn T. 1892-93; White, Reggie 1980-81-82-83 (Capt.); White, Steve 1975; White, Steve 1992-93-94-95; White, W. C. 1921; Whitehead, Mike 1985-86-87; Whitener, Gordon (Mgr.) 1984; Whittle, Matt 1905; Widby, Ron 1964-65-66; Wildman, Charles 1944-45-46-47; Wilkerson, Bruce 1983-84-85-86 (Tri.-Capt.); Wilkinson, Rick 1981-83; Williams, Billy 1993-94; Williams, Bob 1954-55; Williams, Cliff 1956; Williams, Dick 1966-67-68 (Capt.); Williams, Jay 1977-78-79-80; Williams, Johnny 1981-82-83; Williams, Martin 1988-89; Williams, Russ 1974-75-76-77; Williams, Todd 1994; Williams, Tom 1960-61-62; Williams, Tony 1984-85; Wilson, Al 1995; Wilson, Charles 1984-85-86-87; Wilson, Darryal 1981-82; Wilson, Dwight 1980; Wilson, Eddie 1971-72-73; Wilson, James 1989-91-92-93 (Co-Capt.); Wilson, Rollin 1922-24; Winstead, Jid 1956; Winston, D. B. (Mgr.) 1937; Witherington, Sid 1973; Witherspoon, Carl 1971-72; Witt, Roy E. 1926-27-28 (Capt.); Wold, Steve 1968-69-70; Wolfe, Dennis 1976-77-78 (Co-Capt.); Wolfe, Lloyd S. 1914-15-16; Wood, Caroll 1945; Wood, James R. 1891; Wood, Lee 1989-90; Wood, Walter "Babe" 1936-37-38; Woodall, David (Mgr.) 1973-74-76-77; Woodruff, George R. "Bob" 1936-37-38; Woods, Gerald 1963-64-65; Woods, Thomas 1986-87-88-89 (Alt.-Capt.); Woody, James 1968-69-70; Woofter, Jim 1974-75-76; Word, Roscoe 1902-03-04 (Capt.) 05 (Capt.) 07 (Capt.); Wortnam, C. L. 1900; Wright, Gary, 1966-67; Wright, George 1957-58; Wrightman, A. L. 1901; Wyatt, Bowden 1936-37-38 (Capt.); Wyche, Bubba 1967-68; Wynn, Herman D. "Breezy" 1931-32-33; Wyrick, Charles 1960-61.

Y Yanossy, Frank 1967-68-69; Yarbrough, John 1973-74-75; Yatkowski, Paul 1992-93; Young, Bill 1966-68-69 (Capt.); Young, Carroll 1956-57; Young, Ed. B. 1925-26; Young, Eddie 1955; Young, J. R. 1910; Young, Jimmy 1970-71-72.

Z Zander, Carl 1981-82-83-84 (Co-Capt.); Zecchino, Nick 1986-87-88; Ziegler, Kelly 1984-85-86-87 (Co-Capt.); Zontini, Lawrence 1942; Zurcher, Kevin 1989; Zvolerin, Bob 1963.

TRIVIA ANSWERS

1. Jim Hofher (to Cornell, 1990).

2. W.H. Britton, who filled in as head coach for one year (1935) for Robert R. Neyland when Neyland was called back to active duty with the U.S. Army. Tennessee had a 4-5 record.

3. 51.

4. Arkansas (8), followed by Florida State (4) and Army (3), Auburn (3) and Ohio State (3).

5. Georgia, Kentucky, Ole Miss.

6. Georgia (21), followed by Florida (15), North Carolina (12) and Ohio (11).

7. C.D. Brown on a 50-yard run versus Maryville in 1892.

8. According to available records, H. Benton White caught a touchdown pass from Lee Wert in 1907. It covered 70 yards.

9. Though it may have been by C.D. Brown in that very first game (1892 versus Maryville), a verifiable report gives that honor to Strang Nicklin (175 yards versus Central University of Kentucky in 1896).

10. It might have been Benton White in 1908 versus Chattanooga (a 57-0 win), but it also might have been Bowden Wyatt in 1938 (also against Chattanooga) with 98 verified yards on three touchdown receptions.

11. UT first played Vanderbilt in 1892. Others the Vols first played in the 19th century were Kentucky (1893) and Georgia (1899).

12. The University of Chattanooga (now UT-Chattanooga) and UT have played 40 games, the last in 1969. Georgia Tech, a former SEC member, has played UT 43 times.

13. Gene McEver and Herman Hickman played in the East-West Shrine Game in San Francisco in 1932.

14. Guard Herman Hickman (1932-34, Brooklyn Dodgers).

15. Mississippi State (20-0, Oct. 6, 1933).

16. Penn State (1972, UT won 28-21).

17. A tie; 100 yards by Pete Panuska (vs. Maryland in '84 Sun Bowl) and Willie Gault (vs. Pittsburgh in '80).

18. Bert Rechichar; 100 yards (vs. Washington & Lee, 1950).

19. No player has intercepted more than three passes in a game but seven have pulled off 3-"pick" efforts: Bob Lund (vs. North Carolina, 1948); J.W. Sherrill (vs. Kentucky, 1949); Albert Dorsey (vs. Alabama, 1967); Bill Young (vs. Rice, 1968); Tim Priest (vs. Alabama, 1970); Chris White (vs. UCLA, 1985); and Preston Warren (vs. Boston College, 1988).

20. UT defeated Alabama 27-13 in Birmingham.

21. The 1952 Vanderbilt team gained 13 total yards in a 46-0 UT win in Nashville.

22. In 1951, UT ran for 513 yards against Washington & Lee.

23. In 1990, UT passed for 399 yards against Notre Dame.

24. Andy Kelly and Carl Pickens hooked up in 1991 for an 87-yard touchdown against Auburn.

25. Andy Spiva (134 in 1976).

26. Al Saunders (San Diego), Dom Capers (Carolina).

27. Fuad Reveiz (71, 1981-84).

28. John Becksvoort (317, 1991-94).

29. Greg Burke (107, 1990).

30. Fuad Reveiz (60 yards vs. Georgia Tech, 1982).

31. Darrin Miller.

32. Chip Kell (1968-70), Curt Watson (1969-71), Mickey Marvin (1974-76).

33. Sam Bartholomew (1938).

34. Guard Steve DeLong (1964).

35. John Michels (1996)

36. Beattie Feathers (1933).

37. Bowden Wyatt (1956).

38. Black (with orange and white piping).

39. Sewanee (1891).

40. Maryville (1892, 1893).

41. 1907.

42. Estes Kefauver (1922-23).

43. Georgia Tech, 1963.

44. In 1991 against Vanderbilt, "Little Man" Stewart ran for 145 yards; Aaron Hayden, 115; and Mose Phillips, 107.

45. 294 by Chuck Webb vs. Ole Miss (1989).

46. One, his senior season (1994) when he ran for 1,028.

47. Stanley Morgan (201 vs. Hawaii, 1975).

48. Two; the Freres (Rob and Ron, 1972), the McKenzies (Raleigh and Reggie, 1982-84).

49. 73,801 in 1986.

50. Jimmy Elmore (1925-27) was mayor of Knoxville; Hal Littleford (1947-49) was mayor of Johnson City.

51. Condredge Holloway to current Clemson head coach Tommy West (vs. Vanderbilt, 1974).

52. Gene McEver (1929).

53. George Cafego (1940, Chicago Cardinals).

54. Tackles Antone Davis and Charles McRae and wide receiver Alvin Harper.

55. Baylor, Colorado, Dartmouth, Florida State, North Texas State, Pittsburgh, Purdue, Southern Cal, Texas Tech, VMI.

56. Roscoe Ward was captain in 1904, 1905 and 1907; J.G. Lowe was captain in 1924 and 1925.

57. John Barnhill was captain in 1927 and head coach 1941-45; Bowden Wyatt was captain in 1938 and head coach 1955-62.

58. Tennessee shut out all its opponents in a 10-0 SEC championship season (1939), but then lost to Southern Cal 14-0 in the Rose Bowl to finish 10-1.

59. Barnhill in 1944.

60. UT played its first night game at Baton Rouge, La., beating LSU, 13-0, in 1944.

COLLEGE SPORTS HANDBOOKS

Stories, Stats & Stuff About America's Favorite Teams

U. of Arizona	Basketball	Arizona Wildcats Handbook
U. of Arkansas	Basketball	Razorbacks Handbook
Baylor	Football	Bears Handbook
Clemson	Football	Clemson Handbook
U. of Colorado	Football	Buffaloes Handbook
U. of Florida	Football	Gator Tales
Georgia Tech	Basketball	Yellow Jackets Handbook
Indiana U.	Basketball	Hoosier Handbook
Iowa State	Sports	Cyclones Handbook
U. of Kansas	Basketball	Crimson & Blue Handbook
Kansas State	Sports	Kansas St Wildcat Handbook
LSU	Football	Fighting Tigers Handbook
U. of Louisville	Basketball	Cardinals Handbook
U. of Miami	Football	Hurricane Handbook
U. of Michigan	Football	Wolverines Handbook
U. of Missouri	Basketball	Tiger Handbook
U. of Nebraska	Football	Husker Handbook
U. of N. Carolina	Basketball	Tar Heels Handbook
N.C. State	Basketball	Wolfpack Handbook
U. of Oklahoma	Football	Sooners Handbook
Penn State	Football	Nittany Lions Handbook
U. of S. Carolina	Football	Gamecocks Handbook
Stanford	Football	Stanford Handbook
Syracuse	Sports	Orange Handbook
U. of Texas	Football	Longhorns Handbook
Texas A&M	Football	Aggies Handbook
Texas Tech	Sports	Red Raiders Handbook
Virginia Tech	Football	Hokies Handbook
Wichita State	Sports	Shockers Handbook
U. of Wisconsin	Football	Badgers Handbook

Also:

Big 12 Handbook: Stories, Stats and Stuff About The Nation's Best
    Football Conference

The Top Fuel Handbook: Stories, Stats and Stuff About Drag Racing's
    Most Powerful Class

For ordering information call Midwest Sports Publications at:

1-800-492-4043